PUBLICATIONS

Pocket Employer

Related titles in this series:

The Pocket Economist
Rupert Pennant-Rea and Bill Emmott

The Economist Pocket Banker
Tim Hindle

The Economist Pocket Accountant
Christopher Nobes

The Economist Pocket Guide to Marketing
Michael Thomas

The Economist Pocket Guide to Defence
Michael Sheehan and James H. Wyllie

The Economist Pocket Lawyer
Stanley Berwin

The Economist Pocket Entrepreneur
Colin Barrow

The Economist Pocket Guide to Business Numeracy
David Targett

The Economist Pocket Negotiator
Gavin Kennedy

The Economist

PUBLICATIONS

Pocket Employer

Derek Torrington
and
Jill Earnshaw

Basil Blackwell

and

The Economist Publications

Copyright © Derek Torrington and Jill Earnshaw 1988

Jointly published 1988 by
Basil Blackwell Ltd
108 Cowley Road, Oxford OX4 1JF, UK
and
The Economist Publications Ltd
40 Duke Street, London W1A 1DW

Basil Blackwell Inc.
432 Park Avenue South, Suite 1503
New York, NY 10016, USA

All the information in this book is verified to the best of the authors' and publisher's ability, but they do not accept responsibility for loss arising from decisions based upon them. Where opinion is expressed it is that of the authors, which does not necessarily coincide with the editorial views of The Economist Newspaper.

British Library Cataloguing in Publication Data

Torrington, Derek
Pocket employer
1. Personnel management—Dictionaries
I. Title   II. Earnshaw, Jill
658.3′003′21   HF5549.A23

ISBN 0–631–15389–6

Typeset in 10 on 12 Bembo
by Opus, Oxford
Printed in Great Britain by
Billing and Sons Ltd, Worcester

Contents

Preface

This book is to help all those dealing with the management of employment – personnel managers, other managers, proprietors of small businesses, lawyers, journalists, union officials and employees – to understand better what employee management is and to make better use of its specialist expertise. Whatever sort of 'people manager' you are, there should be something in here for you.

The entries range from quite short dictionary-type definitions (like BLACKLEG, LIEU and STATUS QUO) to fuller explanations of features of employment law (like CONTRACT VARIATION, GENUINE MATERIAL FACTOR and RANGE OF REASONABLE RESPONSES), personnel management methods (like ASSESSMENT CENTRES, JOB EVALUATION and MANPOWER PLANNING) and conclusions from academic research (like HYGIENE FACTOR, ORGANIZATION CULTURE and REPERTORY GRIDS). There are references to important institutions and publications, as well as explanations of many mysterious sets of initials. Cross-references are indicated by small capitals in the text or by 'See also' after an entry. There are suggestions for further reading on some of the larger or more complex issues.

We hope there is enough here for you to have better-informed discussions with personnel managers, to appreciate what they can do, to give a clear brief the next time you employ a personnel consultant or employment lawyer, and to be more satisfied with all the work you do yourself in employing, deploying and rewarding those who work with you.

Derek Torrington and Jill Earnshaw
March 1987

Acknowledgements

The publisher and authors are grateful for permission to reproduce cartoons as follows.

Cartoons on pp. 6, 27, 54, 70, 89, 103, 120, 152, 163, 179, 212, 222, 250 are reproduced by kind permission of *Punch*.

The cartoon on p. 139, 'I'm just a number here too', is reproduced by kind permission of *The Wall Street Journal* – permission, Cartoon Features Syndicate.

The cartoon on p. 190, 'The man we need must have guts', is reproduced by kind permission of Hector Breeze.

A

Absence control. Employee absence can be best controlled by observing trends and monitoring initiatives to modify those trends. The standard measures are *lost time*, showing how much is lost over a period, which is calculated as follows:

$$\frac{\text{number of days lost through absence}}{\text{average number of employees} \times \text{number of days in period}} \times 100$$

Frequency shows the number of times people are absent. Frequent short spells can be a bigger problem than fewer long spells and the method of calculation is:

$$\frac{\text{number of absences}}{\text{average number of employees}} \times 100$$

Useful initiatives to reduce irresponsible absence include:

• authorizing absence for acceptable reasons, such as dental appointments;
• notifying employees regularly about their personal absences;
• following up individual incidents to see if some assistance from management might reduce the likelihood of future absence, such as moving to a different shift;
• introducing flexible working hours; improving aspects of working conditions or job design.

Research findings suggest that absence is reduced and kept down more effectively by taking a positive attitude towards the reasons causing employees to be absent, rather than by relying solely on disciplinary action. Disciplinary action can be effective for short periods but the effect fades without constant reinforcement.

ACAS. The Advisory, Conciliation and Arbitration Service is a statutory body set up with the support of the government, employers and trade unions, but independent of them. Its purpose is to assist with a range of industrial relations and employment problems.

The main activities of ACAS are:

- arbitration and mediation, where ACAS appoints one or more people to resolve an issue with the consent of both parties to the dispute, who are not otherwise able to agree;
- advisory services on general matters of industrial relations;
- individual conciliation to seek voluntary settlement of issues involving alleged breaches of individual statutory rights.

The Head Office is at 11–12, St James's Square, London SW1Y 4LA (01 214 6000). There are regional offices in Glasgow, Newcastle-upon-Tyne, Leeds, Manchester, Birmingham, London, Bristol and Cardiff. An annual report is produced each spring and free booklets are available on various employment matters.

Action research, action learning. The aim of action research is not simply to collect data about a situation but also to improve the situation being studied. The argument is that the presence of the researcher is bound to have some impact, so this should be seen as an advantage rather than as a drawback. It is a method that has been extensively used by the Tavistock Institute of Human Relations. Although the process is one involving regular discussion between the researcher and the client organization, the client obviously always has the final decision about action to be taken.

A development of this is the action learning approach to MANAGEMENT DEVELOPMENT, where trainees learn to manage by working on projects provided by organizations having a genuine problem which currently needs an answer. Trainees each have one project, based in an organization other than their own. They are also members of a learning set of 10 or 12 trainees tackling similar projects. The learning set meets regularly for discussion and mutual support, so that the questioning insight of the individual trainee in charge of each problem to be solved is sharpened and developed by the questions of a dozen other people. All the learning is centred on the problem being analysed.

Alcoholism. Drinking alcohol does little harm to most people and its modest consumption releases tension and puts people socially at ease. Alcoholism, however, is the state of physical or psychological dependency on alcohol such that the individual cannot cope with the normal stresses and challenges of life without drinking. Alcoholism used to be a disease mainly of middle-aged men, but the proportion of women and adolescents who are addicted has increased sharply. Many of the women addicts are working women suffering from the stress of their dual roles. Those becoming addicted will benefit from the support and understanding of their working colleagues as well as the more direct assistance they will need from the family, family doctor, clergyman or counselling service. The most valuable contribution from working colleagues will be understanding and acceptance, so that the sufferer sees the problem as a disease that can be cured rather than as a disgrace which must be concealed at all costs. Some organizations have set up their own stress counselling services. Other sources of assistance are Alcoholics Anonymous, 11 Redcliffe Gardens, London SW1 9BG (01 352 9779), and the National Council on Alcoholism, 3 Grosvenor Crescent, London SW1X 7EE (01 235 4182). Both these organizations operate in all parts of the country.

Alienation. This describes the emotional state of those who feel estranged from the society of which they are a part. When people feel alienated from the working organization to which they belong, they may manifest this by apathy, aggression or blind obedience. Marx, who introduced the concept, attributed alienation from work to the division of labour and the capitalist system of property ownership. Other suggested explanations include job specialization, impersonal systems of organization, close supervisory or bureaucratic control and large organizational size.

Originally alienation was seen as a problem for managers because of the uncooperative behaviour it might induce in factory workers, but the work of Harry Braverman (1974) argues that it is an emotional state experienced by many administrative and managerial workers as well, with the uncooperative behaviours being less obvious, but no less serious.

Managers needing to overcome the problems of alienation ought to consider aspects of JOB DESIGN and MOTIVATION. In some

cases it may be more realistic simply to acknowledge the fact that some employees will remain alienated from their work at the same time as performing their duties effectively, just as high-powered executives can make an excellent job of the washing-up no matter how apathetic they feel about it.
H. Braverman, *Labour and Monopoly Capital: The Degradations of Work in the Twentieth Century* (New York: Monthly Review Press, 1974).

Application forms. The main advantage of these to the recruiters is that they organize the required information about a candidate in a way which suits the recruiter. They simplify short-listing, aid selection interviewing and become the basis of the employment record for the appointed candidate. In contrast, letters of application may omit vital details and organize the information in varied ways.

Most organizations now use application forms, although some ask for a letter of application as well, and others ask for a CURRICULUM VITAE. Ideally the form should be designed to suit the specific job for which applicants are being considered, so as to elicit the factors which will of prime importance in the selection and ensure that only the most appropriate candidates are called for interview. This is not often found in practice, although it is becoming more common where organizations are selecting for a *category* (like management trainee) knowing that there will be a large number of applicants. Where standard forms are to be used, there is certainly an advantage in having a number of different forms for use in appointing to the various vacancies.

Among the features of form design are:

• applicants must be identifiable and locatable so the information requested must include name, address, date of birth, telephone number, availability for interview;
• information about educational attainments to be provided must be specific;
• information about working experience should specify what is wanted (for example, posts held and/or skills acquired, dates of starting and finishing, position in hierarchy, nature of responsibilities);

- miscellaneous but vital items such as post applied for, ethnic origin (for later monitoring), the date and the applicant's signature;
- space: the 'boxes' must be big enough to fit in the information you are asking for and there must be empty space for short-listers and interviewers to make notes on the form, adjacent to the information provided by the applicant;
- length: the form must be long enough to be useful, but not long enough to deter the ideal applicant.

The folklore of applicants misunderstanding application forms is considerable. Aspects of misunderstanding we *know* to be true include the following:

Forenames: Mr
Nationality: Roman Catholic
Date of birth: I stand on the Fifth Amendment
Marital status: (a) Royal Navy
                      (b) Expecting
Sex: (a) Awaiting results
     (b) Seldom
     (c) If possible

See also WEIGHTED APPLICATION FORMS.

Appraisal. Also known as performance appraisal, this is the judgement of a person's working performance and potential, carried out with the objective of developing that performance. In some ways similar to the school report, it has various objectives:

- to assess training needs;
- to provide feedback to the employee on how someone else judges the working performance;
- to assess promotability;
- to provide a basis for developing the existing job;
- to provide information for managerial control of sub-ordinates' performance.

These are the most common objectives, although all five are seldom found in a single scheme. Sometimes the system is 'closed', so that the subordinate does not receive any feedback, except by inference, and the use of appraisal to provide managerial control information is rarely acknowledged. Individual schemes sometimes have other objectives, such as determining salary increases.

"Tell me, Smithers, if all the world's a stage, how come all the clowns are employed in this office?"

The main methods are form-filling and interviewing. Forms are used to standardize the questions to be asked about performance and to record the answers. This ensures that appraisers ask questions they would not otherwise think of, or would be diffident about putting. It also makes the appraisal accessible to others – like management development officers – who can take action beyond the scope of the appraiser (such as transfers, training or secondment). Interviewing is used both to obtain the answers to the questions on the form and to generate a discussion between the appraiser and the appraisee about the performance and its context.

Appraisal is most often carried out by the immediate superior, with some element of corroboration from the superior's superior. Less often it is carried out by an independent specialist.

Some appraisal schemes include self-assessment by the employee. Rare schemes include appraisal by subordinates of superiors. Despite its logic and superficial appeal, appraisal is seldom completely successful. It inevitably involves paperwork, which takes time to complete and introduces formality into the working relationship, neither of which are welcome to most managers. Action on appraisals is often not taken for the inescapable reasons of organizational life, such as shortage of resources or the non-availability of facilities, and this breeds cynicism. There is also a tendency to blandness, with appraisers giving everyone 'a good report' in order to avoid problems. Although the level of effectiveness is not high, the use of appraisal is increasing because of the strong belief that it *should* work and that an awareness of the problems helps to reduce their impact. Schemes are gradually being improved in order to cope with the weaknesses mentioned. Also, as G. K. Chesterton said, a thing worth doing is worth doing badly.

See also ASSESSMENT CENTRES, MANAGEMENT BY OBJECTIVES.

C. Fletcher and R. Williams, *Performance Appraisal and Career Development* (London: Hutchinson, 1985).

Aptitude tests. Where a job requires the possession of a specific inherent or acquired ability, it may be possible to test the level to which applicants possess that aptitude. Among the aptitudes for which reliable tests have been developed are spatial judgement, mechanical reasoning, manual dexterity, clerical skill, abstract reasoning, computer programming and language ability,

Tests are usually proprietary products and their validity needs to be checked before use. The British Psychological Society maintains a register of approved agencies.

See also INTELLIGENCE TESTS, PERSONALITY.

Agencies Offering Approved Courses in Psychological Testing (Leicester: *The British Psychological Society*, 1983).

Arbitration. When industrial disputes cannot be settled by voluntary agreement between the parties they may seek arbitration, whereby an external arbiter or panel resolves the matter for them. In nearly all cases arbitration is provided by ACAS, which deals with approximately 200 requests annually on

Sample questions from an aptitude test to test spatial judgement

Which of the four boxes on the right can be folded from the pattern shown on the left? The pattern shows the outside of the box.

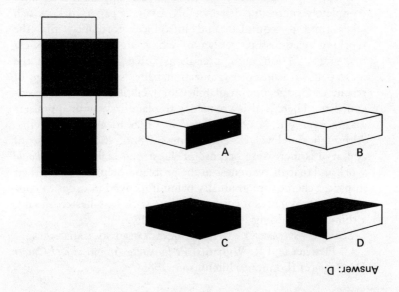

Answer: D.

matters ranging from major national pay claims to individual grievances. They may, where one party requests it and the other party consents, refer the matter to the Central Arbitration Committee (CAC) which sits as a tripartite body, consisting of a chairman and one representative from each side of industry. Such references are infrequent; in 1984 there were only seven.

As a means of settling disputes, arbitration has never enjoyed the same popularity in Britain as in the USA, where it can be legally binding on the parties.

Article 119 of the Treaty of Rome. As a member of the EEC, the UK is bound by Article 119 of the Treaty of Rome which lays down the principle of 'equal pay for equal work'. This phrase was expanded by EEC Directive 75/117 (the Equal Pay Directive) to mean 'for the same work or for work to which equal value is attributed'. UK legislation in the form of the Equal Pay Act provided for a woman to claim equal pay for work of equal value only where her employer had carried out a job evaluation study and rated her work equivalent to that of her male comparator. Infringement proceedings were therefore brought against the UK alleging that it was in breach of its Community obligations in failing to provide a remedy where no job evaluation study existed. As a result the EQUAL PAY (AMENDMENT) REGULATIONS 1983 (see also EQUAL VALUE) were passed.

Article 119 is directly enforceable in the UK and can be relied on by individuals to provide them on occasions with more extensive rights than they enjoy under UK legislation. Thus under the EQUAL PAY ACT 1970 and the SEX DISCRIMINATION ACT 1975 discriminatory provisions in relation to retirement are permitted (but see SEX DISCRIMINATION ACT 1986). However, in two cases taken to the European Court of Justice it was held that the discriminatory benefits in question could be regarded as 'pay', and hence the employers concerned had acted contrary to Article 119.

Assessment centres. A costly, but very effective, method of appraising potential is to use an assessment centre, with a number of candidates being assessed by a variety of means over several days. The objective is solely to determine whether or not a person is likely to to be successful in a position calling for qualities which have not previously been exercised in that person's career. Common applications of this method are for promotions of technical specialists to managment positions or where senior managers are to move into top management. Some organizations also use assessment centres for graduate selection.

These centres are more successful in assessing potential than other methods, mainly due to the variety of techniques which are used: PSYCHOLOGICAL TESTS, in-tray exercises, the use of GROUPS, BUSINESS GAMES and other simulations. A further advantage is that several assessors are used and they tend to assess different aspects of potential individually.

See also APPRAISAL.

Associated employers. Employers are associated if one is a company of which the other has control (that is, voting control), or if both are companies of which a third party has control. The concept has significance in several areas, including:

- where employees are transferred between associated employers, their CONTINUITY OF EMPLOYMENT is preserved;
- under equal pay legislation, applicants may compare themselves with employees working for an associated employer, provided common terms and conditions apply in both that establishment and their own;
- in determining whether the exemption for SMALL EMPLOYERS applies, the number of employees working for associated employers must be counted (except in the case of health and safety legislation);
- in cases of redundancy, potentially redundant employees may be made an offer of 'suitable alternative employment' by their employer or an associated employer. If they accept, or unreasonably refuse, they are not entitled to a redundancy payment (see REDUNDANCY).

Attitude surveys. Attitude surveys are systematic investigations of the attitudes held by a large number of people, where the attitudes (and the anticipated resultant behaviour) are likely to be important to the investigators. They are used to diagnose problems of organization and to assess the likely reaction of employees to specific management initiatives, as well as eliciting suggestions and demonstrating a concern about employees' opinions.

Beware of one aspect: when attitudes are surveyed expectations are raised, so that it is unwise to undertake a survey without being prepared to publish the results and take some action!

Automatically unfair dismissal. A DISMISSAL will be automatically unfair if the reason for it was:

- that the employee was a trade union member;
- that the employee was not a trade union member (but see CLOSED SHOP);
- that the employee was taking part in trade union activities at an appropriate time;

- PREGNANCY, or a reason connected with it;
- selection for REDUNDANCY contrary to an agreed or customary procedure unless there were special reasons justifying a departure from the procedure (or selection on grounds of the first three points above);
- a spent conviction (see REHABILITATION OF OFFENDERS ACT 1974);
- the transfer of an undertaking, or a reason connected with it (see TRANSFER OF UNDERTAKINGS (PROTECTION OF EMPLOYMENT) REGULATIONS 1981).

In respect of the first three points, no qualifying period of employment is required to bring a claim of unfair dismissal (and see also TRADE UNION MEMBERSHIP AND ACTIVITIES).

See also UNFAIR DISMISSAL.

B

Ballots. Legislators have favoured the idea of balloting union members to ensure that the membership concurs with decisions being taken on their behalf. There has been the underlying assumption that members will generally be less inclined to take industrial action than their officials, although there have been many instances where the membership has voted against agreements reached on their behalf. Union officials have been reluctant to extend balloting of the memberships as this much reduces the scope of negotiators in dealings with employers and makes the branch life of unions less important.

Currently there are two legal aspects of balloting; financial assistance in carrying out postal ballots and the need for closed shops to be verified by secret ballot.

The EMPLOYMENT ACT 1980 allows payments from government funds to unions by the CERTIFICATION OFFICER to meet the costs of postal ballots on such issues as the election of principal officers, calling or ending industrial action, accepting or rejecting an employer's offer on terms and conditions of employment, and amending union rules. Some unions affiliated to the TUC have accepted these payments, but most have not.

Under the EMPLOYMENT ACT 1982 a CLOSED SHOP agreement will count as approved only if it has been supported during the previous five years in a secret ballot either by 80 per cent or more of those affected by the agreement or by 85 per cent of those voting. In an approved closed shop it is a condition of employment that employees should be union members, and dismissal for failure to join, or for ceasing membership, is potentially fair. If the closed shop agreement is not approved, all employees will be entitled to normal remedies from a tribunal.

See also TRADE UNION ACT 1984.

Department of Employment, *Union Membership Rights and the Closed Shop* (London: HMSO, 1984); Department of Employment, *Union Secret Ballots* (London: HMSO, 1985).

Bargaining units. These form the basis for COLLECTIVE BARGAINING with trade unions within the organization. It is a group of employees, represented by a trade union official, with which the management negotiates some aspects of terms and conditions of employment. A preliminary step is for management to agree with unions what the boundaries of the bargaining units should be; what grouping of employees' interests is logical for the collective bargaining process. The main considerations are the characteristics of the work group itself: job skills, payment arrangements and general conditions of employment need to be broadly consistent between unit members to make constructive representation through a single channel feasible. Another consideration is the nature of union membership and the organization of management.

At times of technological and organizational change there can be frequent needs to redefine the boundaries between units. There has also been a tendency recently to move towards fewer bargaining units and the HARMONIZATION of terms and conditions of employment across a number of groups which previously had separate bargaining arrangements.

Blackleg. An employee who continues working when the bulk of employees have withdrawn their labour in furtherance of an industrial dispute is sometimes known as a blackleg. The term derives from identification with working miners during the nineteenth century, who had coal-blackened legs.

Blake's Grid. R. R. Blake is an American management expert who has devised a grid as a way of characterizing individual managers. It is a two-dimensional grid with one axis labelled 'concern for production' and the other 'concern for people'. There are nine points on each scale (1=low and 9=high) and five main management styles are identified according to their position on the grid:

● 1.1 shows a low concern for production as well as a low concern for people and is impoverished management;
● 9.2 is a high concern for production but a low concern for people and known as task management;
● 1.9 has the concerns reversed and is called country club management;
● 5.5 is middle-of-the-road management;
● 9.9 is high concern for both people and production.

It is often used in training courses as a means of people identifying their own style and working out how to modify their performance to move closer to the desired 9.9.

R. R. Blake and J. D. Mouton, *The Managerial Grid* (Houston, Texas: Gulf Publishing, 1978).

The Blake and Mouton managerial grid

(High) 9	1.9 MANAGEMENT Thoughtful attention to needs of people for satisfying relationships leads to a comfortable, friendly organization atmosphere and work tempo.						9.9 MANAGEMENT Work accomplishment is from committed people; interdependence through a 'common stake' in organization purpose leads to relationships of trust and respect.		
8									
7									
6			5.5 MANAGEMENT Adequate organization performance is possible through balancing the necessity to get out work with maintaining morale of people at a satisfactory level.						
Concern for people 5									
4									
3									
2	Exertion of minimum effort to get required work done is appropriate to sustain organization membership.					Efficiency in operations results from arranging conditions of work in such a way that human elements interfere to a minimum degree.			
(Low) 1	1.1 MANAGEMENT						9.1 MANAGEMENT		
	1 (Low)	2	3	4	5 Concern for production	6	7	8	9 (High)

Source: Blake and Mouton 1978, p. 11.

Breach of statutory duty. In conducting business an employer must comply with many statutory duties related to safety. These can include the Factories Act 1961, the Mines and Quarries Act 1954, the Construction (Lifting Operations) Regulations 1961 and many others. Breach of these regulations normally constitutes a criminal offence for which the employer may be fined. In addition, where employees are injured as a result of such a breach they may be able to sue the employer for 'breach of statutory duty'. If successful they will be awarded damages as compensation for injuries (but half of certain state benefits received are deducted from the award).

Certain statutory duties make employers 'strictly' liable, that is, they may be liable if a breach occurs even though they have done everything possible to prevent it. Others may oblige employers to follow a course of action 'so far as is reasonably practicable' so that in general no liability arises unless they are in some way at fault. In such cases overlapping claims of negligence and/or breach of statutory duty occur in practice.

See also COMMON LAW DUTY OF CARE, HEALTH AND SAFETY AT WORK ACT 1974).

Briefing groups. These are a method of using the formal structure of the organization to ensure regular face-to-face discussion between managers and their subordinates on matters of organization objectives and strategy. It is believed that this improves the integration of the organization, and the method is often described as team briefing in order to emphasize that aspect. The manager always briefs teams of subordinates rather than briefing individuals and then utilizes the 'cascade' principle, under which each manager briefs immediate subordinates, each of whom then holds separate briefings with their own subordinates, and so on.

Among the principles of team briefing are:

- collective briefing enriches the information exchange;
- cascading enables the initial message to be reinterpreted so as to be relevant to the needs of the listeners;
- meetings are regular and with a regular agenda;
- their purpose is briefing, not general issues or the airing of grievances.

Bureaucracy. The term is frequently used pejoratively to describe administrative inefficiency and delay, with a bureaucrat being seen as an unimaginative figure who shields incompetence behind a mass of rules and paperwork. Human beings are depersonalized because the maintenance of the administrative system becomes more important than the interests and personalities of the people who operate the system or who seek service from it.

Behind the popular distaste lies an important method of organization which is indispensable for the rational attainment of the goals of any organization. The German sociologist Max Weber identified the following characteristics:

- defined areas of duties for each role in an organization; a hierarchy of responsibility;
- appointments and promotions based on technical qualifications;
- a fixed salary paid according to rank;
- a separation of office from office holder so that there is no change in organization when a person leaves or is promoted.

Weber saw this as an ideal type of organization because it freed employees from nepotism and over-dependence on the whim of superiors at the same time as producing a disciplined and ethical mode of conduct, but more recent analysts have pointed out that the need to conform closely to rules leads people to sustain the system rather than serve the people who use it, as we saw in the opening paragraph.

The principles of bureaucracy remain the most common principles for managing organizations, especially those that are large and stable.

C. B. Handy, *Understanding Organizations,* 3rd edn (Harmondsworth: Penguin, 1985); M. Weber, *The Theory of Social and Economic Organisation* (New York: Free Press, 1947).

Business games. In order to find a method of management training that is participative and realistic, trainers frequently use games which replicate a business situation. The games provide teams with information on which a decision has to be based. The decision is then evaluated by comparison with decisions made by competing teams and a fresh set of data supplied which shows the effect on the imaginary business situation of the team's decision in relation to other team decisions. Then a second decision is made, followed by a third and so on. The most common game is one which asks teams to answer specified questions about expenditure in relation to resources, so that the evaluation of the decisions is quantifiable on the basis of parameters built in to the game by the designer and processed by computer.

The advantages of this form of training are that learners work on hard data rather than opinions, the results of their decisions are fed back to them and they are competing with other groups. The disadvantage is that they focus so completely on a single aspect of management: rational decision-making. The team that wins the game might not be able to replicate that success in real life.

Business schools. In the middle 1960s two British business schools were set up in an attempt to follow the American model of, for instance, Harvard, Stanford and Wharton (where complete university faculties are devoted to postgraduate education in business). Within 20 years of this initiative there were many other business schools in Britain, as well as departments of management and business studies with large numbers of both undergraduate and postgraduate students. In 1986 there were over 30 such schools in the university sector alone. In polytechnics and other institutions, under the aegis of the Council for National Academic Awards (CNAA), business studies is the largest generic area of study.

The main vehicle for study in business schools is the Master of Business Administration (MBA) degree, a graduate course which is mainly taught but usually has a small element of personal research. Doctoral programmes and shorter post-experience courses are also available. The business schools have been criticized by some employers for over-emphasizing aspects of company strategy and finance that are beyond the reach of most students when they return to employment. Some pressure has been exerted on business schools by other academics to become more self-financing and less dependent on general university funding.

C

Catering. Virtually every employing organization makes some catering provision for its employees, ranging from a single coin-operated drinks machine through to meals served on damask tablecloths by liveried footmen. The extremes of status differentiation have lessened in recent years, but in large organizations the question of where you eat frequently remains an indicator of your hierarchical position, with the pinnacle being a dining room used by only the most prestigious members.

Vending machines have been used increasingly to provide a service and to reduce the number of individual kettles and 'coffee swindles' that are otherwise maintained by small groups of employees to provide coffee two or three times a day. Machines can be purchased but are usually rented from a supplier who also services the machine by both mechanical maintenance and the regular replacement of supplies. The price charged for drinks is then negotiated between the supplier and the employer. An alternative arrangement is for the supplier simply to install the machine and also arrange the prices.

Contract caterers have grown steadily since the late 1960s, so that now over three-quarters of large organizations use contractors to provide a full in-house catering service to cover coffee breaks, snack service and meals. This devolves the responsibility for the operation to a supplier having all the advantages of professional expertise and economies of scale in purchasing, preparation and staffing. It also has the advantage that the contractor can be changed if the service proves unsatisfactory. The most common type of contract is for the contractor to employ staff and provide the service, presenting an account each month for the difference between income and expenditure. Catering is seldom provided on a break-even basis; usually it is subsidized to some extent.

Certification officer (CO). The role of the CO was created by the EMPLOYMENT PROTECTION ACT 1975, combining the former duties of the Chief Registrar of Friendly Societies and certain new functions. Of prime importance, perhaps, is the CO's task of maintaining a list of trade unions and employers' associations and granting certificates of independence (see INDEPENDENT TRADE UNION). Additionally the CO has a supervisory role over certain trade union matters, ensuring unions maintain proper accounts and submit annual returns, and overseeing their superannuation schemes. In the case of union mergers COs must see that unions comply with statutory balloting requirements, and under the TRADE UNION ACT 1984 they may hear complaints that statutory provisions in relation to ballots for the election of the principal executive committee have not been complied with. Where a union holds a secret ballot for a 'specified purpose' under the EMPLOYMENT ACT 1980, such as the calling or ending of a strike or the election of a member to a position in the union, the CO may reimburse the union for the expenditure incurred (see BALLOTS).

R. Lewis, *Labour Law in Britain* (Oxford: Basil Blackwell, 1986), ch. 10.

Change, organizational. In some ways the implementation of change is the essence of management; taking initiatives, creating precedents and bringing things into being. Often this is impeded by a feature of the organization, which is too slow or inflexible to adapt to a new situation, because people within the structure (always *other* people, of course) are reluctant to change the methods of working with which they are familiar, or where the procedures which they use are no longer suitable to new demands. The problem is exacerbated when necessary change is seen to be against the interests of some individuals or groups, who fear the loss of status, pay or resources in the very insecure world of most modern organizations.

One of the methods of implementing organizational change is restructuring, so that patterns of communication and accountability are altered. This often has no more effect than getting new people into more influential jobs, but a change from one organizational form, such as BUREAUCRACY, to another, such as MATRIX, can be more far-reaching. Another method is piloting, whereby changes are introduced in a small unit as a pilot for the eventual introduction of the changes elsewhere, so that potential problems can be identified and resolved before universal implementation. The likelihood of successful change is enhanced by employee participation in the process, on the principle that people will support that which they have helped to create. QUALITY CIRCLES are one of the best-known recent examples of this approach; ORGANIZATION DEVELOPMENT is another widely used method. Change is often facilitated by the use of a change agent, acting as a catalyst within the system, identifying the goals of change, developing the requisite strategy and assisting the forging of new working relationships. The change agent may be an external consultant, an internal consultant or an employee with a specific change-inducing mission, like an Equal Opportunities Officer.

T. Burns and G. M. Stalker, *The Management of Innovation* (London: Tavistock Press, 1961).

Check-off. The term check-off is used when the employer deducts union subscriptions at source from wages and salaries and then makes a monthly payment to the appropriate union. This overcomes the problem of the union member who falls into arrears with subscriptions and saves the time which might otherwise be spent by union stewards collecting weekly dues. The member will sign a consent form for the deductions to be made and can withdraw that consent at any time.

Closed shop. One of the most controversial features of British industrial life, the closed shop is a place of work where a job can only be obtained and retained if a prospective employee is a member of a specified trade union and retains membership of that union. The union membership is a condition of employment, so that the employer may dismiss an employee whose union membership lapses and decline to recruit an employee who does not have, or obtain, the required membership. Controversy about the closed shop centres on the two questions of individual freedom and the ability of the management to manage. Critics claim that the union membership requirement infringes the rights of individuals and denies employers necessary freedom of action in deploying their personnel. Supporters claim that the closed shop is the most effective way of ensuring employee solidarity in the face of potential exploitation by employers and that it improves management/employee communication and shop-floor discipline.

Since 1971 there have been a series of legal moves to limit the number and scope of closed shops, or UNION MEMBERSHIP

AGREEMENTS (UMAs), and it is now a much less significant aspect of the industrial scene than it was in the early 1970s, when it was estimated that one worker in six was a member of a closed shop.

As a broad generalization, dismissal for non-membership of the union where a UMA is in force will be fair. However, a number of qualifications have been added to this principle with the result that dismissal for non-membership will now be automatically unfair under S58(3)–(8) of the EMPLOYMENT PROTECTION (CONSOLIDATION)ACT 1978 where:

- the employee genuinely objects on grounds of conscience, or other deeply held personal conviction, to being a trade union member or a member of a particular trade union (it is for a tribunal to decide whether a particular objection satisfies this requirement, but it would seem that mere disagreement with a union's policies may be sufficient, as well as more fundamental objections);
- the employee commenced employment before the UMA was entered into and has not been a union member since that time;
- the UMA was entered into after 14 August 1980 and has not been approved by the appropriate ballot (see BALLOTS);
- a UMA (as in the preceding point) has been approved by the appropriate ballot, but the employee has not been a union member since the date of the ballot;
- the employee has been excluded or expelled from the union and that action has either been held to be unreasonable under S4 of the EMPLOYMENT ACT 1980, or proceedings under that section are still pending;
- the employee is a member of a professional body with a written code of conduct which prevents him or her from taking industrial action.

Dismissals for non-membership which are held to be automatically unfair may attract very large awards of COMPENSATION, for which the union may be partially or totally liable (see JOINDER).

Codes of practice. Codes of Practice give practical guidance on what is regarded as good industrial relations practice. They also help to clarify the meaning of often complex pieces of legislation and show how they may be implemented. Codes have been issued:

1 by ACAS, namely:
- Disciplinary Practice and Procedure (1977)
- Disclosure of Information for Collective Bargaining Purposes (1977)
- Time Off for Trade Union Duties and Activities (1977)

2 by the Secretary of State for Employment, namely:
- Closed Shop (1983)
- Picketing (1980)

3 by the COMMISSION FOR RACIAL EQUALITY (1983)

4 by the EQUAL OPPORTUNITIES COMMISSION (1985)

5 by the Health and Safety Commision, namely:
- Safety Representatives and Safety Committees (1978)
- Time Off for training of Safety Representatives (1978)

6 under the Industrial Relations Act 1972. See the Industrial Relations Code of Practice (1972).

Codes do not have the force of law, so that breach of a Code is not itself unlawful. However, the fact that a Code has not been observed can be used in evidence in any subsequent legal proceedings to which it is relevant (like the Highway Code). Thus the fact that an employee has been dismissed in breach of the disciplinary Code may be relied on to show that the employer acted unreasonably (see UNFAIR DISMISSAL). Similarly in criminal proceedings brought under the HEALTH AND SAFETY AT WORK ACT 1974 a failure to observe a Code will be prima facie evidence that the defendant contravened the Act, unless that person can show that he or she carried out his or her obligations in some other equally satisfactory manner.

See also CLOSED SHOP, COLLECTIVE BARGAINING, HEALTH AND SAFETY, SAFETY COMMITTEES AND SAFETY REPRESENTATIVES, TIME OFF.

Cognitive dissonance. Where a person has attitudes or beliefs that are not consistent with each other, or not consistent with behaviour, then there is a dissonance between that person's cognitions: the processes by which knowledge and reasoning are acquired. The problems in working life arising from cognitive dissonance are many, mainly where action that is required from someone is not produced because he or she lacks the conviction to produce the behaviour. For example, people may fail to implement new procedures fully because their anxieties or suspicions about the innovation have not been fully resolved, or a manager may be unable to adopt a new style of leadership when moved to a job where a different style is required.

The middle-aged businessman who responded to a knock on his hotel door in a strange city illustrates the problem neatly. Outside stood the sort of beautiful girl who peoples the wildest fantasies of ageing males. She indicated that she would like to come in and help him relax after a hard day. After a lifetime of careful study he *knew* that such creatures never, ever wanted to do that with *him*. He had the cognitive dissonance block, unable to understand what he was being told, unable to believe it, and lacking the conviction to produce the desired behaviour.

Collective agreements. Collective agreements are those made between an employer or group of employers and a group of workers, usually STAFF ASSOCIATIONS or a TRADE UNION. The agreements are entered into by the parties in order to regulate various aspects of the working relationship between them. These are:

● terms and conditions of employment, such as hours, pay and holidays;
● procedural arrangements for dealing with disagreements, such as GRIEVANCE and DISPUTES arrangements and DISCIPLINARY PROCEDURES;
● mutual undertakings in relation to the operation of the relationship, such as agreeing to defer either LOCK-OUT or INDUSTRIAL ACTION until procedures have been exhausted.

Most collective agreements are presumed not to be legally enforceable, notably those covering the matters listed in S29 of the Trade Union and Labour Relations Act 1974 (see GOLDEN FORMULA). If, however, they are incorporated into individual contracts of employment, they will then be legally enforceable by the employer and employee in question. Express incorporation may take place in a statement to that effect in the contract itself, or in the written statement of particulars (see CONTRACT, WRITTEN PARTICULARS OF). The courts are also willing to imply incorporation where, for instance, there has been universal observance of a collective agreement in the workplace. Where such incorporation has taken place, unilateral termination of the collective agreement by the employer may not affect an individual employee's entitlement under the agreement to, for example, a bonus scheme. Problems may also arise where there is inconsistency between national and local collective agreements. Some terms of collective agreements are not apropriate for incorporation, notably those which are of a 'collective nature' such as redundancy procedures or union recognition.

Collective agreements are the product of COLLECTIVE BARGAINING.

Collective bargaining. This became the cornerstone of British industrial relations in the middle of the twentieth century, although its origins can be traced back to workplace bargaining at the end of the eighteenth century, to district bargaining in the ninteenth and national bargaining by the 1920s. The term was originally coined by Beatrice Webb to cover negotiations in which employees do not negotiate individually with the employer, but collectively through representatives. The formal structure is in COLLECTIVE AGREEMENTS, but the process influences all aspects of the employer/employee relationship.

The main features of British collective bargaining have been:

- an emphasis on 'voluntarism', with the parties settling their own affairs and having minimal recourse to a third party for, say, ARBITRATION;
- it has been a method of job regulation preferred to external arrangements, such as state determination of wages;
- a preference for procedural rules rather than substantive rules in agreements, with much more emphasis on how matters shall be resolved than on specifying employee rights and similar issues;
- minimal legal regulation.

Although championed by most employers, as well as by the trade union movement, the institution of collective bargaining began to crumble by the end of the 1970s as a result of government attitudes and public opinion becoming increasingly disenchanted by what was seen as the inefficiency and irrelevance of much collective bargaining. There has been increasing legal intervention and constraint on the process, and considerable erosion of the traditional areas of strong collective bargaining because of unemployment and technological change.

Legal intervention has also contributed to the erosion. Recognition rights, the Fair Wages Resolution of 1946 and Schedule 11 of the EMPLOYMENT PROTECTION ACT 1975, relating to low pay, have all been repealed. The only remaining duties on employers relate to disclosure of information for purposes of collective bargaining and consultation provisions in the areas of proposed redundancies, transfers of undertakings and health and safety (see CONSULTATION; HEALTH AND SAFETY AT WORK ACT 1974). However, the individual employment rights now to be found in the EMPLOYMENT PROTECTION (CONSOLIDATION) ACT 1978, whilst encroaching on areas traditionally covered by voluntary agreements, also protect individual trade union rights and activities. Employees are entitled not to be deterred from, or penalized or dismissed for, being union members or taking part in union activities. Union members and officials have related rights to TIME OFF for such activities (see TRADE UNION DUTIES/ACTIVITIES). Furthermore the provisions, such as those governing time off, guarantee payments and maternity rights, are perceived to be a 'floor' of rights, which can be built upon, but not detracted from, by collective bargaining.

Commission for racial equality (CRE). This body, established under the RACE RELATIONS ACT 1976, is similarly composed (and has similar functions to) the EQUAL OPPORTUNITIES COMMISSION. Its Code of Practice for the Elimination of Racial Discrimination and the Promotion of Equality of Opportunity in Employment came into force on 1 April 1984 (see CODES OF PRACTICE). It has placed greater emphasis on formal investigations than has the Equal Opportunities Commission, having started just under 50 in nine years.

The address of the CRE is Elliot House, 10–12 Allington Street, London SW1E 5EH (01 828 7022), and Maybrook House (Manchester Regional Office), 5th Floor, 48 Blackfriars Street, Manchester M3 2EG (061 831 7782).

Common law. This term is used to describe that body of law recorded in law reports which derives from decisions of judges in the higher courts, as opposed to the various forms of legislation. It is founded on the doctrine of precedent, which means that a judge in a later case will apply similar principles to those established in an earlier case, where similar facts are in issue. Legislation always takes precedence over common law.

In the employment field areas covered by common law include the question as to whether an employed person is an EMPLOYEE or independent contractor (see CONTRACT FOR SERVICES/INDEPENDENT CONTRACTOR), the torts (civil wrongs) in respect of which IMMUNITY is granted when taking lawful INDUSTRIAL ACTION, and IMPLIED TERMS in contracts of employment. An important aspect of the latter concerns the employer's duty to take reasonable care for the safety of employees (see COMMON LAW DUTY OF CARE).

Common law duty of care. At COMMON LAW a term is implied into every contract of employment that the employer will take reasonable care for the safety of employees. The duty is conventionally divided into three aspects:

- provision of competent fellow-staff;
- provision of adequate plant and machinery (includes maintenance and testing of tools and equipment, and the state of the premises themselves);
- provision of a safe system of working (including the lifting of heavy loads, handling and use of dangerous materials, instruction and supervision of employees).

The duty is merely to take 'reasonable care' and is therefore not broken unless the employer is at fault. There may thus be no breach where, for example, current knowledge does not indicate that a particular practice carries a risk of industrial disease. Similarly employees may slip or otherwise injure themselves in circumstances where the employer has taken all reasonable precautions to prevent such occurrences. The duty is owed to employees individually so that where, for example, an employee has a known susceptibility to disease, greater precautions would be expected.

Three possible consequences flow from a breach of the employer's obligation. First, if the breach is serious, the employee may resign and claim CONSTRUCTIVE DISMISSAL. Second, where an employee is injured as a result of the breach he may sue the employer in the tort of negligence and claim damages (an employee who is guilty of 'contributory negligence' will have the damages reduced proportionately). To ensure that employers can pay the damages, the Employer's Liability (Compulsory Insurance) Act 1969 obliges employers to be insured against liability for injury or disease sustained by employees in the course of their employment. Third, the employer may also be in BREACH OF STATUTORY DUTY.

Employers cannot delegate this duty to others. Additionally, they may be 'vicariously' liable for the wrong-doing of an employee who in the course of employment negligently injures another.

Communications. Communications is a generic term used in management to include not only the specific transmission of messages and information which the term initially suggests, but also working relationships, trust and understanding. Frequently problems of mismanagement are described as failures of communication. *Organizational communication* is the flow of

"I have to be frank with you. Promotion prospects are terrible."

information through the organization structure, both formal and informal, via media such as the organization chart, procedures and drills, reports, written messages, electronic mail and word of mouth. *Interpersonal communication* describes the one-to-one or small group discussions in which managers spend most of their time. Communication is not limited to sending messages: the process is only complete when the message is received and understood.

At the Battle of Balaclava in 1854 the British Commander sent an order to his cavalry: 'Advance and take advantage of any opportunity to recover the heights. You will be supported by infantry which have been ordered to advance on two fronts.' In transmission the order was distorted, so that the last sentence read: 'You will be supported by infantry which have been ordered. Advance on two fronts.' The result of the message not being properly received and understood was the infamous Charge of the Light Brigade.

Organizational communication is made more accurate if a two-way feature is incorporated into processes, such as BRIEFING GROUPS, so that it is possible for both transmitters and receivers of messages to check the accuracy of the information transfer. Frequently, however, the need for speed in disseminating information overrides the two-way feature, with the inevitable misunderstandings, queries and disbelief which unilateralism involves. Among the problems that managers have to contend with are:

- distortion through too many links in a communications chain;
- overload, particularly with written material, so that people will not read all the material provided but seek summaries instead;
- the expectations that people have will lead them to hear what they expect to hear rather than what is intended.

This is exacerbated by such difficulties as COGNITIVE DISSONANCE and the HALO EFFECT. Although frequently distrusted by managers, the GRAPEVINE is an important feature of organizational communication.

Interpersonal communication is made effective by an individual being skilled in interactive behaviours. The person skilled at interaction is likely to have:

- social poise, being at ease in a variety of social situations;
- perceptual sensitivity so that signals from the other person are noticed and accurately interpreted;
- good timing, so that the exchanges are smoothly coordinated;
- 'rewardingness', so that the other person will both respond to and seek the rewards that the skilled communicator can provide.

An apocryphal example of communications failure is of Napoleon in battle in the Middle East. When asked what should be done with 1,200 Turkish prisoners, he was suddenly seized with a fit of coughing and said *'Ma sacré toux!'* ('My damned cough'.) This was understood as *'Massacrez tous!'* ('Massacre them all') and all were executed.

Community Law. UK membership of the EEC in 1972 meant the incorporation of Community Law into its legal system. This was effected by the European Communities Act 1972, as a result of which certain treaties and secondary legislation became part of UK law. In addition, various directives are issued from time to time; these are addressed to member states which are then obliged to implement the directives in their own systems, amending legislation if necessary, to accord with the directive. Thus the enactment of the TRANSFER OF UNDERTAKINGS (PROTECTION OF EMPLOYMENT) REGULATIONS 1981 was a result of the Transfer of Undertakings Directive; similarly the provisions in Part IV of the EMPLOYMENT PROTECTION ACT 1975 on redundancy consultation was the response to the Collective Redundancies Directive (see CONSULTATION). A member state which is not fulfilling its Community obligations may ultimately be faced with infringement proceedings in the European Court of Justice.

Individuals who wish to rely on rights given by Community Law may only bring proceedings in national courts where such Community Law is directly effective. It has, for example, been decided that the Equal Treatment Directive has direct effect where an individual brings an action against the state, but not against another individual. Thus a female employee in the public sector was permitted to claim that the application to her of a discriminatory retirement age was unlawful under the Directive even though permitted by UK legislation (see also ARTICLE 119 OF THE TREATY OF ROME and SEX DISCRIMINATION ACT 1986). Even where Community Law is not directly enforceable, a UK court may be asked to construe its own legislation so as to be in accordance, where possible, with Community Law.

Compensation. An unfairly dismissed employee who is neither reinstated nor re-engaged must be awarded compensation under two heads:

1 the *basic award* (S73 of the EMPLOYMENT PROTECTION (CONSOLIDATION) ACT 1978). This is calculated in relation to the employee's weekly gross pay (up to a maximum of £158 in 1987; these figures are reviewed annually) and number of years' employment (up to a maximum of 20 years), that is:

- years below the age of 22 – half a week's pay;
- years between the ages of 22 and 40 – one week's pay;
- years between the age of 41 and 65 (there are tapering provisions in the sixty-fifth year) – one-and-a-half weeks' pay.

The basic award can be reduced by reason of:

- *the employee's contribution to his or her own dismissal;
- any redundancy payment;
- unreasonably refusing an offer of reinstatement;
- conduct not accounted for by *(for example, conduct prior to the dismissal which only comes to light after it).

2 the *compensatory award* (S74 of the EMPLOYMENT PROTECTION (CONSOLIDATION) ACT 1978). This is calculated on the basis of what is just and equitable to compensate the employee for financial loss attributable to the unfair dismissal. It is awarded under various headings:

- loss of net wages to the date of the hearing;
- estimated future loss of net earnings (but the employee must take reasonable steps to mitigate that loss);
- loss of fringe benefits, for example, a company car or subsidised housing;
- loss of statutory protection, for example, an employee must build up two years' service before unfair dismissal or

redundancy protection is restored – a nominal sum of £100 to £150 is usually awarded;
- loss of pension rights;
- expenses in looking for a new job;
- manner of dismissal – a sum may only be awarded if the manner of dismissal makes the employee less acceptable to potential employers.

The compensatory award may be reduced by reason of:

- the employee's contribution to his or her own dismissal;
- a redundancy payment greater than the basic award.

There is a maximum compensatory award, which was £8,500 in 1987.

If an employer fails to comply with an order for reinstatement or re-engagement, the employee is entitled to an *additional award* of between 13 and 26 weeks' pay (between 26 and 52 if the dismissal is on grounds of sex or race) unless the employer proves it was not practicable to comply with the order.

Where the dismissal is on grounds of union membership, or non-membership, or activities, very high levels of compensation may be awarded, consisting of:

1 a *minimum* basic award (of £2,300 in 1987);
2 a compensatory award;
3 a *special award* where the employee requests reinstatement or re-engagement:

- if the tribunal does not grant the application the amount is one week's pay×104 or £11,500 (in 1987) whichever is the greater (maximum £23,000), or,
- if the tribunal grants the application but the employer does not comply with the order, the amount is one week's pay×156 or £17,250, whichever is the greater (unless it is impracticable to comply).

Interim relief is available in cases of dismissal for trade union reasons where employees claim to a tribunal not more than

---

Calculation of compensation: examples

X commences work for Y Ltd at the age of 30 and is unfairly dismissed at the age of 45, earning £120 p.w. X is entitled to:

Basic award
  1 week's pay × 10 (age 30–40) = £1,200
  1½ week's pay ×   5 (age 41–5) = £ 900
                        _____
                        = £2,100

+ *Compensatory award* (maximum £8,500)

A commences work for B Ltd at the age of 19 and is unfairly dismissed at the age of 26, earning £200 p.w. Only pay up to £158 p.w. can be claimed, therefore A is entitled to:

Basic award
½ week's pay × 2 (age 19–21) = £158
  1 week's pay × 5 (age 22–6) = £790
                      _____
                      = £948

+ *Compensatory award*

M commences work for P Ltd at the age of 22 and is unfairly dismissed at the age of 37, earning £150 per week, for not being a union member. He asks for reinstatement, but this is not granted. M is entitled to:

Basic award
1 week's pay × 15 (age 22–37) = £2,250

But this is less than the statutory minimum of £2,300, so M is entitled to the latter sum.

+ *Compensatory award*

+ *Special award*

1 week's pay × 104 = £15,600

---

seven days after the EFFECTIVE DATE OF TERMINATION: the tribunal can order reinstatement or re-engagement pending the hearing, or suspend on full pay if the employer refuses.

See also JOINDER, REINSTATEMENT, RE-ENGAGEMENT.

Computer based training (CBT). Training is an area in which the computer has made little penetration, yet there is considerable scope for developing training approaches that put learning effectively in the hands of the trainee instead of in the mind of the trainer. CBT is an approach which basically packages units for training so that trainees can run the programmes at their own speed and in their own locations. If there is a change in some aspect of legislation which has to be understood by a hundred managers within a single week, and they are scattered in all parts of the country, a single computer programme can be available to each of their computer terminals. The programme can be updated as required. The initial costs can by very high, for the hardware as well as for the software and expertise, to say nothing of the many false starts that always seem to be involved. The benefits can be considerable, as it is not necessary to bring people together and the trainee's understanding develops only at a personally suitable pace.

Q. Whitlock and C. Dean, *Handbook of Computer Based Training* (London: Kogan Page, 1983).

Conciliation. Conciliation in industrial relations is an attempt by an independent outsider to enable two disputing parties to find a solution to their disagreement. It is the 'C' in ACAS and virtually all conciliation is undertaken through that agency, which receives some 1,500 requests for collective conciliation and 40,000 requests for individual conciliation annually. The majority of individual conciliation requests relate to issues of alleged UNFAIR DISMISSAL, with others relating to equality of opportunity and disputes about employment protection. The origins of this service lie in the Conciliation Act of 1896, and the responsibility was long held by the Minister of Labour or Secretary of State for Employment until the growing significance of union organizaion in the public sector of employment made a move to an independent statutory body necessary.

Individual conciliation is by a single conciliator.

See also ACAS.

Confederation of British Industry (CBI). Established in 1965 by an amalgamation of three previous bodies, the CBI has in membership most of the larger private sector employers as well as the main nationalized industries. It seeks to represent the views of industrial management in a number of ways, including economic, labour, social and legal issues. Its representative voice is heard as a contrast to that of the TRADES UNION CONGRESS by government ministers, and both bodies are strongly represented at meetings of the National Economic Development Council. The CBI has a national secretariat, as well as standing committees and 13 regional councils to coordinate its affairs in different parts of the country. There is a national conference each year.

Confidential information. The courts will imply into a contract of employment an undertaking that an employee will not disclose an employer's trade secrets or misuse confidential information acquired as a result of that employment, regardless of the absence of any contractual stipulation. Lists of customers or their requirements, details of manufacturers and suppliers, prices, designs, the construction of a particular machine, and manufacturing processes are all potentially confidential. The dismissal of an employee who breaches this duty is likely to be fair (see UNFAIR DISMISSAL). It may be that the duty of non-disclosure continues to some extent after employment has ceased, but an employer who wishes to restrain an ex-employee is better advised to do so by means of an express RESTRAINT CLAUSE in the employee's contract of employment. However, the employer may not restrain employees from using information which has become part of their own skills and 'know-how' acquired during employment. The distinction between such knowledge and specific trade secrets which may lawfully be protected is not always clear. Where a lawful restraint clause is breached, the employer may seek an INJUNCTION and/or damages, which can sometimes extend not only to the ex-employee but also to the new employer who may be benefiting from the information.

An employee may always disclose information, whether confidential or not, which reveals 'misconduct' (such as crimes or other unlawful acts) on the part of the employer. However, it must be revealed only to someone having a 'proper interest' in it, and this will rarely include the press.

Conflict. Conflict is an divergence of interests between groups or individuals, or lack of adjustment between the individual or group, on the one hand and the job requirements on the other. It is distinct from competition, which is a situation in which two people or groups are directing their attention towards a goal they both seek. In conflict they are directing their attention towards each other rather than the goal, so that defeating the opponent may be more important than reaching the goal.

Although conflict in and around the workplace can be destructive, as in strikes, demarcation disputes and high absenteeism, it is not always dysfunctional as a degree of conflict is both the cause and effect of change, and the idea of 'constructive conflict' has become increasingly popular in management thinking. There is a useful distinction between conflict which is 'organized' and conflict which is 'unorganized' (as opposed to disorganized), as organized conflict is usually associated with high morale and is expressed through vigorous use of recognized procedures, so that issues are identified, debated and dealt with, often through representatives. Un-organized conflict is haphazard and personal, usually manifested in vague grumbling and negative behaviours which lead to low morale and a poor level of conflict resolution.

A management, and individual managers, both need to have strategies for dealing with conflict. Among those that have been identified are:

- avoidance – behaving as if opposing opinions did not exist and not providing any apparatus, such as procedures, for their expression;
- smoothing – using honeyed words to convince people that their opposing views are appreciated but ill-founded;
- forcing – attempting to stamp out opposing views;
- compromise – splitting the difference between two opposed points of view and making that the accepted solution;
- confrontation – facing up to the issue which divides the parties and trying to work out a settlement which is better for both parties than simple compromise.

C. B. Handy, *Understanding Organizations,* 3rd edn (Harmondsworth: Penguin, 1985), ch. 8.

Constructive dismissal. An employee who resigns because of some conduct on the part of the employer which entitles that employee to end the contract of employment will be treated as having been 'constructively' dismissed. In order to determine whether the employer has been guilty of such conduct it must be asked whether the employer has committed some significant breach of the employee's contract. A trifling breach is not sufficient; it must be something which goes to the root of the contract or amounts to a 'repudiation' of it.

In many cases the breach will be of an *express* term of the contract: for example, where an employee is demoted, or wages are cut unilaterally, or where management attempts to vary the nature of the job. However, tribunals are also willing to find a constructive dismissal where IMPLIED TERMS are involved. Thus a company's failure to investigate an employee's complaint about protective eyewear may amount to a fundamental breach of the employer's implied duty to take reasonable care for the safety of his or her employees. There may be a breach of the implied obligation not to destroy the relationship of mutual trust and confidence if an employer continually and perhaps unjustifiably criticizes an employee's performance without explanation of the criticisms. It has even been held that one could imply a term not to treat an employee 'capriciously, arbitrarily or inequitably'. This is clearly a difficult area for management as the boundaries of such implied terms are by no means sharply defined.

Conduct amounting to constructive dismissal may arise out of one incident, or as a series of events over a period of time where the employee finally feels that 'this is the last straw'. SEXUAL HARASSMENT has been given as an example of the latter. Employees who wish to claim constructive dismissal must act promptly on the employer's breach, and indicate why they are leaving. If they delay, the tribunal may decide they have 'affirmed' the contract: that is, that they have waived the breach by the employer, unless they continually protest about the situation. A restaurant manager who was demoted to waiter but who worked for one day in the new position was precluded from claiming constructive dismissal on this basis.

A finding of constructive dismissal is *not* a finding of UNFAIR DISMISSAL; the employee merely proves he or she has been dismissed. It is always open to the employer to show potentially FAIR REASONS FOR DISMISSAL in the usual way; for example, that the company was forced to vary the employee's contractual terms and conditions following a reorganization, or in the interests of efficiency or advancing technology, and that this amounted to 'some other substantial reason of a kind to justify dismissal'.

Consultants. Management consultants are being used more and more in the employment field, with over 1,000 operating in 1986. They are used mainly as a source of expertise and independent opinion, but can also provide a short-term input of manpower for a project with a limited life. They work mainly in the fields of training, recruitment and selection, management development, computer applications and job evaluation. Consultant charges in 1986 ranged between £200 and £400 per consultant day, so it can be cheaper to employ a consultant for a month than to employ someone full-time and permanently. The costs can, however, mount without careful attention. This is not to suggest that all consultants are pirates who will milk the client ruthlessly, but the poorly specified assignment can take much longer to complete. The irony is that consultants' initiatives usually need internal expertise for effective implementation, so that the employer who hires a consultant due to a lack of internal expertise can get into difficulties.

Problems which can go *out* to the consultant, like executive search or sending someone on a specialized training course, are much easier to control than those which require the consultant to come *into* the organization, like ORGANIZATION DEVELOPMENT or communications exercises.

A suggested approach to using consultants is the five steps shown below.

• Describe the problem. Thinking an issue through may make you realize that what needs to be done is not what is immediately apparent. If the Marketing Manager leaves abruptly your first reaction (get a consultant to find us a replacement) may change to a different solution (promote X) after describing to yourself exactly what the problem is.
• Formulate an approach. Roughly, what do you think you should do? If you have decided to promote X, you may also have decided that you have problems with succession planning or pay policy.

- Decide how you could do it in-house. If you decide against using consultants, consider how you would deal with the problem, what it would cost, how long it would take and what would be the repercussions.
- Find out how it could be done by consultants. If you now approach two or three consultants, they will bid for the business on the basis of your first two steps. If these have been done correctly you should get bids that you can compare. The main questions for the consultant are how would it be done, how much would it cost and how long would it take?
- Decide between the options. You now have the opportunity to compare relative costs, times and outputs. If one of the consultants can produce the best outcome, have you the resources to implement it? If you can save £5,000 by relying on your own staff and time, will the outcome meet the demands you have set?

Names of consultants are available on most managers' grapevines or from the trade association. The address of the Management Consultants' Association is 23 Cromwell Place, London SW7 2LG (01 584 7283).

Consultation. Consultation with employees over issues which affect them is regarded in law as good industrial relations practice. It may therefore be important in unfair dismissal cases in considering the reasonableness of the employer's actions. An employer who contemplates dismissing an employee because that person is incapable of performing the job through ill-health would normally be expected to consult the employee regarding the nature of the illness and the employee's future prospects. Repeated short absences may, however, be more appropriately dealt with as a matter of discipline and the 'warnings' procedure used (see WARNINGS). In situations of impending REDUNDANCY, the 1972 Industrial Relations Code of Practice (see CODES OF PRACTICE) recommends consultation over issues of possible voluntary redundancy schemes, alternative employment, and so on. A finding of unfair dismissal will often result where an employer makes employees redundant without consultation or warning (see also WARNINGS). However, tribunals sometimes hold such dismissals to be fair where they are persuaded that consultation would have made no difference to the final outcome. Alternatively they may find the dismissals unfair but give little COMPENSATION.

The EMPLOYMENT PROTECTION ACT 1975 placed a statutory duty on an employer to consult with recognized independent trade unions before announcing individual redundancies, where the employees whose redundancy is contemplated belong to the category of employee for which the union is recognized. This duty cannot be avoided if those to be made redundant are volunteers, or if they are not union members. The duty is to 'consult' genuinely with officials of the union, which in this context means the employer must:

• disclose certain information in writing (reasons for dismissal, employees affected, proposed selection method, application of any agreed redundancy procedure, and so on);
• consider any representations made by union representatives;
• give reasons if rejecting any of the representations.

Consultation should begin at the earliest opportunity and in particular:

• where 100 or more employees are to be made redundant at one establishment within a period of 90 days or less, at least 90 days before the first of the dismissals;
• where ten or more are to be made redundant within 30 days or less, at least 30 days before the first of the dismissals.

(Notification must also be given to the Secretary of State at these times.) The important question of what is an 'establishment' is decided by tribunals as a matter of common sense. Thus a chain of shops may be a single establishment; where, however, there is considerable autonomy in separate parts of an organization, each may be a separate establishment.

Where an employer fails to carry out these statutory obligations, the union (*not* individuals) may seek a PROTECTIVE AWARD from an industrial tribunal. However, employers who prove there were 'special circumstances' making it impracticable for them to comply need only take such steps as are 'reasonably practicable in the circumstances'. The meaning of 'special circumstances' is for a tribunal to determine, but it generally connotes some unexpected incident like loss of a key order. Insolvency on its own is not sufficient.

There is a similar duty to consult under the TRANSFER OF UNDERTAKINGS (PROTECTION OF EMPLOYMENT) REGULATIONS 1971 when a business is transferred. Either employer (transferor or transferee) must give certain information to the union representative:

- the fact, time and reasons for the transfer;
- the legal, economic and social implications for affected employees;
- any measures expected to be taken in respect of affected employees;
- if he or she is the transferor, measures he or she envisages the transferee will be taking.

This information must be given long enough before the transfer to enable consultation to take place, though no specific time limits are given. Consultation involves considering union representations and replying to them, giving reasons for any rejections, and is required when employers envisage that they will be 'taking measures' (not defined) in relation to employees affected by the transfer. As with redundancy consultation, failure to comply entitles the union to complain to a tribunal, who will award compensation unless a 'special circumstances' defence is raised successfully. The maximum compensation, however, is only two weeks' pay.

See also HEALTH AND SAFETY AT WORK ACT 1974.

Continuity of employment. Most employment protection rights extend only to an EMPLOYEE who has worked for an employer for a certain length of time. Additionally, the length of the period of continuous employment will often affect the compensation awarded for breach of those rights. Continuity of employment is governed by the complex provisions of Schedule 13 of the EMPLOYMENT PROTECTION (CONSOLIDATION) ACT 1978 and involves two questions: first, whether a particular week counts towards continuity, and second, whether continuity is broken by a particular event.

In order for a week to count it must normally be one in which the employee is employed for 16 hours per week or more, or, though employed for less than this number of hours, the employee is governed by a contract normally involving work for 16 hours or more: for example, a week when he or she is on holiday. A week which does not count would generally break continuity. However, the Schedule does allow for a temporary reduction in contractual hours: furthermore, individuals who have worked 8–16 hours per week for at least five years are treated as if working for 16 hours.

By virtue of Schedule 13, para. 9, certain weeks count even though *no contract* is in existence. This may occur where:

- the employee is off sick (maximum 26 weeks);
- the employee is absent because of a temporary cessation of work (a teacher employed on successive academic year contracts relied on this provision to link her contracts by counting the weeks of midsummer holiday);
- by arrangement or custom the employee is regarded as continuing in employment though absent from work (for instance, when seconded to another company);
- the employee is absent by reason of pregnancy (a maximum of 26 weeks is permitted, but this limit does not apply where the woman is exercising her *statutory* right to MATERNITY LEAVE).

Any week during which an employee is on strike (see STRIKES/STRIKING) or is prevented from working by a LOCK-OUT, does not count, but neither does it break the continuity of employment. Other situations where continuity is expressly preserved include:

- where the employee is granted REINSTATMENT or RE-ENGAGEMENT following an unfair dismissal claim;
- where the employee is transferred to ASSOCIATED EMPLOYERS;
- where the business is transferred as a going concern, and the employee is taken on by the new employer (see also TRANSFER OF UNDERTAKINGS (PROTECTION OF EMPLOYMENT) REGULATIONS 1981. Employers are obliged to tell employees in the written statement of terms (see CONTRACT, WRITTEN PARTICULARS OF)

whether any period with a previous employer counts towards their period of continuous employment.

Contract of employment. A contract of employment is defined by S153 of the EMPLOYMENT PROTECTION (CONSOLIDATION) ACT 1978 as a contract of service or apprenticeship, whether express or implied, and whether made orally or in writing. However, the phrase 'contract of service' is not defined, and neither is a statutory distinction drawn between an EMPLOYEE (who works under a contract of service) and a self-employed person or independent contractor who is said to work under a CONTRACT FOR SERVICES. The distinction between these two modes of employment is usually crucial (see EMPLOYEE), and yet certain forms of working, for example, homeworking, may have features of both, so that the distinction is blurred.

As statutory guidance is lacking, the issue is left in the hands of a court or tribunal. Their approach should be to examine all features of the relationship, assessing the weight of those which point towards 'employee' status, and those which suggest an individual is self-employed. Thus payment of tax and National Insurance contributions by the employer, provision of sick pay, payment of wages rather than a lump sum, and a high degree of control over the individual concerned, point to employee status. Where the individual owns the tools or equipment used, can delegate his or her duties to others, and incurs the chance of profit or loss, a self-employed status is indicated. The intentions of the parties themselves as to the form of relationship are relevant but not decisive; the reality of the relationship cannot be altered by the label which is put on it. Recently stress has been laid on 'mutuality of obligation': that is, if there is no obligation on the employer to provide work, or on the individual to do the work offered, a contract of employment is negated. Consistent decisions are not always reached; thus certain homeworkers who were paid wages gross and who could choose not to work for a number of weeks if they wished, were classified as employees. Conversely 'regular casuals' working for Trusthouse Forte in their Banqueting Department (in some cases for 30–40 hours per week, over 50 weeks of the year), who could be 'suspended' for a period for refusing engagements, were regarded as self-employed.

Contract for services/independent contractor. Where a self-employed person or independent contractor is engaged to do work for another, the relationship between them is governed by a contract for services (cf. CONTRACT OF EMPLOYMENT). An independent contractor is liable for his or her own tax and National Insurance contributions and is denied much of the protection granted by recent legislation to those having EMPLOYEE status.

See also LABOUR-ONLY SUBCONTRACTING.

Contract variation. The strict legal view of a contract is that once formed, it cannot be varied without the consent of the other party, or breach of contract will ensue. The relationship between employer and employee is governed by a contract of employment, yet it is often necessary in practice for this relationship to be dynamic rather than static. Difficulties may arise: for example, where an employer wishes to reorganize the business in the interests of economy, or to introduce modern technological methods or greater flexibility, or where either party asserts that the original contract has been varied by CUSTOM AND PRACTICE, or by conduct.

A number of the issues which arise on contract variation can conveniently be summarized, but it should be stressed that it is rarely possible to predict the stance which will be taken by a court or tribunal.

1 Has there been a breach of contract at all? On computerization of the PAYE scheme it was concluded that the job content of the clerical assistants administering the scheme was not sufficiently altered for their employers to be in breach of contract: the employees were expected to adapt themselves to new techniques.
2 Does an admitted variation amount to a REDUNDANCY? A plumber dismissed because the updating of the heating system for which he was responsible meant the need for the services of a heating engineer was found to be redundant; a cosy, middle-aged barmaid who was replaced by a young girl more in keeping with the youthful atmosphere the pub now wished to create was not.
3 If the employer insists on a variation, do employees have the right to resign and claim CONSTRUCTIVE DISMISSAL? In theory, if the breach of contract is not sufficiently serious or fundamental, they would not, though they would not be precluded from

remaining in employment and suing the employer for breach of contract. The latter course was pursued by an employee who was put on to a four-day week which affected his pay, without the agreement of his union.

4 If the employee refuses to submit to a variation and is consequently dismissed, what are the chances of successfully defending a claim of unfair dismissal? Presumably the employer will assert 'some other substantial reason of a kind to justify dismissal' (see FAIR REASONS FOR DISMISSAL), such as the need to reorganize, or to make economies, or to modernize. However, in deciding whether the employer behaved 'reasonably' in the circumstances (see UNFAIR DISMISSAL), the tribunal may question whether dismissal of the employee was 'within the RANGE OF REASONABLE RESPONSES' which management could have made to the situation. (The same principles would doubtless apply if employees showed themselves constructively dismissed as in paragraph 3.)

Contract, written particulars of. In general a contract of employment need not be in writing but S1 of the EMPLOYMENT PROTECTION (CONSOLIDATION) ACT 1978 requires an employer to give a written statement to employees within 13 weeks of their commencing employment. The statement must give the names of the parties, specify the date employment began and whether any employment with a previous employer counts as part of the employee's continuous employment (and if so, when it began). In addition the statement should give particulars of the terms of the employment including the scale of rate or pay, intervals at which it is paid, hours of work, holidays, sickness, pension schemes, notice period and job title. If there are no such terms, that fact must be stated. Disciplinary rules and methods of dealing with employee grievances should also be specified. To comply with S1 it is sufficient if employees are referred to a document containing this information which they have a reasonable opportunity of reading; any change in the written particulars must, however, be notified to them within one month.

An employee may complain to a tribunal on the basis that the employer has not provided a written statement, or that it is incorrect. The tribunal may determine what are the correct particulars but it has no power to enforce them.

In theory the written statement is not the actual contract of employment; it is supposed merely to reflect the terms of the contract. Thus a particular employee whose contract entitled him to a bonus scheme remained entitled to it even though his statement of particulars recited that the bonus would be calculated with respect to a collective agreement which subsequently had been unilaterally determined by the employer. However, where there was an inconsistency between the disciplinary rules in an employee's written statement and a notice posted on the works notice board, a tribunal held that the written statement constituted the terms of the employment.

Cost of living (pay increases). Alterations to pay to account for changes in the cost of living take two forms. The most widespread is an occasional across-the-board adjustment to the pay of all members of a particular occupational group or BARGAINING UNIT to account for a general increase in the retail price index. This is one of the centrepieces of national negotiations between employers and trade unions. By the 1970s a convention had been established that these negotiated adjustments usually took place at yearly intervals. As the pace of inflation has slackened there has been some move to extend the interval. Seldom is negotiation of an increase to compensate for a rise in the cost of living neatly separated from other negotiating issues such as the relationship between the pay levels of the employees under discussion and the pay levels of other groups; see RELATIVITIES.

The other form of cost-of-living adjustment is where the employee is living in circumstances of particularly high living costs. The most common example is a London weighting for those living in the London area.

Counselling. This describes a one-to-one conversation with an employee that enables the employee to find solutions to problems and develop strengths in job performance. The counsellor provides skilled listening and a different perspective on the matter being discussed, so that the employee with the problem develops a better understanding of it. Counselling is not simply giving advice, although some assistance with information and specialized expertise is usually a feature. The

---

Stages in a counselling interview

Counselling interviews develop in many different ways, and cousellor style, warmth and integrity are more important than technique. Here is a useful sequence to experiment with.

1 *Factual interchange:* focus on the facts of the situation first. Ask factual questions and provide factual information, like the doctor asking about the location of the pain and other symptoms, rather than demonstrating dismay. This provides a basis for later analysis.

2 *Opinion interchange:* open the matter up for discussion by asking for the client's opinions and feelings, but not offering any criticism, or making any decisions. Gradually, the matter is better understood by both counsellor and client.

3 *Joint problem solving:* ask the client to analyse the situation described. The client will receive help from the counsellor in questioning and focus, but it must be the client's own analysis, with the counsellor resisting the temptation to produce answers.

4 *Decision-making:* the counsellor helps to generate alternative lines of action for the client to consider and they both share in deciding what to do. Only the client can behave differently, but the counsellor may be able to help a change in behaviour by facilitation.

---

main skills of the counsellor are active listening, questioning to clarify uncertainty, reflecting and summarizing. The most common matters on which employees seek counselling at work are career development and work stress, although other matters include redundancy and problems of working abroad.

All managers are likely to be involved in counselling situations at some time, and all must resist the temptation to be drawn into counselling on matters where they lack proper competence, such as bereavement, marital problems and financial difficulties.

Craft union. This covers a stratum of workers across different industries, so that the logic of the organization is the craft skill possessed by its members, rather than the industry in which they are engaged. These were the first types of trade union to become established and some of the contemporary craft unions, like the engineers, have continuous histories stretching back to the middle of the nineteenth century. This type of union exists because of the pride members have in their craft skill and the contribution of that skill to the social weal. It also preserves the scarcity and value of the skill. The exclusivity of craft unions has, however, been steadily declining and most have member-ships that include many people without an exclusive skill.

Culture. The values, norms and informal rules that guide the behaviour of people in a particular society or organization may be called its culture. Many of these are national, so that there are limits to what aspects of Japanese working practices can be successfully adopted by the British, just as the model of the British Parliament has not proved successful in all the lands where it has been adopted. Other aspects of culture are regional, so that the level of sickness absence in, for instance, South Wales is much higher than that of South-east England, even after taking account of demographic and industrial differences bet-ween the regions. Occupational cultures produce differences, such as doctors working long hours and engineering craftsmen working Saturday morning overtime. Managers need to understand cultural determinants of behaviour to avoid the risk of seeking to change working practices without an appreciation of all the 'irrational' reasons underlying the practice.

See also CUSTOM AND PRACTICE, ORGANIZATIONAL CULTURE.

Curriculum vitae (CV). Literally meaning 'the course of one's life', this Latin term is used to describe an outline of a person's educational and professional history. This is most often used in job applications and it is becoming more common for a CV to be requested instead of an application form for posts where there is scope for the role to be filled in a number of different ways according to the qualities and experience that the incumbent can offer. It has also become widely used as a result of executive redundancy as people seeking employment prepare a CV for use in a wide range of attempts to find appropriate employment. It has both the drawback and the advantage of being idiosyncratic to the writers who will present their history not only in the most favourable possible light, but also in a personal way which will differ from that of other applicants. This makes comparison between candidates harder than where information is presented in standard form, but the presentation will be more informative because of its individual emphasis.

Custom and practice. Rules of the workplace are partly enshrined in formal agreements (see COLLECTIVE AGREEMENTS) and in what the employer lays down as requirements. They are not, however, the only norms that govern workplace relationships and behaviour. There is also the informal system of industrial relations which is in the accepted customs and unwritten rules, often tacit but sometimes explicit, which govern the actual behaviour of people at work.

Such custom and practice has traditionally been a source of contractual terms and conditions to fill 'gaps' left by the express terms of the contract. Thus an established practice of using suspension as a disciplinary measure, and a custom of deducting sums from weavers' wages for bad workmanship, have been held to be part of the individual contract of employment. COLLECTIVE AGREEMENTS may similarly be incorporated by custom. A custom will not become legally enforceable in this way, however, unless it is reasonable, certain and well known; there seems some doubt as to whether ignorance of the custom on the part of the individual concerned is material.

D

Data Protection Act 1984. The Act is designed to protect individuals against the use of data held about them in computer memories. It does not apply to information held and processed manually. A *data user* is an organization or individual who controls the contents and use of a collection of personal data processed, or intended to be processed, automatically. Data users must register with the Data Protection Registrar the personal data they hold, their sources and recipients and the purposes for which the data will be used. There are eight principles by which data users must abide:

- information to be contained in personal data shall be obtained, and personal data shall be processed, fairly and lawfully (anyone providing information should therefore not be misled about its purpose);
- personal data shall be held only for one or more specified and lawful purposes (one implication of this is that data should not be transmitted to a subsidiary company unless this possibility is included in the registered purposes);
- personal data shall not be disclosed or used in a way incompatible with the registered purpose (it should not, for instance, be sold to companies compiling lists for mail order);
- personal data shall be adequate, relevant and not excessive. This raises queries about what sort of questions can be asked about employees or prospective employees. Personal data relating to race or ethnic background is relevant for purposes of complying with the Race Relations Act, but is it relevant to record religious belief or political affiliation?
- personal data shall be accurate and, where necessary, kept up to date;
- personal data shall not be kept for longer than is necessary;
- individuals are entitled to be told what information the data user holds about them, to have access to that data and to be able to have it corrected or, where appropriate, erased. If an employer or a manager wants to keep information about an individual to which the individual does not have access, then that must be held manually;
- data users should take steps to ensure the security of all personal data.

The Act is due to be fully in operation by the end of 1987. Further information can be obtained from The Data Protection Registrar, Springfield House, Water Lane, Wilmslow, Cheshire SK9 5AX (0625 535777).

The Data Protection Registrar, *The Data Protection Act, 1984, Guideline No. 1: An Introduction and Guide to the Act* (Office of the Data Protection Registrar, Wilmslow, 1985).

Day rate. Day rate is a fixed, daily rate of pay to which there is no incentive addition. The term was initially used to distinguish between that pay arrangement and the alternative where the worker received a lower level of basic rate, to which incentive payments were added, when earned.

Demarcation. Demarcation is drawing a boundary round a certain collection of jobs and saying that those jobs can only be carried out by people carrying a specified accreditation. In one way it is a description of specialization and a sensible way of dividing up available work. It can also act as a safeguard for customers and members of the public against incompetence. It frequently produces RESTRICTIVE PRACTICES, which can cause inefficiency and limit employment opportunities. Demarcation is mainly associated with craft unions and professions.

Differentials. Differentials are pay differences within a single negotiating group, where any comparison involves reaching agreement between one set of negotiators representing management interests and another set representing the interests of those being paid. They are distinct from RELATIVITIES, which are pay relationships between different employee groupings and therefore much more difficult to determine satisfactorily.

Dilution. Early in the Second World War there was a shortage of skilled craftsmen in some factories and production was endangered, so dilution agreements were negotiated with unions representing the craftsmen, allowing other workers to be employed on work that had previously been reserved for skilled men. The agreements specified that the temporary workers or dilutees could not be reclassified as skilled workers and would surrender their jobs when skilled men were again available. Later, these agreements were invoked to deny skilled status to adults who had acquired skill at a Government training centre instead of by a traditional apprenticeship.

Disabled employees. Over 400,000 people in the UK are registered as disabled, although the actual number is certainly higher and their employment experiences are often poor. Legislation provides some assistance. The Disabled Persons (Employment) Act 1944 provides a form of positive discrimination through a quota scheme, whereby every employer of more than 20 people has to employ sufficient people who are registered disabled to make up 3 per cent of the total work-force. Lift attendant and car park attendant are designated as reserved occupations to be filled only by disabled people, and all employers of more than 250 people are obliged to include in the Directors' Report a statement of their policy on the employment of disabled people.

The Manpower Services Commission employ a number of Disablement Resettlement Officers (DROs) throughout the country to assist employers in improving the employment facilities for those who are disabled.

Manpower Services Commission, *Code of Good Practice on the Employment of Disabled People* (Manpower Services Commission, Sheffield, 1984).

Disciplinary procedures. Disciplinary procedure is one of the most common of PROCEDURES in the personnel area, with formality reducing the likelihood of managers making inconsistent, *ad hoc* decisions with the consequent risk of a claim for unfair dismissal. The EMPLOYMENT PROTECTION (CONSOLIDATION) ACT 1978 requires employers to inform their employees in writing about disciplinary rules and indicate to whom employees should apply if they are dissatisfied with any disciplinary decision, as well as explaining further steps in procedure for dealing with both disciplinary decisions and grievances (see: CONTRACT, WRITTEN PARTICULARS OF).

Disciplinary procedures should:

- be in writing and specify who is covered by them;
- work quickly and indicate what disciplinary action may be taken in different circumstances;

Outline disciplinary procedure

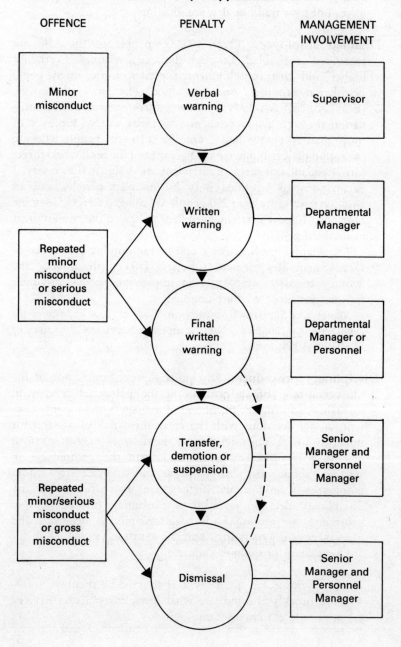

- specify which management levels are authorized to take the various disciplinary decisions and ensure that employees cannot normally be dismissed by their immediate superior without reference to senior management;
- ensure that employees are told of specific complaints against them and provide the opportunity for them to state their case before final decisions are made;
- provide for representation, if required;
- ensure that any investigatory period of suspension is with pay;
- avoid the possibility of dismissal for a first offence unless it is gross misconduct;
- ensure that careful investigation precedes any disciplinary action;
- provide a right of appeal and ensure that any penalties are accompanied by a written explanation.

If an employee is dismissed in a way that breaches disciplinary procedure, such a dismissal will usually be unfair (see UNFAIR DISMISSAL).

See also DISCIPLINE, DISMISSAL, UNFAIR DISMISSAL, WARNINGS.

ACAS, *Disciplinary and Other Procedures in Employment* (Draft Code of Practice) (ACAS, London, 1986).

Discipline. It is a narrow but common management view that discipline is a tedious formality preceding dismissal, its only purpose being to legitimize the final and inevitable action of terminating an employee's contract of employment. A more constructive approach is to see it as part of the process whereby the contribution of the employee is attuned to organizational requirements. It may eventually become necessary to dismiss the employee, but there are many ways of trying to avert that outcome by remedial action as the manager tries to make an unsatisfactory working performance satisfactory. The corollary to discipline is GRIEVANCE, which is how individual employees try to overcome their personal dissatisfaction with the working situation by seeking change in some aspect of management behaviour or decision.

Grievance and discipline require a *framework of organizational justice,* with clear rules, methods of avoiding the rules being broken, information about what the rules are, arrangements for both placement and relocation of employees in work situations that will not expose them to risk of rule infringement, training for the work that is to be done, and understood penalties.

"Oh, by the way . . . according to my teacher I'm suffering from a lack of discipline in the home. See to it, will you . . .?"

Potential disciplinary problems should be identified and a resolution sought by *disciplinary interviewing*. This is an approach of identifying the reason for the unsatisfactory behaviour with the employee and discussing ways in which it may be overcome. The most common reasons for disciplinary infringements are either ignorance of working requirements or external factors, like problems with travel leading to lateness. Sometimes the manager conducting the interview can suggest a way round the problem that the employee could not see alone, like changing to a different shift, and the problem is solved.

If the unsatisfactory behaviour is not overcome by interviewing, there is recourse to *penalties*. These include rebukes, WARNINGS, demotion or disciplinary transfer, SUSPENSION and fines.

An American management expert formulated the 'red hot stove' rule for testing the efficacy of disciplinary action by managers, taking the analogy of touching a red hot stove which produces action that is immediate, with warning, consistent and impersonal:

- the burn is immediate (there is no question of what caused it);
- you had warning (if the stove was red hot, you knew what would happen if you touched it);
- it is consistent (everyone who touches the stove is burned);
- it is impersonal (people are burned not because of who they are, but because they touched the stove).

Another benefit of the analogy is that people who touch red hot stoves always stop!

Disclosure of information. Managers have a major advantage in dealings with trade unions in that they possess information about company performances and finances which is not normally available to their union counterparts. They are usually reluctant to disclose this information except in situations where it strengthens their situation in negotiation (when, for instance, the financial situation is parlous). This general reluctance has been met by various arguments about the need to make negotiations more realistic through linking pay with productivity, the need to increase the level of employee involvement in the business and a general societal move towards greater openness.

The EMPLOYMENT PROTECTION ACT 1975 outlines a legal obligation for employers to provide information, on request, to representatives of an independent trade union for the purposes of collective bargaining. The information has to be:

- information without which the trade union representatives would be to a material extent impeded in carrying on such collective bargaining;
- information which it would be in accordance with good industrial relations practice to disclose for the purpose of collective bargaining.

An ACAS Code of Practice offers guidance on the range of information that would meet the 'good industrial relations practice' criteria. The main topics suggested by the Code are pay and benefits, conditions of service, manpower, performance and financial information.

ACAS Code of Practice 2, *Disclosure of Information to Trade Unions for the Purpose of Collective Bargaining* (London: HMSO, 1977).

Discrimination. Just as we all have to discriminate between right and wrong, so employers spend a great deal of time discriminating between people on the basis of individual differences. They discriminate between different candidates for a post, for training, for promotion, for transfer or for redundancy. The difficulty about discrimination is first, how to do it effectively, so that you single out the most appropriate person, and second, how to do it fairly and lawfully. If you discriminate against someone on the grounds of social class, that may be unfair but would not be unlawful. If you discriminate against someone for being black, that may be unfair but it is certainly unlawful.

Discrimination is defined by the SEX DISCRIMINATION ACT 1975 and the RACE RELATIONS ACT 1976. 'Direct' discrimination occurs when persons are treated less favourably on the basis of their sex, or because they are married, or on racial grounds (defined as meaning on grounds of 'colour, race, nationality or ethnic or national origins'). Motive is irrelevant, so to refuse to employ an isolated woman so as to protect her from SEXUAL HARASSMENT would be direct discrimination.

'Indirect' discrimination is treatment which at first glance seems equal but in fact has an adverse impact on one sex as opposed to the other (for example, a height requirement) or on a particular racial group. Individuals complaining of indirect discrimination have to prove that there was some essential requirement or condition with which a considerably smaller proportion of their sex or racial group could comply, such as a specific number of years' experience in the UK. However, a complaint cannot be made by an individual unless the requirement actually acts as a bar to him or her personally. It would then be up to the employer to show that the requirement was 'justifiable' on non-racial or non-sexual grounds. There has been considerable variation in tribunals' interpretation of 'justifiable', but no doubt one which is 'job-related', such as insistence on the wearing of safety helmets (discriminating against Sikhs), would be more favourably received.

Discrimination by victimization occurs where persons are treated less favourably because they have brought proceedings, given evidence or information or alleged a contravention of the Race Relations Act, Equal Pay Act or Sex Discrimination Act.

Acts of discrimination which are made unlawful cover all aspects of the employment relationship from recruitment through to dismissal. It would therefore be unlawful, for example, to rely unjustifiably on word of mouth recruitment where the work-force was predominantly white, to refuse to promote Asian bus conductors to inspectors in case the public objected, or to choose to make women redundant rather than men on the assumption that men are 'the breadwinners'.

See also EQUAL PAY ACT 1970, REHABILITATION OF OFFENDERS ACT 1974, TRADE UNION MEMBERSHIP AND ACTIVITIES.

Dismissal. A contract of employment may come to an end in one of several ways including dissolution of a partnership, mutual agreement, FRUSTRATION and DISMISSAL. At COMMON LAW a dismissal is lawful if the correct period of notice is given, so that no claim of WRONGFUL DISMISSAL can be made. However, a claim of UNFAIR DISMISSAL under the EMPLOYMENT PROTECTION (CONSOLIDATION) ACT 1978 would not be precluded since employees need only show that they have been 'dismissed'. Under the statute employees are treated as dismissed if:

- the employer terminates the contract with or without notice (see SUMMARY DISMISSAL), or
- the FIXED TERM CONTRACT under which they are employed expires without its being renewed, or
- the employees end the contract because of some conduct on the part of the employer which entitles them to terminate it (see CONSTRUCTIVE DISMISSAL).

An employee who resigns has clearly not been dismissed; but an employee faced with the choice of resignation or dismissal and who chooses the former will usually be regarded as having been dismissed. This will also be the case where an employer uses unambiguous words of dismissal which were in fact intended as mere abuse, but the employee in question acted on them. Where the words are ambiguous, a tribunal should ask itself what a 'reasonable' employee would have understood by the words. There is as yet no clear distinction between employees volunteering to be dismissed (for example, for redundancy) and employees being invited to apply for early retirement, thus ending their contract of employment by 'mutual agreement' with the employer. The former involves a dismissal; the latter does not.

Disputes. These are a collective and formal manifestation of employee dissatisfaction over a management decision, usually taking the form of STRIKES/STRIKING or other INDUSTRIAL ACTION. In the period from 1954 to 1979 the number of stoppages annually varied between 1,937 (in 1966) and 3,906 (in 1970), but since 1980 the average has been 1,258. The disputes have, however, often been longer and the figures quoted only relate to stoppages, ignoring other action such as working to rule.

Occasionally disputes produce such extreme feelings as to become issues of major national concern about public order, allegations of police brutality and the undermining of economic performance. The General Strike of 1926 remains the most widespread dispute in our industrial history, but more recently there have been long-running and very bitter disputes limited to a single employer. In 1977 an acrimonious dispute about union recognition at Grunwick Film Processing Laboratories demonstrated that the united efforts of a trade union movement at the peak of its powers, as well as recommendations from ACAS and a government Court of Inquiry, were powerless to persuade employers to recognize a trade union if they were determined not to. Attempts to introduce new technology into the printing of newspapers were strongly resisted by a strike in Warrington where Mr Eddie Shah started printing his local newspapers by new equipment, but the severity of this dispute was overshadowed by the remarkable incidents surrounding the News International affair at Wapping in 1986, when Mr Rupert Murdoch moved his entire Fleet Street operation to a new location with new equipment and a new work-force. All these were disputes which the employees 'lost'. Those in which the employees may have 'won' recently include the fire service dispute of 1981.

Disputes procedures. There is a theoretical difference between GRIEVANCE PROCEDURES and disputes procedures. The former relate to individuals and the latter are collective. The former may involve trade union representation, the latter always do. In many practical situations this distinction is not made, and a single procedure is used for both types of problem. There are some instances where industrial relations conventions allow for the hybrid of a 'collective grievance'.

Disputes procedures seek to formalize the way in which disputes between employer and employees may be resolved through discussion in order to avoid the problems of breakdown leading to industrial action. Frequently disputes procedure allows for a matter to be referred to bodies outside the particular establishment in which the dispute has arisen, and it is common for procedure to preclude any form of industrial action being taken before the agreed stages have been exhausted and failure to agree has been formally recorded.

See also DISPUTES, STATUS QUO.

E

Early retirement. Early retirement has become a widespread phenomenon of the changed labour market since 1980. In 1949 a Royal Commission on Population described the elderly as a liability because they consumed without producing, reducing the average standard of living in the community. With the increasing scarcity of employment those at the end of the occupational cycle have become expendable, so that the social expectation is not that you will make a greater contribution but that you will make way for others.

The Department of Employment now categorize everyone over the age of 55 who is not working as retired rather than unemployed, even though the retirement pension is still not payable until the age of 60 or 65, and the average age at which people retire has dropped, especially for men.

The extensive 'rationalizations' and 'reorganizations' of the 1980s have shaken out large numbers over the age of 60, many over 55 and some over 50. Provided that the money is right there will be little resistance to early retirement. Many large organizations have been able to make the money acceptable (sometimes by a not-to-be-repeated raid on the pension fund) and the public sector of employment has offered very generous terms, which few have been able to resist.

Early retirement has an interesting effect on the age profile of organizations as the white-haired sage of 63 has been replaced by the grey-haired not-quite-so-sage of 53. People assume significant responsibility in their twenties and middle-aged burn-out can start in one's thirties.

Economic torts. A tort is a civil wrong. A person committing a tort may be sued for damages, and in certain circumstances an INJUNCTION may be obtained ordering that person to cease the unlawful act. A group of torts which potentially would be committed by those organizing or participating in INDUSTRIAL ACTION have been termed the 'economic torts', and are explored below.

1 Inducing a breach of contract or interfering with its performance. Inducing a breach of contract may be committed directly or indirectly.

- **Direct inducement**

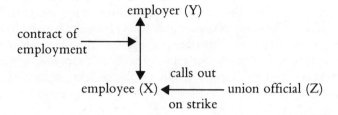

By calling a strike Z induces X to break the contract of employment with Y.

- **Indirect inducement**

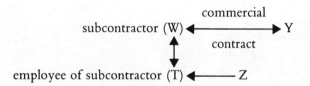

Z induces T not to deliver goods to Y, thereby inducing breach of the commercial contract between W and Y. Indirect inducement is only tortious if unlawful means are used; however, such will often be the case because, for example, in the illustration given Z has induced breach of the commercial contract by pressuring T to break the contract of employment with W.

Where no actual breach of contract results (because, for example, the commercial contract concerned contained a 'force majeure' clause exempting the party unable to perform the contract because of industrial action) the tort of 'interference' with contract may nevertheless be comitted.

2 Conspiracy: this may also take one of two forms.
- Civil conspiracy to injure ('simple' conspiracy); this tort is committed by a combination of two or more persons whose purpose is to damage the plaintiff rather than serve their own legitimate interests even if lawful means are used. A union will therefore not normally be liable unless it does not act out of genuine trade union motives.

- Civil conspiracy to commit an unlawful act or use unlawful means; if an act done by one person would be a tort, such as intimidation, then a combination by two or more persons to do that act amounts to conspiracy. It is uncertain what are the limits of 'unlawful acts' for the purpose of this tort – whether for example, breach of contract is sufficient – but in 1982 it was held that as with 'simple' conspiracy the motive of the defendant must be to injure the plaintiff.

3 Intimidation: this tort was developed by the judiciary in 1964 to cover the situation where trade union officials threatened to call an illegal strike unless the employer dismissed a particular individual. In essence it consists of an unlawful threat to someone to compel that person to do an act which causes damage to that person or to a third person.

4 Interference with trade or business by unlawful means: this tort would encompass points 1 and 3 but is potentially of a much wider and uncertain scope.

IMMUNITY against tortious liability is provided by S13 of the Trade Union and Labour Relations Act 1974 in respect of points 1 and 3 and the subsection on simple conspiracy, but only when the actions taken are 'in contemplation or furtherance of a trade dispute' (see GOLDEN FORMULA). Certain SECONDARY ACTION does not attract immunity, and protection against inducing a breach of contract is lost where a union takes official action without the support of a ballot (see TRADE UNION ACT 1984). Though no specific protection is given against liability for interference with trade or business, 'unlawful means' will not be established if the means used are themselves covered by immunity (for example, inducing a breach of contract).

See also PICKETING.

Effective date of termination. The date on which a dismissal is regarded as taking effect is known as the effective date of termination. It is essential to know this when considering whether an employee has the necessary period of continuous employment to found a claim of UNFAIR DISMISSAL, and in computing statutory redundancy entitlement or the basic award of COMPENSATION for unfairly dismissed employees. It is defined in S55(4) of the Employment Protection (Consolidation) Act 1978 as:

- the date on which notice expires whether given by the employer or the employee; or
- where no notice is given, the date when termination takes effect; or
- the date of expiry of a fixed term contract.

There is, however, a provision to the effect that where an employer gives less than the statutory period of notice to which an employee is entitled, the effective date of termination will be the date on which the correct period of notice would have expired.

Where an employee is summarily dismissed and appeals through an internal appeals procedure then, in the absence of contractual provisions to the contrary, he or she is taken to be suspended without pay, and if the appeal is unsuccessful the effective data of termination will be the date of the original dismissal.

Efficiency bar. Incremental pay scales allow for regular, and usually automatic, progression to higher rates to pay, reaching a ceiling after perhaps five or seven years. One way to stop the progression relying solely on the passage of time is to have a bar beyond which employees only progress after satisfying a test of 'efficiency', which is some assessment of competence and contribution. These are most common on relatively long scales with more than ten steps.

See also INCREMENTS.

Employee. S153(1) of the EMPLOYMENT PROTECTION (CONSOLI-DATION) ACT 1978 defines an employee as 'an individual who has entered into or works under . . . a CONTRACT OF EMPLOYMENT'. Whether or not a given individual has 'employee' status is important because, for example:

- employers are responsible for deducting tax and National Insurance contributions in respect of their employees;

- employers owe a duty to take reasonable care for the safety of their employes (the comparable duty in the case of those working for them under a CONTRACT FOR SERVICES is much more restricted);
- most statutory employment protection rights are restricted to employees (see, for example, GUARANTEE PAYMENTS, ITEMIZED PAY STATEMENT, MATERNITY RIGHTS, REDUNDANCY, TRADE UNION MEMBERSHIP AND ACTIVITIES, UNFAIR DISMISSAL), though protection under the RACE RELATIONS ACT 1976 and SEX DISCRIMINATION ACT 1975 extends to those employed under a 'contract personally to execute any work or labour';
- only employees qualify for social security payments such as unemployment benefit, industrial injuries benefits and sickness benefits.

Employee involvement. Employee involvement has become for some the acceptable, and for others the unacceptable, interpretation of INDUSTRIAL DEMOCRACY. It has legislative emphasis in the Employment Act (1982), which requires all employers of more than 250 people to include in their annual report a statement describing what has been done in the previous year under the following headings:

- providing employees systematically with information on matters which concern them;
- consulting with employees or their representatives on management decisions likely to affect employee interests;
- encouraging employee involvement through shareholding or similar means;
- sharing information on financial and economic factors affecting the company.

Employee participation. The idea of employee participation is that employees have both a need and a right to be involved in management decision-making outside the areas normally covered by collective bargaining. The idea gained momentum during the 1960s and early 1970s, with particular pressure from the EEC and a response to changing attitudes as the so-called deferential society was being replaced by people with less automatic respect for formally constituted authority and greater interest in management by consent. There was also a greater concern for the QUALITY OF WORKING LIFE.

Although there has been little progress in practical terms towards a realization of this ideal, there are trends partly in the workplace and partly at company level.

In the workplace there has been some development of individual autonomy and autonomous work groups. Close supervision has been reduced and greater scope for decisions about the progress of the job has been delegated to the individual employee in JOB DESIGN initiatives. In autonomous work groups responsibility is both assumed and shared between the different members of a working team. Both these approaches enhance the level of participation in matters which most immediately affect the individual.

At company level there has been some widening of the role of collective bargaining, but little direct employee representation at board level. The most significant developments have been in the appointment of SAFETY REPRESENTATIVES, employee representation on PENSION FUND TRUSTEES and participation by employee representatives on JOB EVALUTION panels and *ad hoc* working parties.

See also EMPLOYEE INVOLVEMENT, INDUSTRIAL DEMOCRACY.

D. Guest and K. Knight, *Putting Participation Into Practice* (Aldershot: Gower, 1979); M. Salamon, *Industrial Relations: Theory and Practice* (Hemel Hempstead: Prentice-Hall International, 1987), ch. 14.

Employee relations. The increasing popularity of the term 'employee relations' reflects a change in the field of INDUSTRIAL RELATIONS. It refers to, and concentrates upon, the working relationship between management and employees within the organization and the practices and procedures which structure that relationship. It plays down questions of employee participation in the wider trade union movement and government intervention in industrial matters. It is an activity of which managers are in charge.

Employers' associations. This describes a grouping of employers within a particular industry with a full-time team of officials, who (among other activities) are concerned with the negotiation of terms and conditions for employment within the industry. In 1968 there were 1,350 employers' associations, but this declined to 1,177 in 1973 and to just over 300 in 1984, as individual employers have withdrawn from the industry collectives because of the constraints which the membership imposed. In 1980 only 56 per cent of employers in manufacturing and 20 per cent of employers in distribution and service industries were association members. Among the most significant associations are the Engineering Employers' Federation, the National Federation of Building Trades Employers, the Chemical Industries Association, the Electrical Contractors Association and the Road Haulage Association.

Employment Act 1980. The Act amended legislation of the previous Labour Government and aimed to strike a balance between the rights of employees and the interests of management. Its provisions relate mainly to the following items.

1 Unfair dismissal: a service qualification of two years was introduced for employees of 'small' businesses (employing no more than 20 employees), the minimum basic award of compensation was abolished, the length of a FIXED TERM CONTRACT which permitted waiver of unfair dismissal rights was reduced from two years or more to one year or more, and 'reasonableness' (see UNFAIR DISMISSAL) was to be determined by the tribunal rather than being proved by the employer.
2 Union membership: an employer who was threatened or pressured by the union into dismissing an employee for non-membership of the union, or taking action short of dismissal to compel that employee to become a member, was given the right to 'join' the union if the employee complained to a tribunal (see JOINDER). Where a CLOSED SHOP existed, employees were given the right not to be unreasonably excluded or expelled from the union, and the grounds on which dismissal of a non-union member would be unfair were increased.
3 Industrial action: many forms of SECONDARY ACTION such as sympathy strikes became unlawful, and lawful PICKETING was restricted to an individual's own place of work.
4 Maternity provisions: the Act extended the notice procedure for MATERNITY PAY and MATERNITY LEAVE, gave a new right to

time off for ante-natal care, and weakened the rights of women returning after leave.

5 Guarantee payments: the basis for calculation of entitlement to GUARANTEE PAYMENTS was altered.

See also BALLOTS.

Employment Act 1982. The Employment Act of 1982 mainly concerned provisions relating to the closed shop, the immunity of trade unions, union-only or recognition-only requirements and the definition of a trade dispute.

1 The closed shop: the number of grounds on which dismissal of a non-union member would be fair where there was a CLOSED SHOP were increased further, and high levels of COMPENSATION for employees unfairly dismissed for non-membership of a union were introduced (see also JOINDER).

2 Trade dispute: the definition was altered so as to extend only to disputes between workers and *their own* employer thus excluding inter-union or demarcation disputes. In addition, a trade dispute was henceforth to relate 'wholly or mainly' to certain matters laid down in S29 of the Trade Union and Labour Relations Act 1974 (see GOLDEN FORMULA) rather than being simply 'connected' with them. This tended to outlaw disputes which were partly political.

3 Trade union immunities: the blanket IMMUNITY, which had previously prevented a union from being sued, was removed. Thus where individuals acted unlawfully, the union would be liable if the unlawful act was authorized by a 'responsible person' such as the general secretary or the executive committee. The size of the union determined the maximum award of damages which could be made against it.

4 Union-only or recognition-only requirements: any clause in a commercial contract requiring the recognition of a trade union, or the employment only of persons who were (or were not) members of a trade union, was made void (see also IMMUNITY).

Employment agencies. An employment agency provides a service for both employers and job seekers by matching the complementary aspirations. The agency keeps lists of those seeking particular types of employment together with personal details of experience and qualifications. The employer asks the agency to provide a member of staff or a temporary employee and the vacancy is filled by the agency. The attraction to the employer is that the vacancy can be filled quickly, with some degree of guarantee about the competence of the candidate. Most agencies are profit-making and rely on charging the employer an appointment fee which is usually equal to 2–4 weeks' pay for the appointee. For temporary staff the agency will charge an hourly or daily rate.

Some dubious practices, usually relating to the fact that many of those on the books of agencies are young women, led to the Employment Agency Act being passed in 1973, which requires agencies to be licensed by the Department of Employment and to follow a code of conduct. Among the requirements of the code are that the prospective employer should be provided with a written quotation before work on the assignment is begun and no more than two-thirds of the fee can be charged before an appointment is made.

See also JOB CENTRES, SELECTION COUNSULTANTS.

Employment Gazette. Each month the Department of Employment publishes this *Gazette*. It contains extensive statistical data on all matters relating to employment as well as monthly articles and news. These relate to aspects of government policy and include articles stemming from research carried out at the Department's behest. It is the main source of labour market information.

Employment Medical Advisory Service (EMAS). The HEALTH AND SAFETY EXECUTIVE has ten regional offices which are staffed by members of EMAS, who are available to give advice to employers on any appropriate aspect of health at work, ranging from the provision of first-aid boxes upwards. Addresses and telephone numbers of the regional offices of EMAS can be found in the telephone directories relating to Newcastle-upon-Tyne, Leeds, Luton, Barking, London, Bristol, Cardiff, Birmingham, Manchester and Edinburgh.

Employment Protection Act 1975. The Employment Protection

Act created a 'floor' of individual employment rights relating, for instance, to MATERNITY LEAVE and MATERNITY PAY, GUARANTEE PAYMENTS, and rights in connection with TRADE UNION MEMBERSHIP AND ACTIVITIES. It was envisaged that in many cases employers would provide contractual schemes at least as generous as the statutory minimum entitlement. The Act also established the Central Arbitration Committee (CAC: see ARBITRATION), placed ACAS (see CONCILIATION) on a statutory footing with the power to issue CODES OF PRACTICE, established the role of the CERTIFICATION OFFICER, and created the Employment Appeal Tribunal to hear appeals on points of law from INDUSTRIAL TRIBUNALS. Additionally, employers were obliged to disclose information to the union for the purpose of collective bargaining, and to consult with the union over proposed redundancies (see CONSULTATION).

The individual employment rights were re-enacted in the EMPLOYMENT PROTECTION (CONSOLIDATION) ACT 1978.

Employment Protection (Consolidation) Act 1978. This Act brings together the Redundancy Payments Act 1965, the Contracts of Employment Act 1972, and the individual employment rights contained in the EMPLOYMENT PROTECTION ACT 1975, the TRADE UNION AND LABOUR RELATIONS ACT 1974, and its amendment in 1976. The provisions of the latter Acts not concerned with individual rights, such as the duty of an employer to consult with trade unions over proposed redundancies and the establishment of the Employment Appeal Tribunal, remain unaffected.

Certain sections of the Act were amended by the EMPLOYMENT ACT 1980.

Equal Opportunities Commission (EOC). The EOC, consisting of between 8 and 15 commissioners, was established under the SEX DISCRIMINATION ACT 1975. It has a three-fold duty:

- to work towards the elimination of discrimination;
- to promote equality of opportunity;
- to keep under review the working of the Act and draw up proposals for amendment if necessary.

"The Equal Opportunities Commission have ruined it."

Its activities include assisting individual complainants and giving them advice, undertaking and assisting in research, involvement in educational and other promotional activities, carrying out investigations and conducting inquiries into areas not specifically covered by the legislation. Only the Commission can institute proceedings in respect of discriminatory advertisements or allegations of instructions or pressure to discriminate. In 1985, the Commission issued its Code of Practice for the Elimination of Discrimination on the Grounds of Sex and Marriage and the Promotion of Equality of Opportunity in Employment (see CODES OF PRACTICE).

The Commission's power to carry out investigations is potentially significant in relation to discriminatory practices which may occur on a large scale: in firms, industries or institutions. However, the machinery for carrying out investigations is so cumbersome that they have not had a marked effect. Where the Commission wish to carry out a 'named person' investigation, they must have at least a suspicion that the person named may have committed an unlawful act of discrimination, and the investigation may not be used to examine the firm's employment policies generally. A preliminary hearing must be held if the named person wishes to make representations. If in the course of the investigation the Commission is satisfied that an unlawful act has been committed, it may issue a non-discrimination notice (NDN). The person concerned may appeal against the NDN to a tribunal or court within six weeks. If within five years of an NDN it appears that further unlawful acts are likely to occur, an injunction may be obtained, but contravention of an NDN is not in itself unlawful. Only ten investigations have been begun to date.

The address of the EOC is Overseas House, Quay Street, Manchester M3 3HN (061 833 9244).

Equality of opportunity. Legislation on reducing unfair discrimination mainly seeks to prevent people doing things. Equality of opportunity requires a more positive approach over a wider area, changing attitudes and challenging discriminatory assumptions so that a greater variety of employment opportunities are available to those whose prospects have previously been limited. The main instrument for equalizing opportunity is often the statement of policy, developed by consultation between the employer and union representatives, that tries to prevent lawful actions and decisions which inhibit equal opportunity as well as those which are unlawful. It is quite common, for instance, for equal opportunity policy statements to ban discriminatory action on the basis of sexual orientation. Less frequently discrimination on the basis of age is also banned.

Equal Pay Act 1970/Equal Pay (Amendment) Regulations 1983. The Equal Pay Act was passed in 1970 but became operative only at the end of 1975, theoretically to complement the SEX DISCRIMINATION ACT 1975. Its effect was to entitle a woman to *contractual* terms and conditions (claims invariably relate to 'pay') not less favourable than those of a man with whom she wished to compare herself (and vice versa), in two situations:

- where she was employed on 'LIKE WORK' with him, or

- where her job had been rated as equivalent to his following an analytical job evaluation study.

As a result of a finding that these provisions were not sufficient to comply with COMMUNITY LAW obligations, a third category was added by the 1983 Regulations, namely:

- where her work is of EQUAL VALUE to his.

The two persons being compared must be employed by the same employer or by ASSOCIATED EMPLOYERS. Where the employer has more than one establishment, claims are restricted to the applicant's own establishment unless common terms and conditions apply at another establishment. This restriction raises two problems; first, 'establishment' has no statutory definition, so that tribunals are left to decide whether, for example, a chain of retail shops is one establishment or several. If each is managed autonomously, individual establishments would be indicated. Second, it is unclear to what extent terms and conditions must be 'common' to permit claims between one establishment and another.

Under the Act (as amended by the Regulations) employers have a defence to a claim if they can justify the disparate treatment on grounds unrelated to sex (see GENUINE MATERIAL FACTOR). A claim may be made at any time during employment or up to six months after an applicant leaves the employment; where the tribunal finds it well-founded, arrears of pay for up to two years may be awarded in addition to a declaration that the applicant is entitled to equal pay henceforth.

Equal value. In 1983 the EQUAL PAY ACT 1970 was amended via the EQUAL PAY (AMENDMENT) REGULATIONS 1983 to permit a woman to claim that her work was of equal value to that of a chosen male comparator (or vice versa) and that hence she was entitled to equal pay (see ARTICLE 119 OF THE TREATY OF ROME). 'Value' is defined in terms of the demands made on the job holder under headings such as 'skill', 'responsibility' and 'effort'; it does not mean the value of the job holder to the firm, or their marginal productivity.

An equal value claim entails a more complicated tribunal procedure than claims under the original Act. There is an initial hearing at which claims may be thrown out if the tribunal feels there are 'no reasonable grounds' for believing the jobs to be of equal value, so that it is a hopeless case. Those not rejected are passed to an independent expert who will compare the jobs (*not* the individuals who perform them) in terms of the demands made on the job holder by breaking the jobs down into a number of factors which are then assessed; often as 'high', 'medium' or 'low', though individual experts are free to choose their own method provided they use this analytical framework. Experts can ask the parties to provide relevant information such as job descriptions, and will later send the parties a provisional report of their assessment of the value of the jobs. They take into account any representations made by the parties and finally submit their report to a recovened hearing. The tribunal are not obliged to agree with the expert's conclusion though it is unlikely they will often depart from it.

If an employer (or applicant) wishes to challenge the report factually this must be done when he or she is permitted to make representations, for such factual challenges cannot be made once the report is accepted by the tribunal. Employers (and even some applicants) have chosen to prepare their own expert report as an alternative means of challenge.

Where the expert finds the jobs are of equal value and the tribunal agrees, the GENUINE MATERIAL FACTOR defence is available. However, an employer wishing to rely on such a defence is well advised to raise it at the initial hearing. If this is not done the tribunal may decide not to permit the raising of the issue later (presumably on the basis that if such a defence existed, the time and expense of an independent expert could have been saved).

Employers can only protect themselves from potential equal value claims with reasonable certainty if they have analysed the jobs concerned in a job evaluation study which, like that of the expert, breaks the job down into factors related to its demands. Claims are then excluded unless the applicant can show that the scheme discriminated on sexual grounds, for example, the choice of factors used is not representative of the tasks done by both sexes.

Thus far, successful equal value comparisons include:

- a female packer with a male labourer;

- a female canteen cook with a male joiner, painter and thermal insulation engineer;
- a housemother with a housefather;
- female sewing machinists with male upholsterers.

It should be noted that in principle there are no limits to the jobs which may be compared, so that there is no reason why a manual worker may not choose a clerical assistant as comparator, for example.

See also JOB EVALUATION, POINTS RATING.

Equal Opportunities Commision, *Equal Pay for Work of Equal Value* (Manchester: Equal Opportunities Commission, 1984); Equal Opportunities Commission, *Judging Equal Value* (Manchester: Equal Opportunities Commission, 1984); A. Lester and D. Wainwright, *Equal Pay for Work of Equal Value* (TMS Management Consultants, London, 1984).

Executive search. Often described as 'head hunting', executive search is a form of management selection consultancy which is often strongly criticized as being unethical. Instead of the consultant advertising a vacancy and screening applicants, the list of possible job holders is drawn up first and the consultant then seeks them out to see if they would be interested in a change. The objections to this method are, first, that many aspirants are denied a chance of applying and, second, that people are enticed away from their employer. On the other hand it may be pointless (as well as competitively disadvantageous) to advertise a vacancy for which only a handful of people are regarded as suitable, and people are not likely to be enticed away from an employer unless they want to leave.

Despite the reservations, executive search is now a well-established practice and is widely used for recruiting to very specialized posts and for overseas locations.

Expenses. Coping with expenses is one of the most wearying activities for any employer. Individual employees are enormously attracted to the idea of 'drawing expenses' because they usually seem to amount to slightly more than the actual amount of money expended on the company's affairs and are therefore seen as a fringe benefit. Even greater may be the attraction of avoiding the attentions of the Inland Revenue (and, perhaps, one's spouse). See also SUBSISTENCE ALLOWANCE.

Experienced Worker Standard (EWS). This is the standard of quality and level of output achieved by the average experienced worker. It is used as a benchmark during employee training so that the trainee (and the trainer) can see how close that training has come to reaching the level of full competence. When trainers have experience with a number of trainees preparing for the same job they can also plot a learning curve of the various points on the way to EWS and the time of training which is usually required to reach each point.

Sometimes pay is also linked to EWS, in that the employee does not receive normal weekly earnings until EWS has been reached. An extreme form of this approach was known as Stakhanovism in pre-war Russia; productivity was stimulated by offering incentives to workers who could reach very high standards of efficiency (in other words, much above simple EWS). The model worker was a powerfully-built miner named A. G. Stakhanov, who reached levels of performance far beyond the capacity of all but a few of his colleagues. Soon many Russian factories had 'Stakhanovites' to set the pace, but the pace proved too hot for most other workers to match.

F

Factor comparison. Among the various methods of JOB EVALU-
ATION, factor comparison is regarded by many experts as the one
least prone to human distortion (other experts prefer the term
'human judgement'), and it usually depends on computer analysis
to produce its results. The method is to select benchmark jobs and
analyse each to determine the level of a number of factors, such as
skill, responsibility and working conditions. Each factor is then
ranked and an estimate made as to how much of the present pay
rate is paid for each factor in each job. All other jobs are then
compared, factor by factor, with the benchmarks to produce a
rate of pay for each. In the end the criteria are reasonably
objective, but that relative objectivity is won at the expense of
complexity and mystery to the uninitiated.

See also EQUAL VALUE, JOB EVALUATION, JOB GRADING, JOB
RANKING, POINTS RATING.

Factory Inspectorate. Now part of the HEALTH AND SAFETY
EXECUTIVE, the factory inspectors have a right of entry to any
factory where they may inspect any process to determine whether
or not appropriate statutory levels of working conditions obtain,
especially relating to safety. If they are not satisfied they may
institute a prosecution of the employer. The main statute from
which factory inspectors derive their authority is the Factories
Act 1961.

Fair reasons for dismissal. An employer defending a claim of
UNFAIR DISMISSAL must establish the reason for the employee's
dismissal, and that it was one of the potentially fair reasons laid
down in S57(1) and S57(2) of the EMPLOYMENT PROTECTION
(CONSOLIDATION) ACT 1978.

1 Capability or qualifications. Capability embraces not only skill
and competence but also physical or mental health; the dismissal
of an epileptic who attacks employees whilst having a fit may
therefore relate to capability. A 'qualification' must refer to a
person's aptitude or ability (for example, the possession of a
driving licence). (See also CONSULTATION, WARNINGS.)
2 Conduct. Probably more realistically referred to as 'misconduct', this covers fighting, clocking offences, swearing, absenteeism, lateness, disobedience and dishonesty, but the list is endless.

Misconduct outside the employment may justify dismissal if it affects, or reflects in some way upon, the employer–employee relationship: for instance, an employee in a position of trust and integrity being convicted of an offence of dishonesty. (See also WARNINGS, SUMMARY DISMISSAL.)

3 REDUNDANCY. Though this amounts to a potentially fair reason, it does of course entitle an employee to a redundancy payment. (See also WARNINGS, CONSULTATION.)

4 The fact that the employee could not continue to work in the position held without contravening a statute. The dismissal of a bearded employee working with raw meat and thereby contravening Food Regulations was justified on this ground.

5 Some other substantial reason of a kind to justify dismissal. Commonly referred to as 'SOSR', this reason has been relied on, for example:

• to justify a dismissal consequent on the reorganization of a business which did not legally amount to a redundancy dismissal;

• where local authority employers faced with the need to achieve economies dismissed employees and offered them new contracts on less attractive terms;

• to dismiss fairly the wife of a married couple employed in a pub where the husband had already been dismissed (but probably not so if the wife could have continued the job without the husband);

• where under the terms of a contract between the employer and a third party, an employee could be dismissed at the insistence of the third party.

It should be noted that establishing a potentially fair reason does not constitute a fair dismissal; the tribunal must be satisfied that the employer acted reasonably in the circumstances (see UNFAIR DISMISSAL). In fact it is rare for an employer to be unable to establish a potentially fair reason; the claim is much more likely to fail at the 'unreasonableness' stage. (See also AUTOMATICALLY UNFAIR DISMISSAL, DISMISSAL.)

Feedback. In COMMUNICATIONS a key principle is that feedback improves the quality of the exchanges. The sender of the message receives a range of feedback signals from the recipient, causing him or her to modify the transmission to improve its quality. Examples are looking for signs of incomprehension as a trigger to restating a message in different words, or looking for signs of alarm as a trigger to producing some reassurance. Feedback is not only elicited, it is also provided to improve what is heard, so the selection interviewer will encourage the nervous candidate by nods and smiles, and the puzzled negotiator will furrow a bemused brow when hearing something unbelievable.

In a more general sense feedback is an essential feature of PERFORMANCE APPRAISAL and TRAINING, and can affect the level of both MORALE and MOTIVATION amongst employees.

Felt-fair pay. There is no objective standard of what the correct level of pay is for an individual or group when compared with other individuals or groups, and the pay comparison is one of the key determinants of satisfaction with pay level. There are some useful benchmarks, like the average level of earnings or changes in the cost of living, but no authoritative guideline for deciding that a group should receive payment that is, say, 110 per cent of average earnings. There appears, however, to be a level which is felt by the recipient to be fair. If the pay for that person is within a few percentage points of what is judged fair, then the worker is satisfied. If it is below the felt-fair level, then the worker will be disgruntled and may join with colleagues in industrial action, or simply seek alternative opportunities. If workers feel they are overpaid, their behaviour may also be unsatisfactory as they may create extra work – and staff – to justify their income level, and they may be inhibited from leaving when they have lost interest in the job.

Final salary schemes (in pensions). The most common basis for deciding the level of pension for a retiree is now a link to the final salary. The person due to retire will have accumulated a number of years' entitlement according to the terms of the pension scheme (x 60ths up to a maximum of 40, where x = years of service, is a common formula: a person with 20 years' service would be entitled to 20/60ths or one-third). The pension is then determined by applying that formula to a notional salary figure. In final salary schemes the figure is usually either the salary in the final year of employment, the average of the last three years, or the best of the last three. Less often it is based on the last five years of employment.

See also PENSION SCHEMES.

Fines and deductions. In the absence of contractual agreement or custom, an employer has no power at COMMON LAW to fine employees as a disciplinary measure or for bad workmanship, for example. However, limited provision was made in respect of manual workers and shop assistants by the Truck Act 1896. The area of fines and deductions generally has now been regulated by the WAGES ACT 1986, which repeals all earlier TRUCK LEGISLATION.

The effect of Part I of the Wages Act is that fines and deductions will only be lawful if:

- authorized or required by statute (for example, tax and National Insurance contributions); or
- authorized by a written term of the contract of which the worker has been given a copy prior to the deduction; or
- authorized by any term of the contract (which could be oral, or implied) of which the worker is given a written explanation; or
- the worker has previously agreed in writing to the deduction.

Workers in retail employment are given special protection, for the amount of any deducation or fine imposed on any one pay day is limited to 10 per cent of wages (though the limit does not apply to a worker's final instalment of wages). The provision will no doubt benefit workers such as petrol pump cashiers who have been known to lose in excess of 50 per cent of their wages in respect of till shortages. In addition, employers are only permitted to make deductions in respect of cash shortages or stock deficiencies within a 12-month period of the particular deficiency being discovered (or within 12 months of when it should reasonably have been discovered).

Complaints of unlawful deductions may be made to an industrial tribunal, normally within three months of the deduction. If the tribunal upholds the claim it can make a declaration to that effect and order repayment of the sum deducted.

Protection under the Act is not confined to those of EMPLOYEE status, but extends to those working under a CONTRACT FOR services where there is an undertaking to perform the work personally (unless their services are provided in the course of running a 'profession or business undertaking'). It should additionally be noted that the Act applies equally where, for example, an employer recoups cash shortages by demanding a payment from the worker, rather than by a deduction from wages.

See also ITEMIZED PAY STATEMENT.

First aid. In establishments with relatively low hazards, such as shops, offices, banks and libraries, an employee should be appointed as a first-aider if there are more than 150 people employed. In a factory there needs to be an appointed first-aider when there are 50 employed. All first-aiders should receive training and certification approved by the HEALTH AND SAFETY EXECUTIVE. First-aid boxes should be provided in all sizes of establishment, with contents linked to the number of employees. The minimum requirement is for wrapped sterile adhesive dressings, eye pads, triangular bandages, sterile coverings for serious wounds, safety pins and three different sizes of sterile unmedicated dressings.

Health and Safety Executive, *First Aid at Work* London: HMSO.

Five-fold grading. One of the best-known methods of HUMAN ATTRIBUTE CLASSIFICATION is the five-fold grading method devised by J. Munro Fraser, who suggests that the suitability of candidates for posts can be assessed by reviewing the evidence available to selectors under five headings:

- impact on others;
- qualifications and experience;
- innate abilities;
- motivation;
- emotional adjustment.

J. M. Fraser, *Employment Interviewing,* 5th edn (London: Macdonald & Evans, 1978).

Fixed term contract. This term refers to contracts whose

Selection by five-fold grading

J.M. Fraser has devised a five-fold framework for selection decisions. Use the form below to organize your thinking about candidates, marking A, B, C, D or E in each box, with A meaning much above average declining to E, signifying much below average.

	Candidates			
	1	2	3	4
Impact on others, or the kind of response a person's appearance, speech and manner calls out from others				
Qualifications and experience, or the skill and knowledge required for different jobs				
Innate abilities, or how quickly and accurately a person's mind works				
Motivation, or the kind of work that appeals to an individual and how much effort he or she is prepared to apply to it				
Emotional adjustment, or the amount of stress involved in living and working with other people				

---

duration is fixed by time and not by task, so that a three-year post would be a fixed term contract, but a contract to paint the Forth Road Bridge would not. A provision to terminate the contract by notice before its expiry date does not prevent its being a fixed term contract.

By statute the ending of a fixed term contract without its being renewed constitutes a DISMISSAL, so permitting claims of UNFAIR DISMISSAL and/or redundancy payments. However, employees under fixed term contracts for one year or more may agree in writing to waive their right to unfair dismissal if the contract is not renewed; similarly where the contract is for two years or more, rights to redundancy payments may be renounced. These are exceptions to the general rule that the statutory rights cannot be contracted out of.

Flexible working hours. To avoid a rigid pattern in the working day, some establishments operate a form of flexible working hours with all employees being present for the *core*, say 10 a.m. to 12 midday and 2 p.m. to 4 p.m. but working the remainder of their weekly stint in *flexible time* at the beginning, middle or end of the day. This makes it possible for people to adjust their time to fit in with public travel facilities and other personal arrangements, as well as providing the establishment with the advantage of employee cover over a slightly longer working day.

It is normal for the pattern of hours to be agreed in advance, in order to ease problems of supervision and to ensure a reasonably even level of manning throughout the week, but crises can be well accommodated within the framework. Each scheme has a *settlement period* of a week or a month in which a normal quota of hours has to be worked, so it is not usual for a 35-hour week employee, for instance, to be able to work 52½ hours for two weeks in succession and then have a full week off.

Gradually patterns of working time are becoming much more flexible, with some employees now engaged on annual hours contracts, which allow considerable flexibility to both employer and employee.

See also JOB SHARING, HOURS OF WORK.

C. Curson (ed.), *Flexible Patterns of Work* London: Institute of Personnel Management, 1986).

Fringe benefits. Features of payment other than wage or salary have grown in importance steadily since the 1960s, so that Britain has a level of provision that is not found in other countries, especially for managers and professionals. In the private sector of employment the *company car* is the most significant fringe benefit, being enjoyed by most managers and many other white collar employees. In the public sector of employment *mileage allowance* is more common. *Private medical insurance* is another popular benefit, being provided by over half of British employers to management employees. One-fifth also offer it to manual employees. Other benefits include *free hairdressing, chiropody, loans* (to buy season tickets), the ability to buy *company goods and services at much reduced prices, luncheon vouchers, subsidised meals,* or the *use of the company box at Covent Garden or the company flat in Miami.*

See also EXPENSES, PROFIT SHARING.

Frustration. Frustration is a concept which originates in the law of contract. It envisages the occurrence of an unexpected event for which neither party is responsible, and which makes further performance of an existing contract illegal, impossible or radically different from that originally contemplated. The result is that the contract terminates automatically. Examples of frustrating events have been the burning down of a hired building and the seizing of commercially chartered ships on the outbreak of war.

In the area of employment law the doctrine has been applied where employees have received a prison sentence or suffered some illness which will lead to a potentially long absence from work. If a contract of employment is frustrated there is no need for the employee concerned to be dismissed, and therefore an unfair dismissal claim is precluded. For this reason frustration has been applied reluctantly by tribunals. In the case of a prison sentence, the fact that the employee could be said to be 'responsible' for the event, or 'at fault' does not prevent the *employer* relying on the doctrine, though the employee may not. Should the employer choose to dismiss, he or she would normally allege 'some other substantial reason of a kind to justify dismissal', although if the employee's behaviour had some bearing on the work or the employer–employee relationship the dismissal could relate to 'conduct' (see FAIR REASONS FOR DISMISSAL).

In the case of an unexpected illness (for example, a coronary) it has been held that there is no reason why the doctrine of frustration should not apply, even if the contract is determinable by relatively short notice. Relevant considerations would clearly be the likely length of absence, whether the employment was temporary or permanent, and any provisions as to sick pay. If frustration is not applicable, an employer may well be able to dismiss fairly for 'incapacity' (See FAIR REASONS FOR DISMISSAL).

Further education. A subtle distinction in the world of education is between 'further' and 'higher'. Both forms of education follow schooling, but higher education is generally regarded as that in the university, polytechnic and college of higher education sector where students prepare for degrees, while further education describes the work of colleges of technology and colleges of further education in predominantly vocational courses leading to professional and technical qualifications.

Further education is a responsibility of the local authority, although the MANPOWER SERVICES COMMISSION is now heavily involved in this activity as well.

See also POLYTECHNICS, TECHNICAL AND VOCATIONAL EDUCATION INITIATIVE, YOUTH TRAINING SCHEME.

G

General intelligence. Few words carry such purport as intelligence. In some cases it refers to knowledge or information, as in the Intelligence Corps of the British Army. In another context it means common sense and wisdom ('Any intelligent person would realize that . . . '). In personnel circles the term is used with the prefix 'general' as a statement about an ability to understand, to perceive and comprehend meaning. It is regarded as a natural ability which can be distinguished from both experience and information, and is therefore a useful indicator of potential that in some ways is more accurate than evidence of attainment, such as examination results. It is believed that this ability can be measured for each individual and then compared with the level of ability possessed by the general population, so the individual can be placed at some point in relation to the average. It is also held that the level of general intelligence is normally distributed in the sense described by Gauss, so the number of people in the middle 10 per cent of the distribution is far greater than the number in the top or bottom 10 per cent.

The idea of an intelligence quotient (IQ) was devised by the German, William Stern, to provide an index of mental age related to chronological age. Using the Stanford–Binet test the distribution of IQ scores is as shown in table 1.

Table 1

IQ	Description	% in each group
Above 139	Very superior	1
120–39	Superior	11
110–19	High average	18
90–109	Average	46
80–9	Low average	15
70–9	Borderline	6
Below 70	Mentally retarded	3

The accuracy of intelligence measurements is still not universally accepted and the degree of a person's intelligence remains a highly sensitive issue. 'I am taller than you are' is an unexceptional comment; 'I am more intelligent than you' would be unacceptable arrogance, no matter how obviously accurate the claim.

Genuine material factor (GMF). An employer may defeat a claim for equal pay made under the EQUAL PAY ACT 1970/EQUAL PAY (AMENDMENT) REGULATIONS 1983 if able to prove that the disparity in treatment between the man and the woman is 'genuinely due to a material factor which is not the difference of sex'.

In relation to claims based on LIKE WORK or work 'rated as equivalent' under the 1970 Act, the GMF *must* be 'a material difference between the woman's case and the man's' which objectively justifies the pay differential. Seniority, merit and experience have all been accepted as such differences. Another potential defence may be that the earnings of the comparator are 'red-circled': that is, they are protected at an artificial level because, for example, the employee is no longer capable of doing the original job by reason of ill health, or the job being regraded. (see RED CIRCLING). However, such an argument will not be accepted if sex discrimination has contributed to the situation in the past: for instance, if the higher paid job had been a male-only grade. Lower pay for part-timers will only be justifiable if the employer can show that the differential is reasonably necessary for genuine economic reasons (for example, that machinery is less efficiently used).

Where an EQUAL VALUE claim is made, the Amendment Regulations provide that the GMF *may* be a material difference between the woman's case and the man's, and thus by implication it may presumably be something else. It is thought that the wording will permit defences based on market forces arguments to justify pay discrepancies: for example, that computer programmers must be paid more than their evaluated worth because they are in short supply. It is suggested, however, that the converse would smack of exploitation and should not be acceptable.

It must always be remembered that this legislation addresses itself only to the question of discrimination between the sexes and not to pay levels generally.

Genuine occupational qualification. Both the SEX DISCRIMI-NATION ACT 1975, and the RACE RELATIONS ACT 1976 provide instances of cases where being a member of one sex, or belonging to a particular racial group, is a genuine occupational qualification. In such a case sex or racial discrimination is not unlawful. The issue generally arises at the recruitment stage where the employer for some specific reasons seeks to limit applications for a job.

Examples under the Sex Discrimination Act include occasions when one sex is required for reasons of authenticity in dramatic performances or other entertainment, to preserve decency or privacy (for example, a toilet attendant, or where female employees strip to their underwear to rest during the course of a shift). A genuine occupational qualification similarly applies where the job is one of two to be held by a married couple, and where the job is likely to be performed abroad where the laws or customs would preclude one sex from carrying out the duties. Also included are certain hospital and prison staff.

A more limited list in the Race Relations Act includes requiring persons of a particular racial group for authenticity in restaurants, in dramatic performances (for example, in casting Othello?) or for work as an artist's or photographic model. Personal welfare counsellors are also covered.

The concept of a genuine occupational qualification is clearly designed to prevent absurdities which would arise if no exemptions from the Acts were permitted, but it is for the employer concerned to show that such a qualification exists.

Golden formula ('in contemplation or furtherance of a trade dispute'). Individuals who organize or take part in INDUSTRIAL ACTION are likely to commit certain ECONOMIC TORTS such as 'inducing a breach of contract'. However, they may be granted IMMUNITY from liability for those torts provided they act in contemplation or furtherance of a trade dispute. 'Trade dispute' is given a statutory definition in S29 of the Trade Union and Labour Relations Act 1974 (as amended by the Employment Act 1982); it is a dispute between workers and *their* employers which relates *wholly* or *mainly* to one or more of the following:

- terms and conditions of employment or the physical conditions in which any workers are required to work;
- the engagement or non-engagement or termination or suspension of employment or the duties of employment, of one or more workers;
- the allocation of work or duties of employment between workers or groups of workers;
- matters of discipline;
- membership or non-membership of a trade union on the part of a worker;
- facilities for officials of trade unions;
- machinery for negotiation or consultation and other procedures relating to any of the foregoing matters, including the recognition by employers or employers' associations of the right of a trade union to represent workers in any such negotiation or consultation or in the carrying out of such procedures.

A trade dispute may be in existence before actual confrontation occurs, or even if there is no confrontation at all because the employer yields to the union's demands. A dispute relating to matters abroad is excluded unless workers in the UK are affected by its outcome; similarly political strikes (for example, against apartheid in South Africa) do not fall within S29. However, the line between disputes relating to terms and conditions of employment and those relating to political disputes can be very thin, especially for public employees, or where, for example, employees object to government plans for privatization. In such cases the wording of S29 may be crucial; the dispute must relate 'wholly or mainly' to one of the listed matters.

Clearly, acts 'in contemplation of' a trade dispute may be done before the dispute arises, but it must be imminent rather than a mere possibility. In deciding whether an act is done in contemplation or furtherance of the dispute, the test is a subjective one of asking whether the individual honestly believed that those actions would be in the interests of one of the parties to the dispute.

Golden handshake. When senior officials of an organization are required to leave, convention requires that they be compensated for loss of office. The compensation is a substantial sum of money, most of which will not be taxable as it is not classed as income, unless the amount received exceeds £25,000.

Grapevine. The grapevine is the informal network of COMMUNI-CATIONS within an organization, which mainly conveys rumours that are prurient or alarming. Managers, especially middle managers, tend to dislike the grapevine as subordinates hear news before they do, and part of the appeal of BRIEFING GROUPS is the opportunity of pre-empting the grapevine. However, formal messages can be amplified through the grapevine and it can also be used as a means of testing reaction to an initiative that has not yet been decided, like the government briefing lobby corre-spondents off the record and later deciding what to do on the basis of how the issue has been viewed by the press.

"Know what I really miss? Office rumours."

Graphology. The idea that the analysis of handwriting is a key to character or personality is very attractive to those wishing to fill key positions in their organizations and wanting a means of indicating potential on which they can rely.

Judgement of people on the basis of their handwriting is certainly possible and may be frequently accurate, but producing consistently reliable results is dubious. If, for instance, a person's handwriting sprawls untidily across the page, the reader may interpret this as indicating impulsiveness and poor intellectual organization; while stiff, upright letters may be interpreted as showing strong discipline and firm will.

Analysis requires the identification of components which can be measured, like angle, slope and size of letters, which can then be correlated with personality characteristics, and accuracy can be measured statistically. So far methods providing statistically convincing correlations have not been developed.

Attempts at reliably analysing handwriting have been made for at least 800 years and will certainly continue. The method is used to a limited extent in management selection.

D. Mackenzie-Davey and M. Harris, *Judging People* (Maidenhead: McGraw-Hill, 1982).

Grievance procedure. The last resort for the dissatisfied employee is grievance procedure: a formal request for a complaint to be considered by a manager more senior than the one who has so far been involved. The right to this access is secured by a statutory obligation on the employer to specify in the contract of employment which document contains the name or description of the person to whom employees can apply if they wish to seek redress of a grievance. It is, however, more than a right for the employee: it is also an important management mechanism to monitor levels of employee dissatisfaction and as an early warning on issues that could become serious.

The basic framework of grievance procedure is three steps. The *preliminary* is where the employee advises the immediate superior of a wish to lodge a formal grievance. This is simply serving notice of the wish to have the matter considered by a more senior manager and may often have the effect of the immediate superior, or the management collectively, finding an acceptable solution to the problem which could not be found previously. If the grievance is not withdrawn the second step is

Outline grievance procedure

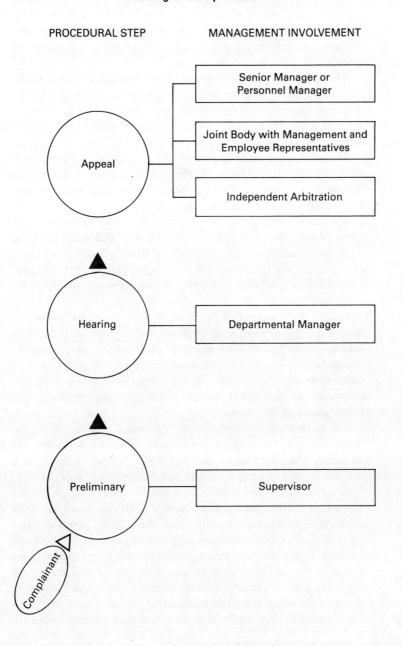

PROCEDURAL STEP   MANAGEMENT INVOLVEMENT

Appeal
- Senior Manager or Personnel Manager
- Joint Body with Management and Employee Representatives
- Independent Arbitration

Hearing — Departmental Manager

Preliminary — Supervisor

Complainant

the *hearing,* where a manager of more senior rank, specified in the procedure, hears the grievance and seeks a solution. If the dissatisfied employee is still not satisfied with the outcome, there remains the possibility of *appeal* to a more senior manager or committee.

Although the basic framework is of only three steps, many organizations have more, which are usually appeals against the outcome of appeals, as well as the possibility of a further stage of procedure involving an external expert, such as an ACAS arbitrator.

Procedures customarily provide the aggrieved employee with the right to be accompanied in the later stages of procedure by a 'friend', who is most often an official of the employee's union, but maybe a colleague or legal adviser. In order to avoid procedure operating too slowly, and therefore failing to cope with grievances when relief is needed, it is also usual for time limits to be incorporated guaranteeing that the hearing will take place within, for instance, four working days of the preliminary, with the appeal following within a further seven working days.

Grievances. Few aspects of managing people are more important than processes relating to grievances: these are real or imaginary wrongs which cause resentment and which may lead to unsatisfactory employee behaviour ranging from grumpiness to industrial action. If these feelings can be uncovered by the employer and remedial action taken, then the dysfunctional behaviour may be averted.

Grievances can be understood by thinking of three stages: dissatisfaction, complaint and grievance. *Dissatisfaction* is anything which unsettles the employee. It usually lasts for a short time and is forgotten by coffee time or by the next day, because so many incidents in a working day can be unsettling and all employees realize that a part of their job is to cope with problems rather than complain about them. Some dissatisfaction persists. The employee cannot cope with an aspect of the job and believes either that the management of the organization is to blame or that the management can deal with the problem. This produces a *complaint* to a member of the management, seeking a solution. In most cases the manager approached will deal with the matter in a way which removes the dissatisfaction, either by taking action or by explaining the situation in a way that was not previously understood. If that does not deal with the matter to the satisfaction of the employee making the complaint, there are two options. One is that the employee's behaviour becomes somehow dysfunctional, such as working without enthusiasm, unsettling colleagues or leaving. The other is that the employee lodges a grievance in the GRIEVANCE PROCEDURE.

Among the ways in which managers can avoid grievances becoming too great a problem are:

- taking complaints seriously and attempting to resolve the difficulties that caused them;
- encouraging the belief that complaints should be aired, despite a general tendency for employees to be reluctant to complain for fear of being dubbed as troublemakers;
- listening carefully to complaints to make sure that there is not a 'real' complaint being hidden behind the problem presented;
- viewing complaints dispassionately rather than as personal attacks.

Groups. Managers are interested in groups because they are sometimes needed to do collectively what the individual members cannot do in isolation. They present problems of leadership and direction which are much greater than those of individual leadership, and most individuals at work ally themselves to a group as a preferred mode of working, even though the degree of dependence on the group will vary considerably. Primary groups are small enough for members to interact with each other informally and face-to-face, like the members of a sports team or a small production unit. Any large organization is a network of primary groups, each having subtly different forms of social structure and roles. Secondary groups are much larger, such as a trade union or professional association, where face-to-face interaction is impractical and relationships are formal and impersonal. In secondary groups members are less concerned with each other as individual persons and more concerned with roles and the function that each member fulfils. Coordination is by formal organization and methods, because custom and tradition are powerful forces to maintain the status quo and significant change can only be achieved through formal mechanisms.

Managers need first to appreciate the existence of both types of group affiliation, as over-emphasis on formality and procedure will not be an effective form of management intervention in the affairs and interrelationships of primary groups. Also over-emphasis on the personal approach will not be effective in dealing with secondary groups.

D. C. Cartwright and A. Zander, *Group Dynamics* (London: Tavistock, 1968).

Group selection methods. When candidates are being assessed in the selection process, group methods are sometimes used to provide data on their ability to interact with each other and to provide the opportunity for candidates to display leadership behaviour.

The normal method is for a group of six to eight candidates to be given a series of communal tasks, such as a leaderless group exercise or group problem-solving activity. Their approach to the task is observed by assessors who make judgements of such qualities as: social skill, leadership, communication effectiveness, poise, coordination, logical thinking, reaction to criticism and attitudes. The method is frequently used in ASSESSMENT CENTRES.

Guarantee payments. Employees who are neither salaried nor paid weekly are liable to be affected financially by lay-offs or by shortages of work. For this reason the EMPLOYMENT PROTECTION (CONSOLIDATION) ACT 1978 obliges employers to pay a guarantee payment to such employees on certain days when they are not provided with work. The day must be one on which they would normally be required to work under their contract of employment. Thus employees who can choose whether or not to work on Saturdays cannot claim a guarantee payment for that day. In addition the reason for the lack of work must be a reduction in the employer's business for the sort of work the employee was employed to do, or some other occurrence which affects the normal working of the business, such as a power failure.

The amount of the payment is the number of normal working hours on that day multiplied by the 'guaranteed hourly rate' (obtained by dividing a week's pay by the number of normal hours in a week). However, this is subject to a somewhat meagre maximum figure of £10.90 per day (as from 1 April 1987, reviewed annually); additionally an employee cannot in any period of three months receive guarantee payments for more than five days. Employers may, however, have more generous private schemes, in which case any contractual entitlement will serve to set off the statutory right. Thus an employee will not be entitled to benefit from a private scheme and *then* claim statutory payments in addition. Employers who are party to a collective agreement covering the question of guarantee payments to the satisfaction of the Secretary of State may be exempted from the statutory provisions.

In order to qualify for the statutory payment an employee must have been continuously employed for one month. However, casual workers employed on fixed term contracts of three months or less, or on a contract to perform a specific task not expected to last more than three months, are excluded unless by the day in question they have actually worked for at least three months.

In three instances the right to a guarantee payment is lost:

• where the failure to provide work occurs because of a strike, lock-out or other industrial action;
• where the employee has unreasonably refused suitable alternative work (which may be work he or she is not contractually bound to perform) for the workless day;
• if the employee fails to comply with a reasonable attendance requirement (for example, where the employer is awaiting essential supplies).

Guide Chart Profile method. Guide Chart Profiles have become popular as a method of job evaluation for application to managerial jobs. Using the method of POINTS RATING, jobs are evaluated on the basis of three factors: problem-solving, know-how and accountability. Evaluations are then checked by employing the method of JOB RANKING. The points score for each job is then plotted on a scattergram against a scale of salaries currently being paid by other employers in the labour market.

This method is a proprietary product of Hay-MSL, who carry out an extensive salary survey in order to provide and update the labour market information, which is one of the main attractions of this particular approach.

H

Halo effect. If you regard a particular person as being very good in all ways as a result of knowing (or thinking) that person to be good in a specific way, then your judgement is influenced by a halo effect: excellence in one way is assumed to imply excellence in many others. There are many well-known examples of historical figures whose followers were so entranced by one outstanding quality – like oratory – that they failed to see other, less attractive characteristics which would have led them to a more balanced judgement of the leader. In everyday working life, however, it is a widespread phenomenon in a less dramatic way. Job applicants who impress in one facet of their self-presentation may find that selectors' judgement is over-influenced by that single feature. In a 1950s film Cary Grant hired Marilyn Monroe as a typist because of the way she walked. When one of his colleagues asked if she could type, he said, 'Anyone can type.' The sour grapes description of people who are rapidly promoted as being 'blue-eyed boys' is another version of the halo effect as those who are *not* promoted cannot accept any alternative explanation. Much of our working day is spent in making quick judgements of other people and the halo effect describes one of the traps into which we may fall.

The opposite is the horns effect, where one unattractive characteristic, like rudeness or unpunctuality, can damn a person.

Harmonization. There are many differences in employment practice relating to the category of employee that have no logical connection with the work done. In Britain, for instance, it has been commonplace for clerical and administrative employees to work shorter hours than manual workers, although the practice in other European countries is the opposite. It has also been commonplace for clerical, administrative and management employees to be paid monthly while manual employees are paid weekly. Harmonization is a process of trying to eliminate all those differences in employment practice that are not logically connected with the requirements of the job, adopting a common approach to pay and conditions and common criteria for all categories of employee.

C. Roberts, *Harmonization: Whys and Wherefores* (London: Institute of Personnel Management, 1985).

Hawthorne experiments. From 1927 to 1932 a series of experiments in working conditions was carried out at the

Hawthorne plant of the Western Electric Company in Chicago by Professor Elton Mayo. The studies were stimulated by the management after they had failed in earlier experiments to correlate the intensity of lighting in the plant and the level of productivity. The results of Mayo's experiments were that productivity increased as a result of a number of different changes in the layout of the workplace, including an increase in productivity when the arrangements were restored to exactly what they had been when the studies began. This led him to the conclusion that the stimulus to enhanced productivity was not the changes themselves but the social factors surrounding the changes. The investigations thus caused a radical development in the understanding of people at work. Previously the orthodox view was to treat each person as an isolated individual who would respond individually to management initiatives and work organization, but this was no longer tenable when the studies had been carried out, demonstrating the importance of social cohesion and the need for management approaches to concentrate on group processes.

See also GROUPS, HUMAN RELATIONS.

Health and Safety at Work Act 1974 (HSAWA). The HSAWA aims to secure the 'health, safety and welfare' of everyone at work, and additionally to protect others who may be at risk through the activities of persons at work. It is a novel piece of safety legislation, for it covers all industries, occupations and professions; it places a duty on employed persons to take care for the *own* safety; and it adopts measures to encourage an awareness of health and safety issues so that accidents may be avoided.

The Act places general and specific duties on employers to be carried out 'so far as is reasonably practicable'. Breach of a duty constitutes a criminal offence, and if prosecuted it is for employers to prove that they did what was reasonably practicable (that is, unusually, the burden of proof is on the accused). The duties are to:

- provide and maintain plant and systems of work that are safe and without risks to health;
- ensure safety in the handling, storage and transport of dangerous articles and substances;

- provide employees with adequate information, instruction, training and supervision to ensure their safety;
- provide and maintain safe means of access and egress;
- provide a safe and healthy working environment and adequate welfare facilities;
- prepare a written safety policy to be brought to the notice of employees;
- consult with safety representatives appointed by recognized trade unions, and allow them to check the adequacy of safety measures.

The employer's duty extends to those living in the vicinity of the workplace, and those who are on the premises but not employed (for example, users of launderettes or self-service petrol stations).

Employees' duties as defined by the Act are:

- to take reasonable care for the health and safety of themselves and others who may be affected by their actions at work;
- to cooperate with employers in observing health and safety requirements;
- not wilfully to misuse or interfere with things provided in pursuance of the statutory provisions.

Manufacturers and suppliers have duties in relation to the design and construction of articles supplied for use at work, their testing and examination and the provision of adequate information on their operation.

The administration and enforcement of the Act are carried out by the Health and Safety Commission and the HEALTH AND SAFETY EXECUTIVE. The Commission is made up of representatives of the Trades Union Congress and Confederation of British Industries and the Department of Employment; it must provide information and advice, make arrangements for appropriate research and training, and may conduct inquiries and investigations. Additionally it has the power to formulate CODES OF PRACTICE, and Regulations which will impose civil liability.

The Health and Safety Executive has the responsibility of enforcing the Act through the Inspectorate who are given new powers in addition to the right of prosecution. They may issue *improvement notices* specifying faults and how they may be corrected, usually with a time limit, or *prohibition notices* ordering a particular practice or operation to stop. In cases of immediate danger they may even seize the source of the danger and destroy it!

Health and Safety Executive. The Health and Safety Executive (HSE) is the executive arm of the Health and Safety Commission (HSC). Its main workforce is the FACTORY INSPECTORATE and the EMPLOYMENT MEDICAL ADVISORY SERVICE. The HSE produces a number of advisory leaflets, which are obtainable from their offices, and some CODES OF PRACTICE. There are 21 regional offices and the head office is at: Baynards House, 1 Chepstow Place, London W2 4TF (01 229 3456).

Hierarchy. A hierarchy is any system of people or offices graded in rank order. In working life the term is usually applied to the upper part of the organizational pyramid and those office holders possessing the greatest power and influence. A significant feature of this power is the responsibility for the actions and decisions of subordinates that is held by the superordinates (or bosses) in the work of subordinates, and a tendency to generate unnecessary administrative work and controls which create a need for extra personnel as well as slowing down decision-making and administrative procedures. There has long persisted the idea that there is an optimum 'span of control', so that no manager should have more than five or six direct subordinates. This idea has been carefully studied by researchers and it is certainly not generally valid. Flatter hierarchies with fewer levels are thought to improve communication and generate greater individual autonomy and responsibility. There can, however, be a case for a steeper hierarchy (and narrower span of control) when problems being encountered are unfamiliar or when subordinates are not fully trained.

See also BUREAUCRACY.

Holiday pay. The amount paid to employees during annual holidays varies considerably. Salaried employees usually continue to receive their normal salary, but manual employees and others with potentially fluctuating earnings will have different arrangements. Some will receive payment at the average level of their earnings in the period prior to their holiday, while others will receive only basic pay and others will receive basic pay plus specified allowances. It is sometimes made a condition of receiving holiday pay that the employee attends for a full shift on the day before the holiday begins.

Holidays. *Public* holidays are those days on which all employees are entitled to holiday with pay. At the moment for England, Wales and Northern Ireland these are:

New Year's Day
Good Friday
Easter Monday
May Day
Spring Bank Holiday Monday
August Bank Holiday Monday
Christmas Day
Boxing Day

In Scotland there are two days at New Year, but Easter Monday and Boxing Day are not normally public holidays.

Anyone required to work on one of those days would normally be paid at a premium rate and would have to volunteer. The employer could only make working on a public holiday a condition of employment if that requirement was written into the contract of employment. There are sometimes extra public holidays for special occasions, like a Royal wedding.

Annual holidays are those days that the individual employee takes for, say, a summer holiday. The entitlement is specified in the contract of employment and the days are with pay. Some or all of these days may be specified by the employer, so that the widespread practice of factories closing from Christmas Eve to 2 January is usually made possible by the employer specifying that two or three days of annual holiday must be taken at that time. Another practice is where an establishment, like a factory, restaurant or shop closes completely for two weeks in the summer and all employees are required to take their holiday at that time. Entitlement to annual holiday usually increases with service, so that few employees with less than 12 months' service will be entitled to a full complement of annual holiday and long service can add extra days of entitlement. Standard entitlement is now between two and four weeks annually, although there are some instances of five and six weeks of entitlement, apart from specialized occupations like school teaching and college lecturing where there is an entitlement linked to teaching terms.

The practice of employees splitting their annual holiday into two or three blocks is growing.

Local holidays are linked to local traditions. In some parts of the Midlands, for instance, there is a practice of working on Good Friday and taking off the Tuesday after Easter Monday instead. In Lancashire a number of towns have one or two Wakes Weeks, so that the town virtually closes down for that period and all annual holidays are concentrated in that short time.

Religious holidays are partly enshrined in public holidays, with the recognition of Christmas and Easter, although Spring Bank Holiday has replaced the traditional Whitsun. With the growing range of faiths represented in the community, most employers will wish to respect the essential requirements of religious observance, but as the annual holiday entitlement increases it becomes less common for days of holiday for religious observance, such as Yom Kippur, to be granted with pay; they will either be without pay or the days will be deducted from annual entitlement.

Although the employee is entitled to annual holiday by the contract of employment, the timing of absence is still at the reasonable prerogative of the employer, who is obliged to allow absence only when it can be accommodated within the requirements of the business.

Homeworkers. By reason of their hours of work or their pattern of working, homeworkers may be excluded from many employment protection rights. Traditionally they have been regarded largely as self-employed (see CONTRACT FOR SERVICES) though there have been instances recently where tribunals have accorded them EMPLOYEE status. The outcome in a given case is likely to be influenced by the length of employment with the company concerned and whether the work has been largely continuous or more sporadic. Employee status alone does not, however, enable claims of unfair dismissal or redundancy pay (for example) to be made. In general a minimum number of hours per week must be worked continuously over a period of at least two years. This may never be achieved by homeworkers who are employed part-time or seasonally.

See also CONTINUITY OF EMPLOYMENT.

"There are, however, some disadvantages to being self-employed."

Hours of work. There are few statutory provisions governing an individual's hours of work; in general they are determined by COLLECTIVE BARGAINING. However, employers are under a statutory obligation to include details of terms relating to hours of work in an employee's written statement (see CONTRACT, WRITTEN PARTICULARS OF). This may be done conveniently by referring in the statement to the appropriate COLLECTIVE AGREEMENT.

Protective legislation does exist in relation to young people, whose hours and times of working are restricted by Acts such as the Factories Act 1961 and the Mines and Quarries Act 1954; the corresponding restrictions on women's employment under those Acts has been lifted by the SEX DISCRIMINATION ACT 1986. Additionally there are some statutory limitations on the working hours of people employed in specific jobs such as mining, sheet glass-working and the driving of certain classes of vehicles.

A working week of at least 16 hours (or between 8 and 16 hours over a period of five years) is an essential factor in determining entitlement to many statutory employment protection rights, whether or not those rights also depend on establishing a period of continuous employment (see CONTINUITY OF EMPLOYMENT and, for example, TIME OFF, ITEMIZED PAY STATEMENT).

House journals. One of the most extensively used means of providing information to employees is the house journal, a publication prepared by and for members of the organization or 'house'. It is a vehicle for conveying hard information about the business and its progress, human interest stories and the more general type of material intended to produce team spirit and a sense of corporate identity.

Although expensive to produce, house journals are usually prepared by a public relations department or consultant and published between four and six times a year. The significance of the house journal has been partly eclipsed by the growing practice of providing employees with reports of business progress under the general umbrella of EMPLOYEE INVOLVEMENT.

Human asset accounting. A development of the general management anxiety to quantify decisions about people and their achievements has been the method of human asset accounting, which examines the people in an organization as human assets with an ascribed value in accounting terms, the depreciation or appreciation of which can be measured. The main reservations about this approach have been that it tends to reduce to too small a range of attributes the potential usefulness of a person to the organization. It may be possible to estimate and 'price' changes in ability and capacity, but changes in interest and motivation may be much more significant than an increase in capacity through the acquisition of new skills or understanding.

Introduced in the early 1970s, human asset accounting found few advocates and faded from view. The more recent development of HUMAN RESOURCES MANAGEMENT incorporates some of the same thinking.

Human attribute classification. Selection and assessment is made easier if there is a language that can be used consistently and systematically to describe people being assessed and compared. The most popular method of doing this is to use a list of attributes which all candidates will possess to a varying degree, so that their relative strengths and weaknesses can be discussed. The most widely used system of human attribute classification is the SEVEN-POINT PLAN; another is the FIVE-FOLD GRADING METHOD.

The decision as to which system to use is largely one of personal preference, as it is merely a method of introducing consistency into judgements, but there is value in persisting with whichever method is chosen as effectiveness increases with practice.

Human relations. Apart from the obvious meaning, human relations describes a school of management thought that developed after the HAWTHORNE EXPERIMENTS, with the basic tenets being that:

- workers respond to interest by management in their work and their opinions about the work;
- the informal social organization of the workplace is a key determinant of behaviour and productive efficiency.

Although these ideas were an over-simplification of the Hawthorne results, they dominated management thinking for a quarter of a century and remain a significant element of the more complex nature of contemporary management thinking.

Human resources management. The concept of human resources management represents a major shift of emphasis in the employment of people, moving away from the traditional emphasis of PERSONNEL MANAGEMENT on conciliation, propitiation and motivation of employees as a potentially uncooperative *cost* towards the idea that people at work need less goading and supervision, but more scope and autonomy. They are seen not as a cost, but as an *asset* in which to invest, so adding to the inherent value.

In most instances the use of the term 'human resources management' is no more than playing with words to sound vaguely fashionable, but in the small number of cases where the concept has been worked through into employment practice there have been significant changes, especially in management training and the types of contract offered to prospective employees. There tends to be a greater investment in training managers and a wider choice of contracts offered to employees, especially short-term contracts rather than permanent contracts, part-time rather than full-time, and CONTRACTS FOR SERVICES rather than CONTRACTS OF EMPLOYMENT.

See also HUMAN ASSET ACCOUNTING, PERSONNEL MANAGEMENT.

G. S. Odiorne, *Strategic Management of Human Resources* (Jossey-Bass, Los Angeles, 1985).

Hygiene factor. The term was coined by American psychologist Frederick Herzberg to describe aspects of working which his research suggested dissatisfied people. The factors were: company policy and administration, supervision, salary, working conditions and interpersonal relations. In medicine the lack of hygiene will cause disease, but hygiene itself will not cause health, so Herzberg argued that dealing with the hygiene factors at work would not satisfy people: it would merely remove dissatisfaction. This means that the hygiene factors have to be dealt with to avoid 'disease', but then managers need to concentrate on motivators to produce 'health': achievement, recognition, work itself, responsibility and advancement. Hygiene factors and motivators are different; both need management attention if workers are to be motivated.

See also MOTIVATION.

I

Immunity. In the UK there is no right to strike, picket or take other INDUSTRIAL ACTION (see STRIKE/STRIKING and PICKETING). The law works by providing immunity against civil liability for certain ECONOMIC TORTS which would otherwise almost certainly be committed in the course of industrial action. However, whether in respect of individuals or (since 1982) unions, the immunity is limited to acts done in contemplation or furtherance of a trade dispute (see GOLDEN FORMULA). In addition, the Employment Acts of 1980, 1982 and 1984 withdrew the immunity in specific instances. Thus acts done in the course of PICKETING, other than within a very narrow sphere, and most SECONDARY ACTION, became unlawful. Similarly immunity was removed from action in support of union-only or recognition-only practices, and from certain acts done by unions without a ballot (see TRADE UNION ACT 1984). Immunity does not extend to torts such as defamation or nuisance, and neither does it extend to criminal acts.

Where individuals or the union act outside the statutory immunity they may be sued for damages or an injunction may be obtained. Furthermore the union may be vicariously liable for individuals' acts if they were authorized or endorsed by a 'responsible person', such as the president or general secretary, the principal executive committee, or certain employed officials.

Implied terms. In any contract there may be terms which the parties themselves have not expressly agreed upon, and which must therefore be implied into the contract if they are to be enforceable. Terms will sometimes be implied by the courts on the basis that they reflect the presumed intention of the parties, for example 'to give such business efficacy to the transaction as must have been intended' (The Moorcock (1889) 14 PD 64, p. 68). A recent development has been to ask whether the implication of, say, a term relating to sick pay would be 'reasonable'. Other terms will be implied regardless of the parties' intentions because it is felt that they are a necessary adjunct to any contract which is a contract of employment. They include:

1 an implied obligation on the part of the employer that he or she will take reasonable care for the safety of the employees (see COMMON LAW DUTY OF CARE);

2 an implied duty of fidelity: namely, that the employee will not disclose the employer's trade secrets or misuse CONFIDENTIAL INFORMATION (note: the employee may be expressly restricted by a RESTRAINT CLAUSE);

3 an implied duty of cooperation; that is:

• on the part of the employees, that they will obey the reasonable orders of the employer, or 'serve the employer faithfully with a view to promoting those commercial interests for which he is employed' (*Secretary of State for Employment* v. *ASLEF* (no. 2) [1972] 2 All ER 949, p. 971) (see also INDUSTRIAL ACTION);

• on the part of the employer, that he will not damage the relationship of mutual trust and confidence by, for instance, victimizing the employee, using foul and abusive language to him, treating him in a demeaning manner, accusing him of theft on scanty evidence or failing to investigate a genuine safety grievance. Breach of such terms may entitle an employee to walk out and claim that he has been dismissed (see CONSTRUCTIVE DISMISSAL): for example, the secretary whose boss said of her in the presence of another employee, 'She is an intolerable bitch on a Monday morning.'

A term may also be implied by statute; thus the EQUAL PAY ACT 1970 operates by implying an 'equality clause' into the contract of employment. A woman being paid less than a man for LIKE WORK, for example, would then claim breach of the equality clause.

See also COLLECTIVE AGREEMENTS, CUSTOM AND PRACTICE, WORKS RULES.

Incentives. Incentive payments remain one of the ideas which fascinate managers as they seek the magic formula that will link payment to performance so effectively that their movements will coincide, enabling the manager to leave the workers on automatic pilot while attending to more important matters, such as strategic planning or going to lunch.

The most common incentive scheme is PAYMENT BY RESULTS. More recently there have been a number of *productivity schemes* which stimulate general productivity, rather than individual or group performance, by 'buying' changes in working practice.

During 1983 Perkins Engines of Peterborough introduced a scheme in which a Business Performance Index was calculated each quarter by the following formula:

$$\text{Business Performance Index} = \frac{\text{number of engines invoiced in the quarter}}{\text{number of production hours in the quarter}}$$

Thus incentive payments were based entirely on saleable production.

A long-standing incentive method is *commission*, whereby the employee receives a percentage of the value of material sold. This is still quite common where the product is high volume with a steady turnover, as in retailing. It causes considerable problems in sales of high-technology equipment, where months of preparation may be needed to produce a single sale.

Executive schemes are similar to productivity schemes, with the individual executive receiving a bonus payment linked to the profitability or value-added of the business.

See also PAYMENT BY RESULTS, SHARE OWNERSHIP.

I. Smith, *The Management of Remuneration* (London: Institute of Personnel Management, 1983).

Increment. Incremental pay scales provide for salary to increase by pre-determined amounts annually, regardless of any other adjustment which may be made for changes in the cost of living; a typical arrangement could be a starting point of £10,000, with ten annual increments of £400 rising to a maximum of £14,000. The idea of increments is to provide salary growth without the need for promotion. In some schemes the progress is automatic, but in others the progress is at the discretion of management depending on the individual's performance during the year. There are two other variations to note. *Acceleration* is where a person can move up by more than a single incremental step in one year by being judged worthy of an extra increment. The *efficiency bar* is a device whereby salary movement can be halted if an employee is judged not to merit further progress. This would be at a fixed point on the scale, like a hurdle, where a judgement has to be made as to whether the employee should go on or be held at that point. See EFFICIENCY BAR.

Independent trade union. A listed trade union may apply to the CERTIFICATION OFFICER for a certificate of independence which, if granted, will confer legal rights on both the union and its individual members, namely:

- the right to CONSULTATION over redundancy;
- the right to appoint safety representatives under the HEALTH AND SAFETY AT WORK ACT 1974;
- rights to TIME OFF for trade union officials and trade union members;
- rights to information for the purposes of COLLECTIVE BARGAINING;
- only an independent trade union can be a party to a UNION MEMBERSHIP AGREEMENT;
- the right to use the employer's premises for secret ballots, and to obtain refunds of the cost from the CO;
- the right to be consulted about occupational pension schemes;
- CONSULTATION rights under the TRANSFER OF UNDERTAKINGS (PROTECTION OF EMPLOYMENT) REGULATIONS 1981.

An 'independent' trade union is defined in S30(1) of the TRADE UNION AND LABOUR RELATIONS ACT 1974 as one which:

- is not under the domination or control of an employer or a group of employers or of an employers' association; *and*
- is not liable to interference by an employer (arising out of the provision of financial or material support or by any other means) tending towards such control.

In exercising their discretion to award a certificate, COs take into account such factors as whether or not the union has received employer support in the recent past, whether it is a single employer union, whether the finances are strong, the degree of reliance on employer-provided facilities, and to what extent members play a full part in decision-making processes free from employer interference. A union which is refused a certificate has a right of appeal to the Employment Appeal Tribunal.

Indirect workers. The logic of traditional incentive payment schemes has required the division of manual workers into two classes: direct and indirect, with the indirect workers being those whose efforts did not actually increase production, but merely enabled direct workers to do so. Direct work could be measured but indirect work could not. In a shoe factory, for instance, people employed in making shoes would be 'directs', while those maintaining the machinery on which the shoes were made would be 'indirects'. Any incentive payments made to indirect workers were linked to the production achieved by direct workers, and there was always a tension between the two groups.

Induction. The new recruit is ill at ease in the unfamiliar situation of a strange organization and does not know the basic information about the organizational system and conventions. This can lead to inefficiency. Induction is the process of taking a management initiative to reduce the difficulties of the settling-in period. To some extent there is an induction crisis in the first few weeks of employment, during which the employee may leave because of feeling ill-suited to the job, and an induction initiative can either prevent that happening at all or can clarify the intention to leave by clearing up uncertainties. Thorough initial selection can also reduce induction problems.

One induction method is the *programme,* in which recruits are introduced to the organization by a series of lectures, tours and demonstrations. These have the advantage of the recruits meeting others with the same uncertainties, but there is a tendency for the programmes to concentrate on exhortation about general matters like team spirit, rather than specific and immediate matters like the location of the nearest shops. *Attachment* methods are informal and attach the new recruit either to the supervisor or to a working colleague, so that information and orientation is provided steadily and within the context of ordinary conversation and in the context of actually doing the job for which the employee has been recruited. For executives there can be periods of *reading in and briefing* with the appointee shadowing the person to be replaced for a few days, or weeks, and reading up all the memoranda and meeting minutes that describe events of the recent past. These arrangements carry with them the assumption that newly recruited executives will be socially self-assured and need less orientation on general matters (like the location of the shops).

The main aspects of effective induction are:

- to concentrate on providing information and orientation that is essential before providing what is useful;
- to locate induction in the context of the job to be done rather than in the general organizational context, as the recruit will have many more anxieties about being able to do the job than about the organization;
- to remember that induction lasts longer than the bewildering first day, and what on the first day was only useful information – and therefore not covered – will soon become essential, and should now be covered;
- to make induction a responsibility of everyone in a department, rather than a specialist job for one person. Those inducted most recently will have most expert knowledge about what is essential.

A. Fowler, *Getting Off to a Good Start* (London: Institute of Personnel Management, 1983).

Industrial action. Most forms of industrial action, notably STRIKES/STRIKING or refusing to perform particular duties, involve a breach of the contract of employment. This may be so even in respect of a work-to-rule or a go-slow since the employee may be held to be in breach of the implied duty of cooperation (see IMPLIED TERMS). Overtime bans will only be a breach of contract if overtime is compulsory.

By virtue of S62 of the Employment Protection (Consolidation) Act 1978, employees who are dismissed whilst striking or participating in 'other industrial action' (or during a LOCK-OUT by the employer) are generally precluded from claiming UNFAIR DISMISSAL. However, if the employer acts selectively by not dismissing all those taking action (or in the case of a lock-out, those 'directly interested' in the dispute), or by re-engaging some (see RE-ENGAGEMENT), but not all of those dismissed within three months of their dismissal, claims may be made in the usual way. No clear answer can be given to what may be the crucial question for an employer, namely whether or not a given individual's actions amount to 'participation'. Tribunals are left to decide the issue as a question of fact, but it has been established that an employee's motives for participating, such as fear of abuse, are irrelevant.

Employers are not obliged to pay employees who are on strike; furthermore they may be entitled to withhold a proportionate part of the employee's remuneration where there is a refusal to carry out specific duties. In addition those made redundant while taking industrial action which involves a breach of contract are denied the right to a redundancy payment.

Where 'official' industrial action is contemplated, a ballot must be held if the union and individuals concerned are not to lose their IMMUNITY from civil action in respect of certain ECONOMIC TORTS (see TRADE UNION ACT 1984).

Some statutory restriction on industrial action exists in relation to particular groups of workers, notably the police, the armed forces, merchant seamen and postal workers.

See also GOLDEN FORMULA, GUARANTEE PAYMENTS, PICKETING, SECONDARY ACTION.

Industrial democracy. Of the various forms of EMPLOYEE PARTICIPATION that are advocated from different sources, industrial democracy is the most radical as it involves the employees taking control of the business either totally or in collaboration with other groups, such as shareholders and management. The logic and moral justification for this idea is that those who personally produce the wealth of the business have the greatest stake in that business and should control what is done with the fruits of their labour. Counter-arguments include the view that ownership should rest with those who risk their money by investing in the business, that management should be free to manage and the democratic process invariably hampers that necessary freedom of action, and that the viability of the business always depends on external factors in the various marketplaces, so that sometimes decisions have to be made which would not be democratically acceptable.

There are very few successful British businesses run on democratic lines, with John Lewis being the best-known example, although there have been many attempts, most recently through worker cooperatives. The Mondragon project in Spain is probably the most successful form of large-scale industrial democracy in Europe, although Germany has for some time operated a system of companies having two-tier boards, with a conventional board of management having responsibility for overall strategy and a supervisory board running day-to-day internal matters. In 1977 a Committee chaired by Lord Bullock produced proposals for main boards with a tripartite structure of management representatives, union representatives and independents. These ideas were not implemented.

Lord Bullock, *Report of the Committee of Inquiry on Industrial Democracy* (London: HMSO, 1977).

Industrial psychology. This describes the study of human behaviour in situations related to the production, distribution and use of goods and services. The National Institute for Industrial Psychology was founded in 1921 to carry out research into matters such as fatigue, employee selection and training and methods of work. A strong centre for this study has been Birkbeck College in the University of London, where the 'Birkbeck Philosophy' was propounded of fitting-the-job-to-the-man and fitting-the-man-to-the-job. This stimulated research into individual differences, ergonomics and the social context of human work. The field of investigation then evolved into occupational psychology and organizational psychology.

Industrial relations. Industrial relations is used to describe the complex of relations between employers and employees in an industry, in a company, in an establishment or individual workplace. To some extent it also covers relations between labour and capital in the economy as a whole, especially through the representative activities of the CONFEDERATION OF BRITISH INDUSTRY and the TRADES UNION CONGRESS. Government and government agencies are frequently seen as being an essential feature of this set of relationships, both because of the influence of government on the social and economic context in which industrial relations operates, especially in the public sector, and because of the legislative arrangements governing collective as well as individual employment relationships.

The central mechanism of industrial relations is COLLECTIVE BARGAINING, with the products of bargaining – *rules* – being the means whereby both parties to the bargain expect change in the workplace to be brought about. This reliance on bargaining also produced a significant emphasis in British industrial relations that has not been much copied in other countries: *voluntarism*. The idea of voluntarism is that workplace arrangements are best produced when the employers and unions are left to make their own agreements with minimal intervention by government and with the minimal legal framework. By the 1970s this long-cherished belief had lost adherents in government and among many employers, so a legal framework has been developing – with several changes of shape and direction – since that period.

Industrial relations is no longer the 'frightener' for managements that it had become by the late 1970s. The reasons cited for this change vary according to the sympathies of the person providing the analysis, but usually include antipathy towards trade unions by government, economic recession and high unemployment. In most private sector organizations the level of trade union membership has declined and the level of trade union activity has been curtailed. This has been largely due to the reduction of employment in manufacturing. Areas of expansion, like retailing, have a tradition of lower union membership density and the growth of union membership in those areas is slower than the growth of employment. For managements the emphasis has shifted towards EMPLOYEE RELATIONS. Although less pronounced, a similar shift can be seen in the public employment sector, but union membership remains high and union activity is relatively confident.

Industrial Society. Supported by both employers and trade unions, the Industrial Society provides advice, publications and consultancy about matters of employment. It runs regular conferences and courses with a strong practical flavour and an impartial approach. The Society was founded by The Reverend Sir Robert Hyde as the Boys' Welfare Association. In 1918 the name was changed to the Industrial Welfare Society, and in 1965 to the Industrial Society. The main thrust of the Society's work is in the areas of leadership, management/union relations, communication and consultation, conditions of employment, and the development of young people, concentrating on poor working conditions.

The headquarters are at Robert Hyde House, 48 Bryanston Square, London W1H 8AH (01 262 2402).

Industrial Training Boards. Under the Industrial Training Act of 1964, the Secretary of State for Employment set up a series of Boards (ITBs) to ensure provision of adequate training within their industries. The Employment and Training Act of 1981 made it possible to abolish ITBs as well as to establish them, and 16 were quickly abolished so that now only some 30 per cent of the employed population are in organizations within the scope of an ITB.

Industrial tribunal. These tribunals were originally set up in 1964 with a very limited jurisdiction, but the latter was greatly increased by the EMPLOYMENT PROTECTION ACT 1975. They now hear claims relating to UNFAIR DISMISSAL, EQUAL PAY, REDUNDANCY, SEX DISCRIMINATION and other employment protection rights. Their aim was to provide a cheap, speedy and informal procedure for settling claims, without too much legalism.

A tribunal consists of a legally qualified chairman and two lay members, one from each side of industry. The parties may present their own case, or choose a representative to act for them, but legal aid is not available. Other than in exceptional cases, a successful party will not be awarded his or her costs (see LEGAL COSTS). The decision of the tribunal will often be given orally at the end of the hearing with written reasons being sent to the parties afterwards, though sometimes it will be reserved until a later date. A majority decision is always possible even if this means the lay members outvoting the chairman.

An appeal may be made against the decision to the Employment Appeal Tribunal on a point of law (where the tribunal has misapplied or misunderstood the law, or misdirected itself in law) or where the decision is 'perverse' in the sense that no reasonable tribunal, properly directed, could have reached such a decision. Questions of fact, such as whether an employee was constructively dismissed, or whether the employer acted 'reasonably' in dismissing an employee, cannot be the subject of appeal. Further appeals on points of law can be made with leave to the Court of Appeal and, with further leave, to the House of Lords.

The address of the Central Office of Industrial Tribunals (COIT) is 93 Ebury Bridge Road, London SW1 8RE (01 730 9161/7).

Injunction. Where unlawful INDUSTRIAL ACTION takes place an employer may sue the individuals concerned, or in some cases the union itself, for damages. Alternatively an injunction may be sought which, if granted, will order the defendant to cease the unlawful action. 'Interlocutory' injunctions, which in theory take effect pending the trial of the action, can be obtained very quickly; in extremely urgent cases they may be granted 'ex parte' (without notice to the defendant) even before a writ is issued. In practice once an interlocutory injunction is obtained the matter rarely proceeds to trial, for the employer has achieve his or her aim. The principles on which a court will decide whether or not to grant the interlocutory injunction is therefore an important issue. It would seem that a plaintiff need only show 'an arguable case fit to go to trial' or that there is a 'serious question to be tried'; there will not be a detailed determination of the merits of the case. If the plaintiff succeeds in this, the court should then consider the 'balance of convenience': that is, whether the plaintiff will suffer more damage if the injunction is not granted in the meantime than will the defendant if it is. In industrial cases this will normally be decided in the plaintiff's favour since he or she will be able to demonstrate potentially large financial losses, whereas the defendant may be able to point only to loss of morale. The court should, however, take into account the likelihood of the defendant's being able to demonstrate at the trial that the relevant actions were protected by the statutory immunities (see IMMUNITY).

An injunction granted against a union may be a valuable weapon, since failure to comply with it amounts to contempt of court for which the union may be fined. If the fine is not paid the plaintiff may apply for sequestration of the union's assets. Nevertheless, in contemplating the use of an injunction, management will have to balance the enforcement of their legal rights against the industrial relations consequences which may ensue.

See also PICKETING.

Institute of Personnel Management (IPM). The IPM was

founded by 34 industrial welfare officers in 1913, but has grown to be the largest personnel organization in the world, with a membership (1985) of over 25,000.

The IPM has five main aims:

- to promote the professional standing of members through exchanging knowledge and experience;
- to develop personnel knowledge and expertise to meet changing circumstances;
- to maintain standards of professional competence among practitioners;
- to present a national, representative view of personnel issues;
- to encourage research on personnel management.

Corporate membership is limited to those who have passed the IPM's examinations and satisfied criteria of experience and professional standing. There are 40 local branches, an information and library service at the head office and a range of publications. In addition to being one of the largest management book publishers in Britain, the Institute has two monthly publications, *Personnel Management* and *IPM Digest*. There are a number of courses and conferences, including the annual national conference at Harrogate, which is the largest management conference in Europe.

The head office is at IPM House, Camp Road, Wimbledon, London SW19 4VW (01 946 9100).

L. E. Mackay and D. P. Torrington, *The Changing Nature of Personnel Management* (London: Institute of Personnel Management, 1986).

Instruction. LEARNING that requires the mastery of drills and procedures involving minimal background understanding by the trainee is usually accomplished by instruction, so that the trainee is taught a series of physical actions. When those actions are practised, skilled performance is achieved. Eunice and Meredith Belbin (1973) described five types of learning: comprhension, reflex, attitude, memorization and procedural (CRAMP). Comprehension involves theoretical understanding of subjects, knowing how, why and when things happen; attitude development requires people to alter their attitudes and social behaviour. For neither of these types of learning is instruction appropriate: you cannot *instruct* someone to understand thermo-dynamics or to be more self-confident. In reflex learning the trainee is acquiring skilled movements or perceptual capacities (such as those of a sewing machinist), in memorization information (for instance, the sequence of colours in the spectrum) is being learned, and in procedural learning the trainee is finding out which drill is to be followed in a range of situations. For these three instruction is an appropriate form of learning.

Among the methods of instruction are first *progressive part* methods, where the trainee learns a small part of the job and practises until competent before moving on to the second part, which is practised until competence is achieved before practising parts one and two together, then part three is learned, and so on until EXPERIENCED WORKER STANDARD is achieved.

Cumulative part method is similar except that the different parts of the job are not practised separately before being added to the existing body of knowledge, because it is not possible. (In juggling, for example, it is pointless to practise juggling with the second ball on its own after practising with the first ball on its own!) Memorization is usually aided by *mnemonics* or jingles. The initial letters of the colours of the spectrum are ROYGBIV, which are easier to recall as Richard Of York Gave Battle In Vain. Procedural learning also uses jingles quite often, but an alternative is the simple *rule of thumb,* such as 'I before E except after C'. Every maintenance engineer has a series of such rules which are applied to fault-finding.

E. and R. M. Belbin, *Problems in Adult Retraining* (London: Heinemann, 1973).

Intelligence tests. In everyday usage the word 'intelligence' is associated with accomplishment and the ability to learn by experience. For this reason the idea of intelligence tests is inhibiting to many people, who fear that the outcome will suggest they are incompetent. There is also a reluctance to accept that intelligence can be measured, which makes of it a value-laden concept. The statement 'You have dark hair' is construed as a statement of fact, while the statement 'You are intelligent' is construed as flattery. A different, and more technical, view of intelligence is the faculty of understanding and the degree to which a person has developed the cognitive aspects of mental functioning, the ability to conceptualize and to see relationships.

"I wonder how long it will be before we can start testing its IQ?"

Intelligence tests were first developed by the French psychologist Alfred Binet (1857–1911) for use among children, but they have been gradually developed in an attempt to measure the intelligence level of adults also, including attempts to measure different aspects of intelligence. The results of tests taken by subjects are compared with a distribution for a given population, such as the general population, the graduate population, and so forth. This data is often used in employee selection, but it is important that users appreciate that only intelligence in the technical sense is being measured, so the results will be more relevant for posts where that faculty is important, such as computer programming, than in other posts, such as selling, where social skills will be more significant. Most selection consultants who use test results combine the evidence with that gained from tests of PERSONALITY.

See also APTITUDE TESTS, PSYCHOLOGICAL TESTS.

P. E. Vernon, *Intelligence: Heredity and Environment* (San Francisco: Freeman, 1979).

Interviewing. Talking with people is the main activity in which managers engage, as information is the stock in which they trade, and they are likely to spend at least three-quarters of their time talking with others. Many of these interpersonal exchanges are interviews, with the manager questioning – and answering questions from – the other party. Ineffectiveness in interviewing usually stems from one of two problems: either interviewers regard it as just another conversation without appreciating its special characteristics, or they believe there is some specific procedure that will guarantee success but no one has told them about it.

Conducting a selection interview

1 *Opening:* seat the candidate comfortably and then 'tune in' to each other by inconsequential discussion about the weather or a similar neutral subject. Explain what is to happen and offer plenty of smiles and nods. Relaxed candidates are more informative then terrified ones.

2 *Information exchange:* Move to a more businesslike pace to obtain information and answer questions. Use a logical sequence for the interview, such as going through the stages of the working record. Use an opening question that will be easy to answer and informative, like 'Can you give me an outline of your present duties?'. Concentrate on enabling the candidate to be frank and informative. Check key points from the application form that need clarifying.

3 *Listen to the candidate:* at all times; make notes; control the interview.

4 *Closing:* Explain what happens next. Check that the candidate has no more questions.

5 *Review job and candidate information:* read through: job description, candidate specification, application form, interview notes, references (if any) and test scores (if any). Decide whether or not the candidate fits the job and the implications of any poor fitting.

6 *Decide between candidates*: complete a fivefold grading form for all candidates who fit the job. Consider how each would fit the relevant working group. Guard against unlawful discrimination. Decide to whom the offer should be made and on what terms.

Effective interviewers are likely to have *poise*, knowing what they are talking about and being able to talk with different types of people in a relaxed and self-confident way, without being either overbearing or ingratiating. They will also be skilled at *listening* and able to concentrate on what the other person is saying or asking. This is what prevents poise from becoming egocentric, as the interviewer constantly listens for feedback to signal understanding or uncertainty. A third feature of interviewing skill is *synchronizing,* picking up the natural conversational rhythm of the other person and adjusting to that rhythm so that exchanges are both comfortable and efficient. Finally, interviewing requires a *plan,* with the interviewer thinking out beforehand what has to be achieved and how the objective is likely to be accomplished. A selection interview, for example, has a plan in the application form, where applicants have set out their achievements and qualifications to date. That record will suggest questions to the interviewer of points which need to be elaborated, or gaps which have to be filled in. Furthermore it has the value of being in a chronological sequence that both the applicants and the interviewer can follow.

It is important that this should not be inflexible, as (in the words of an apocryphal Chinese general) no plan of campaign survives the first encounter with the enemy, and the structure of the interview will be developed in the situation as it unfolds.

See also INTERVIEW TYPES.

Interview types.

1 SELECTION: this is the most common type of interview, where a candidate's potential ability to fill a specific post is being assessed at the same time as the candidate is assessing the post and the general context in which the work will be done. This interview has strong ritual features with the candidate demonstrating (however subtly) deferential behaviours and responding to questions, while the interviewer demonstrates (sometimes subtly) social superiority and poses questions. The most effective approach is to follow the biographical principle in reviewing what the candidate has done so far and how this forms an adequate preparation for what the job in prospect requires. There is the advantage of an APPLICATION FORM, which is the ideal starting point for questioning that will fill out the bare details supplied on the form. To make the best use of the

interview the selector should defer judgement until after the interview is complete in order to avoid being unduly influenced by first impressions. One of the methods of HUMAN ATTRIBUTE CLASSIFICATION can be used to make decisions after the interview.
2 COUNSELLING: this interview is well-developed in professions such as social work, but little used in management, although consultants may be used to deal with specific counselling requirements, such as redundancy, stress or alcohol dependency. The most important difference between counselling and selection is that its purpose is to discover and understand a problem, not simply to exchange information. The exchanges are therefore more analytical; the counsellor will offer understanding and assistance with the expression of unfamiliar feelings. Counsellors make great efforts to avoid deferential behaviours in the client.
3 DISCIPLINE: disciplinary interviewing frequently has similarities with counselling, as it is an attempt to find out what is causing unsatisfactory behaviour at work and then to find solutions to the problem. The exchanges usually involve disapproval and warnings of what will happen if the behaviour does not change, but good interviews then continue to analyse causes of the disciplinary problem, as they can sometimes be resolved simply by some reorganization of the work or workplace.
4 Performance APPRAISAL: perhaps the most demanding of all interviews at work is the review of performance. Norman Maier has described three basic approaches. First is *tell-and-sell* in which the appraiser tells the appraisee the result of the appraisal, including any suggestions about how performance needs to be improved, and tries to sell it to the appraisee so that the required action is taken (rather like a disciplinary interview). *Tell-and-listen* is where the interview is again used to pass on the judgement, but this time the reaction of the appraisee is carefully listened to and the appraisal may be altered as a result. Maier's third type is *problem-solving,* in which problems are discussed openly, as in a counselling interview, on the assumption that job performance will improve as a result of greater understanding.
5 ATTITUDE SURVEY: occasionally interviewing is used to find out the views of a large number of employees on a particular issue, like arrangements for Christmas holidays or a change in the

payment system. The method here is to have a highly structured interview, similar to a questionnaire, with a pre-determined list of questions which are always put in the same way.

N. R. F. Maier, *The Appraisal Interview: Three Basic Approaches* (La Jolla, California: University Associates, 1976).

Itemized pay statement. Every employee working more than 16 hours per week is entitled by virtue of S8 of the Employment Protection (Consolidation) Act 1978 to receive a written pay statement itemizing:

- the gross pay;
- any variable or fixed deductions;
- the net pay;
- where different parts of the net amount are paid in different ways, the amount and method of each part payment.

In the case of fixed deductions such as union contributions, the employer need only give a standing statement, reissued annually. If the employer fails to provide an itemized statement, the employee has the right to complain to a tribunal, which may make a declaration to that effect. Additionally, where the tribunal finds that unnotified deductions have been made in the 13-week period preceding the complaint, it may order the employer to pay a sum not exceeding the aggregate of the unnotified deductions.

See also FINES AND DEDUCTIONS.

J

Job analysis. This is the process of systematically examining the details of a job to isolate the components and then produce a JOB DESCRIPTION. The most common applications are in payment, where it is used as a basis for JOB EVALUATION to justify pay differentials, and in SELECTION, where the job description aids the thinking of the selector as well as providing information to the candidate. Other applications are in TRAINING, to produce the training manual as well as the job description, and in PERFORMANCE APPRAISAL, to assist the comparison of performance with expectation.

Job-and-finish. Although most employees work for a set period of time, some are allowed to finish work when the assigned quota of work is complete. An example could be a brewer's drayman with a number of deliveries to make during the day. When the deliveries are complete he finishes work and goes home: job-and-finish.

Job Centres. These are the chain of offices run by the Employment Division of the Manpower Services Commission to match the requirements of job seekers and employers. They have an open-plan lay-out and displays of job opportunities so that those seeking work can browse through the advertised vacancies before asking for assistance. Employer contact is usually by telephone and particulars of the vacancy can be given over the telephone or in writing. The Commission for Racial Equality urges employers to use Job Centres for recruiting rather than relying on word-of-mouth recommendations and unsolicited letters of application as Job Centres are likely to produce a better-balanced group of applicants.

Job description. The first product of JOB ANALYSIS is a description of a job, which will vary according to the application to which it is to be put. At the moment job descriptions are used most extensively in payment systems as a basis of justifying pay DIFFERENTIALS, though their other applications, in training, selection and performance appraisal, are better documented. The most common method of preparing job descriptions is to follow a check-list. Page 127 starts with an example for application in employee selection.

Part of a job analysis check-list for use in job evaluation

1   Job title ....

2   General statement of duties ....

3   Level of education required
    a Basic secondary ....☐   b 4–6 GCSE ....☐
    c 2 GCE A levels.......................☐   d Degree in ....☐
                e Postgraduate/professional qualification ....☐

4   Amount of previous similar or related work experience necessary for a person starting this job
    a None.....................................☐   b Less than 3 months ....☐
    c 3 months to 1 year ....☐   d 1 to 3 years............................☐

5   How much supervision does the job require?
    a Frequent...............................☐   b Several times daily................☐
    c Occasional ....☐   d Limited..................................☐
    e Little or none.........................☐

6   Number of people supervised by job holder
    a None.....................................☐   b 1...☐
    c 2–5.......................................☐   d 6–20......................................☐
    e 21–50....................................☐   f 51+.......................................☐

7   Cost to organization of errors made by job holder
    a Under £25 ....☐   b £25–£100...............................☐
    c £100–£500.............................☐   d £500–£5,000..........................☐
    e More than £5,000...................☐

8   How often is the possibility of such errors checked?
    a Daily ....☐   b Weekly ....☐
    c Monthly................................☐   d Quarterly...............................☐
    e Annually................................☐   f Not regularly checked............☐

9   Contacts with other people, initiated by job holder

	Constantly	Often	Occasionally	Never
In own department				
In other departments				
With suppliers				
With customers				
With civic authorities				
Other				

10   Aspects of the job involving confidentiality/security
....

11   Disagreeable/dangerous aspects of job
....

12   Resourcefulness or initiative required
....

1 Job title.
2 Duties and range of responsibility:
- what has to be done;
- relationship of job to rest of organization;
- extent of responsibility;
- overall purpose of the job.
3 Relationships:
- job holder reports to . . . ;
- reporting to job holder are . . . ;
- nature of these and other contacts.
4 Physical environment:
- where job is done;
- hours and days of work;
- health or accident hazards.
5 Conditions of employment:
- salary;
- salary review provisions;
- pension and sick pay;
- fringe benefits.
6 Future prospects.

Job design. Job design is the process of getting the best possible fit between what the organization requires from the individual employee and the individual's need for satisfaction from the job. Frequently the management approach to job design is to make the job as simple as possible, reasoning that the simpler the job, the quicker it will be finished. Although this may improve the level of output, it does little for the other side of the equation – employee satisfaction with the job – and raising production may be accompanied by increases in absence, alienation, industrial action and mental illness. More recently attempts have been made to mitigate these unfavourable employee reactions by improving the context of the work, such as the nature of supervision and the ergonomics of the workplace, and by altering the content of jobs. Job wholeness can produce departmental efficiency, economical staffing and satisfied employees.

Two approaches to improving job design are *job enlargement* and *job enrichment*. Job enlargement increases the range of jobs to be performed by one person, while job enrichment gives people more responsibility to set their own pace, decide their own methods and correct their own mistakes.

Job enlargement and enrichment will only motivate those who seek personal fulfilment through work, and personal fulfilment will only be sought through work if the employee can see prospects of real personal growth by that means. Without that prospect they may continue to seek personal fulfilment outside work.

See also MOTIVATION.

R. M. Steers and L. W. Porter (eds), *Motivation and Work Behaviour,* 2nd edn (New York: McGraw-Hill, 1979).

Job evaluation. Job evaluation is a systematic method of analysing the demands of a number of jobs to establish the appropriate pay differentials between them. Jobs are grouped into JOB FAMILIES and then JOB DESCRIPTIONS are prepared. Evaluation is then carried out to obtain a ranking of the jobs on the basis of which should have the highest rate of pay, which the lowest, and how the remainder are ranked in relation to those two. Pay rates are then fitted to that ranking. It is a process that produces no more than a structure for basic rates; it does not provide an incentive element and does not eliminate collective bargaining as the pay level is not determined by the process (but see GUIDE CHART PROFILE METHOD). It has become especially important in the resolution of EQUAL VALUE questions.

Conventionally methods of job evaluation are divided into analytical and non-analytical, with POINTS RATING being the main example of an analytical method while JOB GRADING and JOB RANKING are the main examples of non-analytical schemes.

ACAS, *Job Evaluation, Advisory Booklet No. 1.* (ACAS, 1980).

Job families. In JOB EVALUATION a preliminary step is to sort jobs into appropriate families, so that like is compared with like. A common basis for this sorting is to use a BARGAINING UNIT as a job family, but it is also quite common to have a bargaining unit which includes a number of different job families, such as one for clerical and administrative staff and another for computer personnel. The deciding factor is for the jobs to have sufficient common features for comparison to be feasible.

Job grading. This is a non-analytical method of JOB EVALUATION, which starts by producing a set of pay grades that represent value or worth to the firm. When the grade descriptions have been prepared an evaluation committee considers each job and slots it into one of the grades. It is a method that has the advantage of being easy to understand and simple to operate, but is only suitable for simple jobs which are easy to classify.

Job ranking. The simplest method of JOB EVALUATION requires that jobs are considered as complete entities without any attempt to identify different factors or components. The evaluation committee considers the job description (or sometimes just the job title) and puts all the jobs in rank order before assigning them to a pay grade.

Job sharing. Where a single job can be readily divided into two, it may be shared between two people with, for instance, one working every morning and the other working every afternoon. This specialized version of part-time working depends on the existence of job sharers who are mutually dependent and supportive in maintaining a viable whole job. The approach has been advocated by the Equal Opportunities Commission, but there are few examples of its successful application.

Equal Opportunities Commission, *Job-Sharing: Improving the Quality and Availability of Part-time Work* (Manchester: Equal Opportunities Commission, 1981).

Joinder. Where a union (or an individual) exerts industrial pressure on an employer to dismiss an employee for non-membership of the union, the provisions of the Employment Act 1982 mean that the union may be liable for some or all of the potentially large sum of compensation if a claim of unfair dismissal is upheld (see COMPENSATION). As introduced by the Employment Act 1980 the *employer* was given the right to 'join' the union to the action, and the tribunal could then make an award of compensation against the latter, totally or in part, at its discretion. The 1982 Act extended this right of joinder to the dismissed employee, who might be thought more likely to exercise it than managers wishing to avoid industrial confrontation. The right applies whether or not a CLOSED SHOP is in existence, and to action short of dismissal as well as DISMISSAL itself (see TRADE UNION MEMBERSHIP AND ACTIVITIES).

Joint consultation. If members of management consult with their employees about a proposed course of action, they are able to take the opinions into consideration when shaping their final decision but are not under any obligation to do so. Many trade union members regard this management strategy as spurious because the right to decide is reserved by the management and employee views can be ignored, leading to a pre-determined management decision being imposed. There are, however, many examples of management proposals being abandoned or considerably modified after joint consultation and many organizations have joint consultative committees for this type of regular discussion.

See also CONSULTATION.

Joint Industrial Council (JIC). JICs were set up in many industries following the report of the Whitley Committee on Relations between Employers and Employed in 1918; some are referred to still as Whitley Councils. The objective is to secure the greatest degree of joint action in determining pay and conditions of employment in the industry through the medium of trade union and employers' association representation as JIC members.

L

Labour markets. When filling vacancies it is becoming increasingly useful to understand the operation of the particular labour market in which the prospective employees are to be found, as each labour market has slightly different conventions and characteristics. The *local labour market* is the travel-to-work-area, a few miles in circumference, which contains a number of employers and a number of actual or potential employees, so that those employers are in competition with each other for many categories of employee who are seeking employment only within that local labour market. Crucial factors will be relative levels of pay and conditions, transport facilities, housing and schools, with the intensity of the competition greatly influenced by the local level of unemployment. An *occupational labour market* has different boundaries, not now exclusively geographical but also including aspects such as career opportunity, organizational prospects, business prospects and a more elaborate bundle of pay and conditions. Prospective employees are more likely to come from a wide area and may therefore need greater inducement to come, and the number of competing employers is greatly multiplied. For some posts there is an *international labour market,* with prospective employees moving from, say, Texas to the North Sea or the Persian Gulf. It is not only the highly paid technical specialist who makes this sort of move, but also Third World labourers who move from the Caribbean to Europe, from Sri Lanka to Dubai or from the Philippines to London. A quite different version of this is the more recent phenomenon of moving the work to the labour, as manufacturing operations are set up in Seoul or Manila to take advantage of low labour costs.

Dualism in labour markets describes a growing tendency for people to operate in one of two different types. Primary labour markets are for those of relatively high skill and adaptability, with marketplace conventions that produce high pay, attractive conditions, fringe benefits and permanent, secure employment. Secondary labour markets are for those with less bargaining power due to lack of skill or mobility or union organization. Here the conventions of the marketplace increasingly emphasize temporary work that is not well paid and provides little organizational involvement.

Labour-only subcontracting. Labour-only subcontracting is a form of self-employment which occurs particularly in the building industry. In its commonest form, labourers working individually or in gangs supply their labour to a main contractor and are paid in a lump sum (hence the practice of 'the lump'). Frequently such workers also spend intermittent periods of time working under a CONTRACT OF EMPLOYMENT but performing the same work. The advantage of labour-only subcontracting to an employer is that he or she thereby escapes potential liabilities such as claims of UNFAIR DISMISSAL, or for redundancy payments (see EMPLOYEE). However, the main contractor is responsible for Class I National Insurance contributions and, as a result of widespread tax avoidance, is now generally obliged to deduct tax at source.

Labour turnover. Labour turnover is the rate at which employees leave the organization. If this is too low the organization is likely to become stodgy with few prospects for promotion and little input of fresh ideas from outside. If the level is too high, the organization risks inefficiency through instability and inexperience in the work-force, probably exacerbated by low morale ('If so many people are leaving, there must be something wrong with me for staying here . . . ').

There is no efficient level that applies universally. Some organizations have annual turnover rates which regularly exceed 100 per cent, while in others the percentage is in single figures. Also the level usually has a seasonal pattern. It is therefore necessary for the employer to monitor turnover trends carefully, to see if they are rising or falling, to see if there is a pattern in one department that is diverging from the general organizational pattern and to investigate the reasons for disconcerting trends, which could be caused by a range of reasons from poor pay rates to overbearing supervision.

The conventional measures are, first, the *separation index,* which is normally calculated weekly or monthly:

$$\frac{\text{number of leavers}}{\text{number of employees}} \times 100$$

Second, the *stability index:*

$$\frac{\text{number of employees with more than 12 months' service}}{\text{average number of employees}} \times 100$$

The first of these gives the overall measure, while the second measures underlying stability, on the assumption that many people leave within the first few weeks of employment without ever settling.

In considering turnover there are a few general comments to make about variations in behaviour between different categories of employee:

- those with scarce skills change jobs more often than those lacking shortage skills, partly because of quickly-shifting pay rates;
- those with readily-transferable skills (like typists) move more often than those with organizationally-specific skills (like most middle managers);
- the unskilled move more often than the semi-skilled;
- expanding industries have much higher levels of turnover than static or contracting industries;
- conditions of employment which make the employee unusually dependent on the employer, like generous fringe benefits and much-above-average pay, depress the level of turnover;
- under the age of 35 men with degree-level qualifications change jobs more frequently than women with similar qualifications.

Last-in-first out. The most common criterion for REDUNDANCY is that those with the shortest length of service should be the first to be made redundant, on the basis that they have acquired less entitlement to continued employment: last-in-first-out.

Lay-off. When an employer temporarily has no work for a group of employees to do, they may be laid off for a short period, during which they receive no payment providing that their contracts entitle the employer to withold payment. In certain circumstances an employee who is laid off may resign and claim a redundancy payment (see SHORT TIME WORKING). Sometimes the term is used (incorrectly) to describe dismissal.

See also GUARANTEE PAYMENTS.

Leadership. The idea of leadership (which many people find very appealing) is that there is a combination of personal qualities and skills which enables some people to elicit from subordinates a degree of effective commitment to the task that other people in the same situation cannot achieve. There are many examples from history to support this idea, but it is problematical because it emphasizes rare personal qualities. The practicalities of organizational life require ordinary people to provide some element of leadership in everyday situations, with the *situation* largely determining the type of leader that is needed. Individual managers can change their personal style only slightly. Autocrats will remain autocratic and free-wheelers will remain free-wheeling, as the style stems from personality; it is therefore necessary to change the manager to fit a new situation or change the situation to fit the manager. Fiedler (1967) has produced the most comprehensive theory of leadership effectiveness and suggests that there are three factors determining effectiveness: how well is the leader accepted by the subordinates, are the jobs of the subordinates routine and precise or vague and undefined, and what formal authority does the leader's position confer?

Managers wanting to maintain close ties with their subordinates and regarding these ties as important are likely to be effective in situations where relations with subordinates are good, jobs are undefined and formal authority is not strong. Managers more interested in getting the job done and less concerned about reaction from subordinates are more effective with strong formal authority and well-defined tasks for subordinates.

See also POWER.

J. Adair, *Action-Centred Leadership* (Aldershot: Gower, 1982); F. E. Fiedler, *A Theory of Leadership Effectiveness* (New York: McGraw-Hill, 1967).

Learning. Gagné (1975) has identified a chain of eight events in the learning process:

● motivation: the learner must want to learn, to achieve what the learning will produce;

- perception: the material to be learned must be clear and specific;
- acquisition: the material learned is related to other things the learner already knows;
- retention: the material learned is retained in the long-term memory;
- recall: the learner is able to summon up material from memory, when necessary;
- generalization: the learner is able to apply what has been learned to situations other than that in which the learning has taken place;
- performance: what has been learned is now done;
- feedback: the learner receives feedback on whether or not the performance was satisfactory.

Anyone teaching or coaching someone else needs to remember these eight steps as failure could occur at any one of them.

For some jobs a *learning curve* has been identified, showing that learning proceeds at different speeds according to the stage that has been reached, with some periods of rapid progress followed by plateaux where progress is slower. This can help compare learning rates between trainees and can help in the counselling of trainees at times when they lose motivation because their progress is slowing down.

There is considerable evidence that the motivation to learn is stimulated more effectively by rewards than by punishments.

See also INSTRUCTION.

R. M. Gagné, *Essentials of Learning for Instruction* (New York: Holt, Rinehart & Winston, 1975).

Legal Costs. The general rule is that costs are not awarded (the loser is not ordered to pay the winner's costs) in industrial tribunal cases. However, the tribunal may award costs where one party has in its view acted frivolously (knowing, for example, that the claim has no substance), vexatiously (from improper motives) or otherwise unreasonably in the course of bringing proceedings (see also PRE-HEARING ASSESSMENT). Conduct at the time of any dismissal is not considered. Any award made would be given as compensation to the winner for what it has cost that person to get justice; considerations of punishment are irrelevant. Where the tribunal has postponed or adjourned the hearing on the application of one party, and the other has incurred costs, an award may also be made. In two situations an award of costs is mandatory:

• where an employee has communicated a wish for RE-ENGAGEMENT or REINSTATEMENT to the employer at least seven days before the hearing and the employer causes an adjournment or postponement;
• when the employer seeks an adjournment or postponement in a case where he or she has failed to permit an employee to exercise the statutory right to return to work after pregnancy (see MATERNITY LEAVE).

When making an order for costs, the tribunal has power to order a specific sum as opposed to assessing them ('taxing' them) in the normal way. Being awarded costs is not, of course, to be equated with obtaining them, especially from an impoverished ex-employee.

Costs are to be distinguished from allowances which are awarded to litigants and witnesses out of public funds in respect of attendance at the hearing. The tribunal may order a party against whom an award of costs has been made to repay all or part of the allowances; the party to whom costs are awarded will not obtain allowances and costs in respect of the same expenses.

Where there is an appeal to the Employment Appeal Tribunal, costs are only awarded if:

• the proceedings are unnecessary, improper or vexatious; or
• there has been unreasonable delay or other unreasonable conduct in bringing or conducting the proceedings.

In the higher courts costs are awarded in the usual way for civil cases.

Letter of appointment. Applicants offered employment will expect a letter of offer. This is not the same as the CONTRACT OF EMPLOYMENT, or its written particulars (see CONTRACT, WRITTEN PARTICULARS OF) but it is an offer of employment that should specify the main terms and conditions, including the job title, rates of pay, holiday and hours, with the starting date and the date by which the offer should be accepted. The employer will probably also wish to indicate that the offer will lapse if not accepted by that date. A common practice is for the employer to send a brief letter of offer, enclosing a draft of the contract of employment.

Lieu. The lieu bonus, or lieu payment, is a fixed amount paid to an employee to compensate for the lack of opportunity to earn an incentive payment. It is most common in situations where a group of employees paid on a PIECE-WORK or similar measured output basis can only achieve their level of output by dependence on the work of other employees, whose input cannot be measured (such as maintenance staff and labourers). These other employees may then be paid a lieu bonus to keep their earnings in step with the piece-work earners.

Like work. Where a woman is engaged on 'like work' with a man in the same employment, under the EQUAL PAY ACT 1970 she is entitled to contractual terms and conditions not less favourable than his (and vice versa) unless the employer proves a GENUINE MATERIAL FACTOR defence.

'Like work' is work which is the same or broadly similar, and tribunals have been encouraged to apply a broad brush, non-pedantic approach in making the comparison. On this basis, a female cook making 10–20 lunches in the kitchen of the director's dining room was held to do like work with assistant male chefs producing a much greater number of meals in the works canteen. Where differences between the two jobs do exist, a tribunal should ask whether these are of practical importance in relation to terms and conditions of employment; in other words, whether one would expect these differences to be reflected in a difference in pay, for example. It is important that the jobs are compared in terms of what is performed in practice (including how *often* differences occur) rather than by reference to the employment contract or a job specification. A requirement to work overtime which is rarely implemented, for instance, should therefore be ignored. However, where the duties are similar but one of the jobs involves greater responsibility because the consequences of a mistake are potentially greater, a tribunal may be justified in failing to find 'like work'.

Lock-out. A lock-out is a form of industrial action taken by management, but rarely resorted to until recent years (notably in the newspaper and printing industry). It involves shutting down the workplace during a dispute, normally as a retaliation to strike action; alternatively, the employer may suspend those taking action. CONTINUITY OF EMPLOYMENT is not broken by a lock-out, but any week during which an employee was locked out would not normally be counted as a week of employment.
See also GUARANTEE PAYMENT, INDUSTRIAL ACTION.

M

Management. Management has a variety of connotations. First, it
is a part of the social and economic fabric, in contrast to the
workers; second, it is the term used to describe the group of
people running a particular business; third, it is the process of
running that business, and fourth, it is a job for an individual
person to undertake. Raymond Williams (1983) traces the
derivation of the word to two roots. From the Italian *maneggiare*
comes the idea of handling and directing (especially horses,
apparently) and from the French *menager* comes the idea of
careful housekeeping. Both these elements are present in the
bulk of management jobs, although the emphasis varies considerably.

"I'm just a number here, too, Smith. I'm Number One."

Management jobs are differentiated by two sets of adjectives,
one relating to *function* and the other to *level*. Functional
differentiation is by describing managers according to their
technical specialism, such as Operations Manager or Sales
Manager. Differentiation by level describes top managers as

those at the apex of the organization having few but vital responsibilities, such as merger, acquisition and closure. Senior managers are concerned with policy formulation and implementation. Middle managers complete the process of implementation and try to resolve the unintended consequences of the policies themselves. Junior managers, or supervisors arrange for the day-to-day work actually to get done.

Kotter (1982) has defined the core behaviour of managers as being first to set agendas for action and then establishing and maintaining networks for the implementation of agendas. Agendas are lists of things to be done, ranging from elaborate plans to *ad hoc* initiatives. Networks are the elaborate set of contacts, not only direct subordinates and close colleagues, that a manager builds up inside and outside the organization who will help the manager get things done.

J. Kotter, *The General Managers* (New York: The Free Press, 1982); H. Mintzberg, *The Nature of Managerial Work* (New York: Harper & Row, 1973); R. Williams, *Keywords: A Vocabulary of Culture and Society* (London: Fontana, 1983).

Management by objectives (MBO). This is an approach to running an organization which involves agreeing objectives for individuals to attain over a period of (usually) 12 months. At the end of the period the achievement of those objectives is reviewed and fresh objectives set. In the intervening period the manager has relative freedom from supervision in order to get on with what has been agreed. This approach is based on the principle that target-setting is an incentive for the individual and a means of integrating the objectives of the individual with the needs of the business.

MBO is a method which has to be used with care and without expecting too much from it. It provides an invaluable basis for discussion rather than a neat yardstick of success or failure, as many desirable objectives cannot be precisely specified and circumstances beyond the control of the manager for whom the objectives have been set may undermine the plan.

Management development. Central to the idea of management development is that the effectiveness of an individual manager can be only partly developed by education and experience. Competence derives from those components coupled with an ability to be socially skilful in an organizational context. One of the most influential concepts in management development has been the ACTION RESEARCH/ACTION LEARNING approach of Revans (1982). In this method the individual manager or potential manager becomes a member of a group or set. Each member has a specific and complex problem to solve in a real situation and they use the group as a base and as a source of mutual support and assistance in working through solutions via discussion. By this means the trainee develops the questioning insight, called Q, which Revans regards as an essential addition to the traditional programmed knowledge (P).

See also BUSINESS SCHOOLS, LEADERSHIP, MANAGEMENT BY OBJECTIVES (MBO), MANAGEMENT EDUCATION, MENTORING, ORGANIZATION DEVELOPMENT.

Management Education. In a very short time education for management and business has become widespread. The first British undergraduate course in management sciences was established in 1965, but 20 years later some 10 per cent of all first degree students were pursuing courses in management or business studies. In addition to the growth in the university sector, there has been an even more rapid expansion in polytechnic degrees in business studies.

The courses vary in nature according to the tradition of the academic department in which they are based. Some are in departments of economics, with that subject dominating the course. Others are in departments with a strong accountancy emphasis and others specialize in operations research. Most courses are, however, multi-disciplinary, with introductory studies in accountancy and the social sciences, followed by a range of specialist options in the functional areas of management and some more academic subjects.

As with all higher education the main value of these courses lies in the capacities they develop rather than in the knowledge they convey. Students acquire the ability to appreciate arguments presented from a variety of points of view and consider the purpose as well as the methods of the business organizations they are likely to join. It is a truism that senior managers like proposals presented 'on one side of A4'. The management graduate should be well able to digest and interpret a great deal of material in order to present just such a concise, well-grounded document.

Masters' courses are mainly conversion courses, taken by students with a first degree in a single discipline (for instance, economics or sociology) who are broadening their range of understanding by a one-year management course.

Most management departments have a strong research emphasis with some students pursuing Ph.D. qualifications.

Management work. The work that managers do can be usefully considered under three headings: technical, administrative and managerial, all of which have to be kept in balance if the manager is to be effective.

Technical work is that done by the manager as a result of some previous training or experience. It is probably done by the subordinates also and is done in spite of, rather than because of, being a manager. It is the engineering manager making stress calculations, the charge nurse caring for a patient, the headmaster teaching children, and so on. *Administrative* work is done to keep the organization running in the way it is used to, checking reports, making returns, providing routine information, keeping records. *Managerial* work is creating precedents and taking initiatives, altering the status quo in some way.

All managers need to do all these three to be effective, but they frequently abandon their technical work too easily in favour of administration, thus losing contact with the main task of the organization. Middle managers frequently fail to appreciate the extent to which they can, and should, do managerial work.

Manpower costs. At least some manpower costs can be calculated and monitored. It is possible, for instance, to review regularly the costs of salaries and National Insurance contributions. It is not possible to measure the costs of low morale, even though there may be secondary indicators, such as rising LABOUR TURNOVER, to demonstrate a costly problem. A regular analysis of those costs which can be reliably calculated, and their assignment to cost centres, provides managers with an instrument of control over their operation. The areas where calculation is most likely to be useful are:

- payment: salaries and wages, direct fringe benefits, statutory costs, pension and sick pay provision;
- selection and assessment: recruitment, search, selection, induction, performance appraisal and assessment;
- training and development: training materials, fees and expenses;
- separation: redundancy and similar payments, legal fees, redundancy counselling, pre-retirement training;
- health, safety and welfare: medical facilities, catering, social facilities, house journals;
- manpower administration: consultancy fees, computing and data protection, committee expenses, stationery, postage and telephone.

Although monitoring is useful, over-preoccupation with costs can produce a negative attitude towards the employment of people that can impair the vigour of the business as well as the employees. See HUMAN RESOURCE MANAGEMENT.

J. Cannon, *Cost Effective Personnel Decisions* (London: Institute of Personnel Management, 1979).

Manpower planning. Manpower planning is a general term used to describe a company strategy for acquiring and developing the human resources needed to meet the organization's needs in the future: 'the right people in the right place at the right time'.

Problems in manpower planning stem from the nature of the manpower resource, which is so different from others: people are different from each other and relatively immobile; surplus is a drain rather than a benefit; and people are dynamic and unpredictable. Because of these problems there is always a heavy reliance on managerial judgement, although the basic method is to extrapolate trends from the past into the future. The demand for manpower is calculated on the basis of marketing predictions of business growth, which are then converted into the numbers of people involved, when they will be required, and the skill range that will be needed. This is compared with an analysis of the supply: the numbers and skill range of people already employed, and estimates of turnover in different categories.

As with all business plans it is important to use a manpower plan and not to be mastered by it. Things do not always go according to plan, and we have to remember that the reality is what is happening, not what the plan says *should* be happening.

M. Armstrong, *A Handbook of Personnel Management Practice*, 2nd edn, (London: Kogan Page, 1984), ch. 10; Department of Employment, *Company Manpower Planning*, Manpower Papers No. 1, (London: HMSO, 1968).

Manpower Services Commission (MSC). The MSC was set up under the Employment and Training Act of 1973 and has since become the central agency dealing with employment issues, including measures to mitigate unemployment, and the development of training. It has taken over some activities, like JOB CENTRES, from the Department of Employment and some, like the TECHNICAL AND VOCATIONAL EDUCATION INITIATIVE, from the Department of Education and Science. Its best-known initiative is the YOUTH TRAINING SCHEME, but there have been many others, such as the Community Programme, which provides work opportunities for the long-term unemployed in community service projects.

Others are:

- PROFESSIONAL AND EXECUTIVE RECRUITMENT;
- the Skillcentre Training Agency, which provides training either in local Skillcentres or on company premises;
- the National Priority Skills Scheme, which funds industrial training for adults;
- the Open Tech Programme;
- the Industrial Language Training Service, which improves the language and communication skills of ethnic minorities;
- Information Technology Centres specializing in computers and electronics;
- the New Enterprise Programme, for those aiming to start their own business.

The headquarters is at Moorfoot, Sheffield S1 4PQ (0742

753275). There are 55 area offices to which inquiries should be directed. Addresses and telephone numbers are in local telephone directories.

Manual workers. Since the repeal of the TRUCK LEGISLATION, the distinction between manual and other workers has become less significant and even more difficult to define. The idea, however, that those who work with their hands are in a different category from other employees dies hard. Despite HARMONIZATION initiatives, there remain a number of ways in which manual workers are likely to be treated differently from other employees:

- pay: although some manual pay rates are now higher than those of many white-collar employees, the overall average for manual work remains lower than that for white collar jobs;
- careers: there is little scope for manual careers in the sense of moving up through the organizational hierarchy, and jobs seldom contain any significant incremental element, performance appraisal or training (see INCREMENT);
- pensions and sick pay: the number of manual employees covered by occupational pension and SICK PAY schemes has increased considerably in the 1980s, but provision remains more generous for those in white collar work (see PENSION SCHEMES);
- FRINGE BENEFITS and allowances: as non-salary elements of the 'remuneration package' for management and white collar employees become more generous and elaborate, those for manual employees remain few and are usually only those regarded as essential;
- TRADE UNION MEMBERSHIP and ACTIVITIES: union membership and participation are higher for manual employees than for other employee categories.

All of these differences emphasize the divided nature of organizational life, with some employees seeing themselves (and being seen as) a part of the business, while others see themselves as just being there to do the work.

Maternity Leave. The maternity leave provisions give a woman a basic right to return to work at any time up to 29 weeks after the week in which her child is born provided that she:

- continues to work until at least the eleventh week before the expected week of confinement, and
- has been continuously employed for two years at that date (see CONTINUITY OF EMPLOYMENT).

A similar notification to that for claiming maternity pay is required, but additionally:

- it must be in writing;
- it must state the expected week of confinement;
- it must indicate an intention to return to work.

Since there will inevitably be women who state that they intend to return to work even if they are undecided, employers may now ask a woman to confirm her intention. They may write to her not earlier than 49 days after the beginning of the expected week of confinement, and she must reply in writing within 14 days. The letter from the employers must tell her that failure to confirm will mean the loss of the right to return.

The employee must notify the employers in writing of her intention to return at least three weeks before the day on which she proposes to return. On her return she is entitled to her original job, and on terms and conditions not less favourable than would have been applicable to her had she not been absent. 'Job', however, is defined in relation to the woman's *contractual* duties, so she may not have the right to exactly the same work in exactly the same place if her contract permits some variation.

Normally an employee who is not permitted to return will be treated as having been unfairly dismissed on her notified date of return, and can claim to a tribunal accordingly (see UNFAIR DISMISSAL). However, the 1980 Act, supposedly to balance the interests of employers, provides that this will not be the case in two circumstances:

1 (a) where immediately before her absence the number of employees employed by her employer (or any associated employer) did not exceed five; and

(b) it is not reasonably practicable to reinstate her in her original job or to offer her suitable alternative employment (S56A(1) of the Employment Protection (Consolidation) Act 1978);
2 irrespective of the size of the firm it is not reasonably practicable to reinstate her in her original job, and suitable alternative employment is offered, and she either accepts or unreasonably refuses that offer (S56A(2) of the Employment Protection (Consolidation) Act 1978).

The latter provision envisages a situation other than redundancy, in which case a suitable alternative employment on terms not less favourable than the original job must be offered. If no such job exists the employee is entitled to a redundancy payment.

Maternity pay. The current scheme of statutory maternity pay, administered by employers, came into effect on 6 April 1987. It is payable for a maximum of 18 weeks, beginning no earlier than the eleventh week before the expected week of confinement. A woman who has been continuously employed (see CONTINUITY OF EMPLOYMENT) for two years is entitled to be paid nine-tenths of her week's earnings for six weeks, followed by a flat-rate payment for a further twelve weeks. Women with between six months and two years' service are entitled simply to the flat rate for eighteen weeks (provided their earnings are not less than the lower earnings limit for payment of National Insurance contributions). Employers recover the payments in the same way as with STATUTORY SICK PAY. A woman who does not qualify for statutory maternity pay may be able to claim maternity allowance, payable through the DHSS.

In order to claim payment the employee must tell her employer that she intends to stop work because of her pregnancy at least three weeks (or if this not reasonably practicable, as soon as is reasonably practicable) before stopping. Her employer is entitled to request this notification to be in writing, and to require the employee to produce medical evidence of the date the baby is due.

Employer's Guide to Statutory Maternity Pay NI. 257, available from local offices of DHSS.

Maternity rights. The EMPLOYMENT PROTECTION (CONSOLIDATION)

ACT 1978, as amended by the EMPLOYMENT ACT 1980, contains provisions entitling women to MATERNITY LEAVE and paid TIME OFF to keep anti-natal appointments. Entitlement to MATERNITY PAY is governed by the Social Security Act 1986, which came into effect on 6 April 1987.

These statutory rights (particularly in relation to maternity leave) involve strict adherence to a fairly complex procedure of written notices. Employers may provide more generous contractual schemes which do not require such formal procedure.

Mentoring. Mentoring is a form of coaching which tries to reproduce in an organization the working relationship of skilled worker and apprentice by attaching a new recruit to an established employee to induct, guide and coach the recruit while full competence is developed. In some ways it is similar to the arrangement of the medical houseman. One set of suggestions for a mentor's relationship with a protégé is:

- *M*anage the relationship;
- *E*ncourage the protégé;
- *N*urture the protégé;
- *T*each the protégé;
- *O*ffer mututal respect;
- *R*espond to the protégé's needs.

D. Clutterbuck, *Everyone Needs a Mentor* (London: Institute of Personnel Management, 1985).

Moonlighting. In Britain the practice of people holding a second job, typically in the evening (working by moonlight), is growing. This is a product partly of a desire to increase income, partly of a desire to have varied employment and lessen the sense of dependency on a single employer, and partly as a means of the employer (especially the small employer) being able to use specialist expertise without any great commitment to the employee. The arrangement usually has the further attraction to the unscrupulous that the employee avoids income tax and the employer avoids National Insurance contributions.

Morale. Morale is an important yet nebulous quality that all groups need to have, providing a sense of confidence in what is being done and self-respect as a result of doing it.

A conclusion of the HAWTHORNE EXPERIMENTS was that high morale was linked to high productivity, yet subsequent studies have shown that high productivity can be achieved in spite of low morale. High morale in a group does not necessarily mean high commitment to organizational goals, as a group might develop high morale in its attempt to resist management initiatives which are seen as hostile. One feature of group behaviour which often assists high morale is appropriate LEADERSHIP to help express and focus feelings within the group.

See also MOTIVATION.

Motivation. To most employers the secret of motivation is the most prized of all discoveries. What does the employer do to get people to work effectively? This is a very crude view of motivation as the employer can usually do very little: the motives are within the people rather than in the hands of the employer. There has, however, been a great deal of research on this topic and some suggestions can be made. One of the difficulties is that theoretical explanations vary, but two of the best-known are *expectancy theory* and the *two-factor theory*.

Expectancy theory was first formulated by the American, Tolman, in the 1930s and argues that behaviour is directed by the conscious expectations that we have about our behaviour leading to expected goals. If we expect high productivity to lead to high earnings but the disapproval of our workmates, then we will only work hard if we want high earnings more than we want the approval of those we work with. In 1964 Vroom developed this theory by the addition of valence (or personal preference for a particular outcome) and produced the expectancy equation of:

$$F = E \times V$$

where F is the motivation to behave, E is the expectation that the behaviour will be followed by a particular outcome, and V is the valence of the outcome. This explanation takes account of the extent to which individuals are motivated differently from each other and assumes that we are all sufficiently rational to calculate both our goals and our behaviour.

The two-factor theory was propounded by another American, Frederick Herzberg, who suggested that satisfaction and dissatisfaction are caused by different factors, so that eliminating dissatisfaction does not necessarily produce satisfaction. The 'dissatisfiers' are company policy and administration, salary, supervision, working conditions and status. Herzberg described these as HYGIENE FACTORS, using the medical analogy on the grounds that satisfaction with work was not possible if any of these factors were perceived as incorrect by the job holder. Eliminating dissatisfaction by cleaning up the hygiene factors does not produce satisfaction. This comes from motivators, which are achievement, advancement, growth, recognition, responsibility and the work itself, so employers need to work on those factors to develop the job satisfaction and then the effectiveness of employees. Herzberg has been heavily criticized by academics because of his research methodology and on the grounds that his explanation may work for middle-class Americans, but is less applicable to other groups. Nevertheless it has an instant common-sense appeal and his ideas have been very influential, especially with the emphasis on the job itself, which provides a helpful counterpoint to some of the headier ideas about personal leadership being the way to produce results.

The employer's approach to improving employees' motivation lies in JOB DESIGN, a useful framework for which is the formulation of Robert Cooper (1973) suggesting that managers (or other designers of individual jobs) should concentrate on:

- *variety,* the pace, place and nature of the work;
- *discretion,* the amount of choice available to the worker in connection with the job;
- *contribution,* the significance of the employee's work in shaping the final product or service;
- *goal characteristics,* the clarity and difficulty of the goals set for the employee in carrying out the job.

R. Cooper, 'Task characteristics and intrinsic motivation', in *Human Relations,* 26 (August 1973), pp. 387–408; F. Herzberg, 'One More Time: How do You Motivate Employees?' in *Harvard Business Review,* January–February 1968; V. H. Vroom, *Work and Motivation* (London: John Wiley, 1964).

N

National Insurance. National Insurance contributions are payable jointly by the employer and the employee to finance a range of benefits such as unemployment benefit and retirement pension. The lowest levels of income incur no liability for contributions, and there is then a sliding scale of contributions. The figures shown in table 2 are the contribution levels applying in April 1986.

Table 2

| Employee income (weekly) | | Contribution (%) | |
At least:	Less than:	Employee	Employer
	£ 38	0	0
£ 38	£ 60	5	5
£ 60	£ 95	7	7
£ 95	£140	9	9
£140	£285	9	10.45
On that part of pay above £285 weekly		0	10.45

Those over normal retirement age are exempted from these contributions, as are students, those drawing benefit through unemployment or incapacity and a dwindling number of married women who exercise the right to the married woman's election to pay industrial injuries insurance only.

Details of National Insurance change frequently but particulars are always available from a post office or from the local office of the Department of Health and Social Security, most of which provide an excellent advice service by telephone.

Natural wastage. Employees leave organizations of their own will, through retirement, ill-health, family reasons and a desire for a change. When an organization needs to reduce the number of personnel in its employ, there is always a degree of reduction that can be calculated as a result of natural wastage through these causes, involving no expense and no enforced redundancy. It is therefore always the first calculation to be made.

Negotiation. This is one of the most important, and the most stylized, of face-to-face encounters in the field of employment. It is typically between representatives of management and representatives of trade unions working out details of pay and conditions acceptable to both parties, starting from the premise that the interests of the parties to some extent CONFLICT. Most negotiations result in a mutually unsatisfactory compromise, but the ideal product is a mutually satisfactory arrangement which has resulted from confronting the issues dividing the parties and finding a resolution to which both parties are committed because it represents a solution that is better than either could have envisaged before the negotiation began: the negotiation process has itself developed possibilities and initiatives that the parties could not think of or implement without the negotiation taking place.

"Aha! Trying to buy us off with huge salaries and great working conditions, huh?"

Before negotiation takes place the parties need to agree the agenda for their discussions and the sequence in which matters will be taken. They also need (separately) to collect and organize the information they will need and agree their objectives and the roles that each team member will fill. The negotiation itself follows a ritual pattern:

- interparty antagonism. Statements from both sides emphasize that they have a strong case from which they will not be moved. They also articulate exactly what their case is and where they stand. Statements are relatively long and formal, expressing a collective rather than personal view.
- interpersonal probing. The opening mode will eventually break as one of the two lead spokesmen (quickly followed by the other) will move into a different type of statement, much more personal and non-committal, tentatively exploring possibilities of movement from the positions indicated by the opening statements. Interparty antagonism was needed to clarify the two positions, but interpersonal probing begins testing out the possibility of mutual accommodation.
- decision-making. Gradually the negotiators piece together an agreement which secures concessions from both sides, but with the advantages to both sides outweighing the disadvantages.

This type of negotiation is different from others (for instance, in the commercial field) because the parties cannot escape from each other. It may be that one party can abandon negotiations and force a settlement by other means, but they cannot change the protagonists. The seller can choose a different customer and the buyer can choose a different supplier, but in employment negotiations the union can only negotiate with the employer it has and only in extreme circumstances will an employer dismiss a work-force and recruit afresh. The great value of negotiation in employment matters is that it is the most effective way in which to introduce major change in the workplace.

D. P. Torrington and L. A. Hall, *Personnel Management: A New Approach* (Hemel Hempstead: Prentice-Hall International, 1987), ch. 26.

New technology agreements. Since the advent of the computer and the visual display unit (VDU) working practices have been altered for many categories of employee, and a number of employers sign agreements with unions representing their employees regarding the introduction of new technology to ensure that new working practices will not be impeded. The main features of these agreements relate to training and redeployment, but they may also provide for employees to share in the economic benefits of new technology. The most specific features relate to health and safety aspects of working with VDUs.

The three possible health hazards are radiation, eye strain and posture. The possibility of radiation hazard is remote, but eye strain is more common, especially with small, monochrome screens. Some people may have to wear glasses just to operate a VDU and a new technology agreement might include an undertaking from the employer to pay for such spectacles and for an annual eye test. Employees with a history of migraine, photo-sensitive epilepsy or severe nervous disorders should not operate a screen-based system without a prior medical examination. VDUs should be positioned to ensure background illumination in the range of 100–300 LUX.

Posture problems can cause back-ache and neck-ache so that VDU operators should be provided with chairs which can be adjusted to suit individual requirements.

Although VDUs are a source of non-iodizing radiation, it has not so far been scientifically or statistically possible to prove or disprove that they present a hazard to the reproductive capacity of either men or women. There is, however, a widespread popular belief that a pregnant woman working at a VDU could be putting her unborn child at risk and there is at least one tribunal case (*Johnston* v. *Highland Regional Council,* 1984) where it was found that the dismissal of a woman who refused to work at a VDU while pregnant was unfair. The trade union SOGAT have suggested that the right to transfer to non-VDU work, without prejudice, should be available both to women who are pregnant and to those intending to become pregnant.

Normal retiring age. Employees who have reached the normal retiring age at the EFFECTIVE DATE OF TERMINATION are precluded from bringing claims of UNFAIR DISMISSAL. The presumption is that the contractual retiring age is the normal retiring age. However, if there is some higher age at which employees in the position of the individual in question regularly retire, that age will be their normal retiring age. 'Normal retiring age' is determined at the date when the employee is dismissed. This means that where management effect a change in retirement policy prior to dismissing an employee, the normal retiring age will be governed by the new policy and not by the employee's original expectations.

Where evidence shows that the contractual retirement age has been abandoned and employees retire at a variety of ages, there is no normal retiring age. The statutory retirement age then bars unfair dismissal claims.

See also SEX DISCRIMINATION ACT 1986.

O

Occupational Pensions Board. Occupational pensions are those linked to a specific occupation for the benefit only of those engaged in that occupation. This is in contrast to national schemes, linked to National Insurance contributions. In order to ensure the probity of these occupational schemes, the Occupational Pensions Board was set up in 1973 to supervise contracted-out schemes. These are occupational pensions organized by an employer to cover employees in preference to participation in the STATE EARNINGS RELATED PENSION SCHEME. The Occupational Pensions Board reviews these schemes and issues contracted-out certificates where these are appropriate. The Board also ensures equal access of both sexes to contracted-out schemes and the preservation of pension rights.

See also PENSION SCHEMES.

Occupational stress. Stress is a demand made on our mental or physical energy. When this demand is felt as excessive it can lead to such physiological symptoms as irritability, depression, headaches and chest pains. However, what is stressful to one person may not be stressful to another, as we have different personalities, expertise and abilities ('One man's meat is another man's poison'), and too little work for one person may be just as stressful as too much work for another.

The six main sources of stress at work are:

- an aspect of the job itself;
- uncertainty about what to do, including conflicting demands being made;
- relationships at work, especially where there is mistrust;
- under-promotion or over-promotion;
- organizational climate;
- conflicting demands between home and working life.

Among the strategies to cope with stress are physical exercise which will use up the adrenalin that stress produces in the body. a change of scene, therapy and self-help groups, and family support and listening.

It is a misapprehension that those in managerial positions are particularly prone to occupational stress. Symptoms are more common among those lower in the hierarchy. The American psychiatrist Holmes has devised a scale of life incidents which produce varying levels of stress risk (the higher the points the higher the risk). A change of responsibility at work scores a mere 29 points, compared with 50 for getting married, 73 for divorce, 40 for pregnancy, 45 for retirement and 20 for moving house.

C. L. Cooper and J. Marshall, *Understanding Executive Stress* (London: Macmillan, 1978).

Off-the-job training. Training off the job is appropriate when it is possible to simulate the activity for which the trainee is preparing and where time is needed for explanation, discussion and practice to develop competence. It has all the advantages of work being organized for the purpose of training, rather than training being fitted into a work routine organized for another purpose.

Methods of training off the job include the company training centre, where there is likely to be a steady flow of employees requiring training that can be standardized, such as the training of apprentices. An alternative is day release or block release to a technical college, a commercial agency or a Skillcentre. For managers there are courses run by business schools and consultants, although short periods of attachment to other companies are becoming more common.

See also ACTION LEARNING.

On-the-job training. Training off the job may not transfer easily to the real working situation, so some learning has to take place on the job to reinforce what has been learned elsewhere. This is a key element in the training of most professionals and is the dominant mode of MENTORING and the YOUTH TRAINING SCHEME.

Open learning. Traditionally learning is located at the same place as the teacher: in the workshop, the classroom, the lecture theatre or the training centre. This has a number of problems, mainly the difficulty of providing learning that is equally available to all. For many years a partial solution to that problem has been the correspondence course, whereby the student learns through correspondence with a tutor, but the potential of television and the microcomputer have increased the range of possibilities and methods of delivery available, so that a learning programme can be built up from a range of different elements and based on the learning needs of the individual rather than the limitations of an academic institution.

The Open University was founded in 1969 to provide study facilities by means of television and radio lectures, correspondence, audio and video tapes, local counselling and summer schools. It has recently extended its range to a number of courses in the Open Business School. Open Tech was established in 1985 to provide more directly vocational training under the auspices of the MANPOWER SERVICES COMMISSION. Some large businesses have short training courses packaged and available to branches via the on-line computer terminal from a centre at head office. If there is a new development (for instance, a change in currency regulations that will affect all bank staff) it is possible for a training course to be prepared at the centre, and those at the periphery call up the programme and run it on their terminal at any moment when they have time available. This saves the time and expense of hundreds of staff having to visit the company training centre over a period of months until all have been processed.

Manpower Services Commission, *An 'Open Tech' Programme: A Consultative Document* (Manchester: Manpower Services Commission, 1981).

Organization. Organization is both the act of organizing and the state of being organized. For managers it is therefore the process of getting things done by orchestrating resources and conducting the work of other people. For all employees it is the state of being part of a social group that is created and maintained for the purpose of achieving specific objectives which can only be achieved by the corporate activity of people holding different yet complementary roles. Organization involves specialization, coordination and hierarchy.

See also BUREAUCRACY, ORGANIZATION CULTURE, ORGANIZATION DESIGN, ORGANIZATION DEVELOPMENT, ORGANIZATION STRUCTURE, POWER.

J. Child. *Organization: A Guide to Problems and Practice,* 2nd edn (New York: Harper & Row, 1984).

Organization culture. Organizational culture refers to a set of shared values held by members of an organization, which have the effect of distinguishing that particular one from other organizations. The value of this idea to employers is that it shifts the emphasis of organizing away from ORGANIZATION STRUCTURE, on which perhaps too much reliance has been placed in the past. Peters and Waterman (1982) found that companies they regarded as excellent had the following emphasized values:

- a bias for action;
- closeness to the customer;
- autonomy and entrepreneurship (activities encouraged for all employees, not just those in high places);
- productivity through people;
- hands-on, value driven (meaning that those in senior positions were closely involved with the main task of the organization and practised the values they espoused);
- stick to the knitting (meaning that the organization diversified only with care, so that it operated in fields where it had expertise);
- simple form, lean staff (so that the organization was simple and there were few people in support roles);
- simultaneous loose–tight properties (meaning that there was tight management control of the operation accompanied by autonomy as mentioned above).

T. J. Peters and R. H. Waterman, *In Search of Excellence* (New York: Harper & Row, 1982).

Organization design. Designing the organization is creating the structure or changing it. The first requirements are *differentiation* and *integration*. Differentiation is making the arrangement for an individual job or task, while integration is coordinating the output of all the individual jobs so that the whole task is completed satisfactorily. There are four fundamentals in organization design:

- task identity and job definition: deciding what jobs need to be done, making clear what the jobs consist of, how they adjoin other jobs, and avoiding gaps or duplication;

- structure: grouping together different jobs into groups or departments, using the bases of function, territory, product or time period (a further structuring device is HIERARCHY);
- decision-making complexes, where organizational affairs are pushed along by decisions which cannot be made by individuals but only by groups of people representing different interests and areas of expertise;
- PROCEDURES, those administrative devices for putting plans and policies into operation.

See also BUREAUCRACY, ORGANIZATION STRUCTURE.

D. P. Torrington and L. A. Hall, *Personnel Management: A New Approach* (Hemel Hempstead: Prentice-Hall International, 1987), ch. 4.

Organization development. This represents an approach to developing the organization and its people systematically and at the same time, with the emphasis on innovation, using the argument that both organization and people have to develop and change to meet fresh challenges, and the development of one will be fruitless without the development of the other. This has had the effect on MANAGEMENT DEVELOPMENT of moving attention away from developing the individual in isolation and towards developing the individual within the context of the work group, and the work group within the context of the organization.

The method of organization development is usually to use a consultant as catalyst. This person may be internal or external, but the role is the same: to stimulate and enable change. This is done by commenting on what is taking place, interpreting events and helping members of the organization to find the strategies for change in which they believe and which they will be able to implement.

Organization structure. The most common type of organization structure is the *bureaucratic,* which is formal and mechanistic, exhibiting the characteristics of BUREAUCRACY.

Where the organization has a need to move fast and make major decisions which depend more on flair and judgement than on the measured weighing of alternatives, then the structure will be *centralized,* relying on key, powerful figures with all decisions made in the light of central expectations.

When there is reliance on diverse professional specializations and well-established functional expertise, then the bureaucratic structure will be *decentralized,* with greater use of procedures and committees and less dependence on precedents. There may be one of two emphases: function or product. In functional organization, people are grouped according to the expertise they share in a function (such as marketing or personnel). In a product organization people are organized around product lines first, functional specialization second.

The *matrix* form of organization attempts to overcome some of the inflexibility inherent in bureaucracy by combining a functional structure with a product structure. There are two sets of overlapping hierarchies, one at right angles to the other. The vertical hierarchy is the orthodox ranking and reporting relationships of functional specialization, while the horizontal hierarchy links together people from different functions to share full responsibility for a particular project requiring skills from each. This was first advocated as a way of making organizations more accountable, but it is a form that has tended to lose favour because of high support costs and unwieldy administration.

See also ORGANIZATION CULTURE, ORGANIZATION DESIGN.

C. B. Handy, *Understanding Organisations,* 3rd edn (Harmondsworth: Penguin, 1985).

Overtime. Overtime is time worked beyond the agreed hours to meet fluctuations in demand, although it is also frequently worked as a mechanism of increasing earnings. In manufacturing industry over one-third of all operatives worked approximately nine hours' overtime a week during 1985. The lowest figure in recent years was 26.6 per cent of operatives working an average of 8.2 hours a week in 1981, so the institution of overtime has remained proof against economic vicissitudes. It is customary for overtime hours to be paid for at an enhanced rate.

P

Panel interviews. These are usually selection interviews, although panels are occasionally used for appraisal or discipline, where three or more selectors interview candidates at the same time. Theoretically this reduces the risk of individual prejudice or bias. In practice, however, the panel interview is a very difficult interview to run, as individual selectors can be more aware of each other than they are of the candidate and sometimes are more concerned to score points off each other than they are to form a clear view of the applicants. There is a likelihood of questions being haphazard and not allowing for development or discussion, and many candidates are overawed by the extreme formality of the occasion. The best use of panels is after a series of one-to-one interviews during which tentative opinions have been formed and there may be several specific and important matters on which the interviewers have formed conflicting opinions or have elicited contradictory evidence. Then the panel can deal with these outstanding matters in a way that can satisfy all interviewers.

Parity. The notion of parity is a specialized form of concern about differentials or pay relativities when a group of employees seek to justify increasing pay or reshaping pay structures to achieve the position of being equal in rank to another group, who are regarded as receiving more favourable treatment.

Participative management. Participative management is a style of leadership or supervision which aims to increase the commitment of subordinates to management objectives by actively encouraging their participation in the making of decisions which directly affect them. This can improve both the quality of the decisions made and the commitment of the subordinates to implementing the decisions.

See also EMPLOYEE INVOLVEMENT, JOINT CONSULTATION, LEADERSHIP, MANAGEMENT STYLE.

Part-time working. This method of working has grown significantly in the 1980s: 21 per cent of all employees had part-time contracts by 1981. This increase is related to the increasing number of women (especially married women) in the work-force, 90 per cent of the recent rise in part-time working being female. This calculation is based on the Department of Employment figure of those working less than 30 hours a week, although those working at least 16 hours a week have the legal status of full-time employees.

See also JOB SHARING.

Paternalism. An attitude or policy whereby the manager behaves like a father, having the best interests of the employees at heart but usurping their individual responsibility and liberty of choice, is known as paternalism. The attitude is best illustrated by a remark attributed to the first Lord Leverhulme, who introduced profit-sharing in his company decades before it was even contemplated elsewhere. When it came to the question of how the money was to be spent he said: 'It will not do you much good if you send it down your throats by buying bottles of whiskey or fat geese at Christmas. If you leave the money with me, I will use it to provide schools, hospitals and all the things that make life pleasant, Anyway, I am not disposed to allow profit-sharing on any other basis.'

"He always rewards good work . . ."

Paternalist employers tended to resist union recognition and are sometimes accused of providing benefits only as a means of control. It remains an approach that is adopted in modified form by some large organizations and many individual managers.

It is interesting that the word 'maternalism' is never used in this sense.

Payment. Employees are paid for the work they do; this is central to the contract of employment. Employers constantly seek to manipulate the payment arrangements to influence the performance of the employee, through such modifications as INCENTIVES or SHARE OWNERSHIP, and employees seek to manipulate the arrangements to enhance their security and sense of fair play, through devices such as JOB EVALUATION and provision for PENSION SCHEMES and SICK PAY. Above all else, payment is the device for regulating the supply and demand of people and jobs. It is an imperfect regulator but there is a tendency for payment to improve when there is a shortage of people and to stagnate when there is a shortage of jobs. Payment is also the most tangible indicator of status, which is why so much energy is expended in mounting or resisting pay claims. 'How much?' is an important question, but 'How much more than . . . ?' (or 'less than') is more significant. For this reason the dominant principle relating to payment is fairness: 'a fair day's pay for a fair day's work' even though this makes change difficult.

Employers and employees always view payment differently, as indicated by the Tyneside story of the labourer struggling with a heavy load in the works yard. It was wet and windy and the labourer was handicapped by the sole of his boot flapping loose. The manager appeared on the other side of the yard in smart suit and shining shoes. 'Oh, Joe,' he said to the labourer, 'We can't have you struggling with a boot like that.' Whereupon he pulled a roll of banknotes from his pocket and Joe's eyes gleamed. Carefully the manager removed the rubber band from round the notes and passed it over to secure the flapping boot sole.

Payment by results (PBR). In PBR schemes, payment is related directly to the results attributable to the worker. Schemes are widely used although many newer jobs are not suitable to this form of payment arrangement. Between one-quarter and one-third of employers use some PBR arrangement for manual workers, although less than 10 per cent use such schemes for other employees.

Most often used is *individual time saving,* whereby a standard time is derived for a specific work sequence and the employee receives additional payment for the time that is saved in completing a number of such operations. When the worker is stopped due to shortage of materials or similar circumstances beyond the worker's control, then the time involved is not counted at the end of the day when the PBR calculations are made (see WAITING TIME). The standard times are derived by method study (a technique to find the most efficient way of performing a task) and work measurement (measuring the time taken to complete the task).

Group incentives are the same principles applied to group rather than individual activity. This is logical in situations where jobs are interdependent, as on an assembly line, but they can put considerable strain on the social cohesion of the work group.

Measured daywork operates the other way round. A daily or hourly quota is determined and a sustained rate of pay is paid all the time during which that level of output is maintained. Thus the incentive element is stable and the level of output is predictable. These PBR schemes have become more popular than individual or group time-saving.

Pendulum arbitration. In normal ARBITRATION the arbitrator usually produces a solution that is a compromise between two positions. This may deal with the problem but there is always the risk that this splitting of the differences dissatisfies both sides (see CONFLICT). Pendulum arbitration requires the arbitrator to choose between one of the two final positions, so that one side 'succeeds' and the other 'fails'. The advantage of this approach is that it induces a greater willingness of the parties themselves to seek out the middle ground and settle the matter themselves. This method has been adopted to only a limited extent in Britain, mainly in agreements by the Electricians' and Engineering Unions concluded with foreign-owned, high-technology companies.

Pension Fund Trustees. Pension scheme contributions go into a fund which is independent of the employer's control. A trust deed makes trustees responsible for managing the fund and the investments made with the fund monies. The trustees may be appointed by the management or the employees or both, but their powers are as defined in the trust deed; they do not have the power to alter the scheme or negotiate about its membership conditions. Trustees safeguard the fund against illegal use by the employer, but the employer is still largely responsible for it and has great interest in it. In extreme cases the employer could wind it up.

Pension schemes. The basic pension for retired people is the state flat-rate pension to which employed people acquire an entitlement through NATIONAL INSURANCE contributions during their working lives. The amount of pension is set according to the size of the household. In November 1985 the figure was set at £38.30 for a single person and £61.30 for a married couple; the figure is adjusted annually in line with the cost of living. An additional amount linked to lifetime earnings is the STATE EARNINGS RELATED PENSION SCHEME.

The majority of employees are now also members of an occupational pension scheme. This is linked to employment in a particular organization or in a particular occupation, with regular contributions being made by the employer and the employee, although some schemes run on employer contributions only. The level of contribution varies considerably, but a typical arrangement would be 7 per cent of earnings contributed by the employee and 12 per cent by the employer, although there are instances of the employer's contributions being more than double those of the employee. Both these contributions are, of course, in addition to the National Insurance levy.

The most common type of benefit is the *final pay* scheme, where the pension is a proportion of the final pay at or shortly before retirement. Pension will be paid at some fraction of the final pay, according to the number of years of contribution. If the proportion is 1/60th per year, 20 years' service would produce 20/60ths, or one-third, of final pay as pension. If the proportion is 1.25 per cent, then the same service would produce 25 per cent of final pay as pension. Final pay also varies in interpretation from one scheme to another. It may be the average of the final 12 months, the average of the last five years, the actual final salary figure, or some other variation.

Average earnings schemes are less attractive as the pension is linked to average earnings throughout the period of employment, so that the actual pension is the total of the amount of pension earned in each year.

Money purchase schemes start by determining not the pension but the contribution. The contributions are then paid in, year by year, and the accrued benefit is used on retirement to buy a pension most closely linked to the individual's personal needs.

Few people remain in the same employment for all their working lives, so the Social Security Act 1985 secures the rights of early leavers, who are entitled to one of the following:

- a refund of their own contributions, but only on service up to April 1975;
- a preserved pension, which is the pension due on the contribution made so far but which will not be paid before normal retirement age;
- a transfer value paid over to the pension arrangements of the next employer;
- a transfer value paid to an insurance company which will issue the early leaver with a policy or an annuity.

The Inland Revenue have strict rules regarding pension funds, which includes one that the pension should not exceed two-thirds of final pay, and another that employee contributions should not exceed 15 per cent of pay. Contributions cannot be refunded except on death or leaving and if the scheme allows for a lump sum payment on retirement, as an addition to the pension, this should not exceed one-and-a-half years' final pay. Compliance with these rules earns tax relief on the contributions.

Information about pensions can be obtained from The Company Pensions Information Centre, 7 Old Park Lane, London W1Y 3LJ (01 409 1933/4).

See also NATIONAL INSURANCE, OCCUPATIONAL PENSIONS BOARD, PENSIONS FUND TRUSTEE, STATE EARNINGS RELATED PENSIONS SCHEME.

Performance appraisal. See APPRAISAL.

Perquisites. A perquisite (or 'perk') is an incidental benefit derived from a certain type of employment, like free meals in restaurants for catering staff and discount purchase of company products by employees. Recently it has taken on a slightly different connotation from FRINGE BENEFITS, which are seen increasingly as a salient feature of the employee's 'remuneration package' (and more likely to be subject to taxation), while perquisites remain an incidental benefit of the employment.

Personality. Although it initially sounds ponderous, the most succinct definition of personality was produced by Gordon Allport in 1937: 'Personality is the dynamic organization within the individual of those psychophysical systems that determine his unique adaptations to his environment.' It is thus the way in which each one of us puts together a number of bits of ourselves to cope with the circumstances in which we are placed, especially the circumstances in which we interact with other people. The assessment of personality is of interest to employers because of its close connection with behaviour and because personality is a product of heredity, culture and learning, which alters little in adult life. There may be minor changes but neurotics remain neurotic and autocrats remain autocratic. If, as an employer, you know the personality of the person with whom you are dealing, you can at least begin to understand their behaviour. Some personality attributes are particularly useful for predicting behaviour.

1 Locus of control: those who believe they are masters of their fate are known as *internals,* while those who see themselves as the pawns of fate are called *externals.* Research shows that externals are more likely than internals to be alienated from their work, more often absent, less satisfied with their jobs and less involved with their colleagues. Internals are more motivated to achieve and will succeed in jobs requiring initiative, while externals will succeed in jobs that are well structured and routine, involving compliance and a willingness to follow instructions.

2 Needs achievement: similar to the external is the person with a *need to achieve* (nAch), constantly striving to do things

better and overcome obstacles by their own efforts. However, nAch personalities are best suited only for jobs with an intermediate level of challenge. Easy jobs will not stimulate them, but neither will very difficult jobs as they will fear failure and the lack of achievement which that will represent, so they are best in posts providing rapid feedback on performance, control of the situation and a 50/50 chance of success.

3 Authoritarianism: the belief that there should be status and power differences between members of an organization varies considerably. The highly authoritarian are intellectually rigid, deferential to superiors and exploitative of subordinates, distrustful and suspicious of change. This type of person should succeed in jobs which are highly structured and require close adherence to the rules. Where the job requires tact and an ability to adapt to changing situations, they will be less effective.

4 Machiavellianism (Mach): a person who rates highly on Mach believes that the ends justify the means. Mach personalities remain emotionally distant from colleagues and manipulate a great deal. They can be very successful in winning and persuading providing that they can deal with people face-to-face in a situation where there are few rules and where they can remain emotionally detached.

5 Risk-taking: we all differ on how willing we are to take risks and how much information we will gather before taking a decision. Stockbrokers need a high risk-taking propensity, while auditors need to be low on this attribute.

Judgements about personality are most often made by personal, on-the-spot assessment or after long experience with a person, and they are likely to eschew classification like the above in favour of comments like 'strong' or 'weak'. An alternative is PERSONALITY TESTING.

S. P. Robbins, *Organizational Behaviour: Concepts, Controversies, and Applications,* 3rd edn (Englewood Cliffs, New Jersey: Prentice-Hall, 1986), ch. 3.

Personality testing. Measurement of personality causes even more controversy than measurement of intelligence, largely because some of the earlier attempts involved the judge interpreting activities performed by the person being assessed in a way which the layman could not readily appreciate. The thematic apperception test, for example, presented a person with a series of pictures and asked for a story to fit them. The Rorschach inkblot test required a person to interpret an inkblot. Both were obviously open to manipulation. Rather more satisfactory is the 16PF test of R. B. Cattell, who has identified through research 16 personality factors which are reasonably steady and constant sources of behaviour, so that an assessment of the factors in an individual can predict that person's behaviour in a range of situations. Each person taking the 16PF test is eventually rated at a point on each of the following 16 factor ranges:

1 Reserved...Outgoing
2 Less intelligent.....................................More intelligent
3 Affected by feelings .... Emotionally stable
4 Submissive .... Dominant
5 Serious ....Happy-go-lucky
6 Expedient.. Conscientious
7 Timid.. Venturesome
8 Tough-minded... Sensitive
9 Trusting .... Suspicious
10 Practical.. Imaginative
11 Forthright ....Shrewd
12 Self-assured .... Apprehensive
13 Conservative... Experimenting
14 Group-dependent..................................... Self-sufficient
15 Uncontrolled .... Controlled
16 Relaxed .... Tense

The main value of this test is that large numbers of people have now taken the test and the results have been analysed to suggest what profile is likely to produce success in a particular type of job.

Personality testing is now much used in assessment of potential for management or professional jobs, but tests should only be administered and the results interpreted by people trained for the task.

See also APTITUDE TESTS, INTELLIGENCE TESTS, PERSONALITY.

R. B. Cattell, *The Scientific Analysis of Personality* (Harmondsworth: Penguin, 1965).

Personnel management. The personnel function of management is directed mainly at the organization's employees; finding and training them, arranging for them to be paid, explaining management's expectations, justifying management's actions, satisfying employees' work-related needs, dealing with their problems and seeking to modify management policy and action which might otherwise produce an unwelcome employee response. It covers a range of activities and approaches present in all management jobs. Sometimes there is a specialist personnel management group, who undertake some aspect of all the above duties. That specialist group is never totally identified with management interests, as it becomes ineffective when it is not able to understand and articulate the aspirations and views of the work-force. For this reason it is always to some extent in between the management and the employees, mediating the needs of each to the other. Underpinning personnel management are the twin ideas that employees need a degree of looking after while at work, and that they are only effective when their needs are being met.

See also HUMAN RESOURCES MANAGEMENT.

Personnel policy. Statements of personnel policy are declared courses of action to be taken in the future by the management of an organization. The actions of the management can then to some extent be judged by the implementation of the policy, which becomes the yardstick of success or failure. The advantages of such policy statements are:

- clarification to colleagues, employees and public;
- reducing dependence on individuals carrying precedents and expertise in their heads;
- producing consistent management behaviour;
- responding to legal and other external pressures.

Statements of policy are not, of themselves, sufficient to bring about the action that they describe and there have been some bitter disappointments about the effectiveness of, for example, policies on equal opportunity that have failed to deliver the change their protagonists sought. Personnel policies must be devised for, and relevant to, the situation in which they will be implemented; they need effective PROCEDURES and determined management action to make them work. Policies also need to be monitored and updated to ensure, first, that they are achieving what they are supposed to achieve and, second, that they have not been overtaken by events.

See also PERSONNEL STRATEGY.

Personnel records. Personnel records excite few people, but are the essential basis of effective personnel management, providing the data to monitor employment trends as well as answering individual queries. The growing tendency to store records on computer disc means that greater amounts of information can be stored and the data can be manipulated by modelling, which is asking the computer questions about the future which can be answered by interrogating the data base and making a prediction. Typical questions are about the number of employees needed in a particular category at some time in the future and the effect of applying a pay rise of x per cent to a group of employees.

The computerization of personnel records also raises difficult questions about confidentiality. (See DATA PROTECTION ACT.)

Personnel specification. In systematic staff selection a JOB DESCRIPTION is followed by a personnel specification. Having described the job to be done, the selector then specifies the appropriate type of person to do it. The job is known and can therefore be described: the person is as yet unknown and can only be specified by stating the type of knowledge, skills and experience required for the job holder. A simple form of specification is the matrix:

Job title ....

	Essential	Desirable	Dangerous
Education and qualifications	....	....	....
Knowledge and skills	....	....	....
Working experience	....	....	....
Disposition	....	....	....
Aptitudes	....	....	....

Circumstances	....	....	....
Attitudes	....	....	....
Age	....	....	....
Car driver	....	....	....
Union member	....	....	....

P. Plumbley, *Recruitment and Selection,* 4th edn (London: Institute of Personnel Management, 1986).

Personnel strategy. There are widely differing ideas about what constitutes personnel strategy, as distinct from personnel policy. It lies somewhere between policy and procedure and deals more with the 'what?' than the 'how?' A military analogy could be of a strategy to capture a city within the framework of a policy not to execute any prisoners taken in the process. If an organization has a sudden major development, such as the opening of a new branch requiring 200 employees, there would probably be a strategy (to acquire and train 200 new employees) to be put into operation within the personnel policy framework and using agreed procedures.

See also PERSONNEL POLICY.

Picketing. Traditionally, picketing involves groups of workers gathering at the entrance to a workplace and attempting to persuade any BLACKLEGS or substitute workers to refrain from working in support of a dispute. Increasing features of modern industrial conflict have been mass picketing which effectively blockades the employer's premises, and 'secondary' picketing. Secondary picketing involves workers picketing places of work other than their own (for example, so-called 'flying pickets'), or picketing their own place of work in support of strikers elsewhere even though they themselves are not in dispute with their own employer.

'Lawful' picketing is very narrowly defined by S15 of the Trade Union and Labour Relations Act 1974, which provides that it shall be lawful for persons in contemplation or furtherance of a trade dispute (see GOLDEN FORMULA) to attend:

• at or near their *own* place of work;

- for the purpose *only* of peacefully obtaining or communicating information, or peacefully persuading any person to work or abstain from working.

The 'own place of work' rule has three qualifications:

- trade union officials accompanying a member they represent may attend at or near their member's place of work;
- those who work at more than one place (for example, lorry drivers) or where the location of their workplace makes picketing impracticable, may picket any of the premises where they work or from where their work is administered;
- those dismissed in connection with the dispute may picket their former place of work.

Pickets who act within the boundaries of S15 are granted IMMUNITY from civil liability for inducing breaches of contracts, whether contracts of employment or their employer's commercial contracts. Clearly secondary picketing at premises of other employers does not attract immunity; neither does the picketing of other plants in a multi-plant company. Secondary picketing at a picket's own place of work is only lawful if it satisfies the requirements for permitted SECONDARY ACTION in S17 of the Employment Act 1980.

S15 does not give pickets the right to stop vehicles, and neither does it protect them from civil liability for nuisance or trespass, for example. Furthermore the use of violence or threatening, abusive behaviour will constitute a criminal offence, as will obstruction of the highway, criminal damage, obstruction of police in the execution of their duty, conduct likely or intended to cause a breach of the peace, 'watching or besetting' a person's house or business to prevent that person doing something he or she has a right to do (under S7 of the Conspiracy and Protection of Property Act 1875) and behaviour related to the old offences of unlawful assembly and riot (now contained in the Public Order Act 1986). Clearly such behaviour will occur with greater frequency in mass picketing but, even where it does not, mass picketing is unlikely to be lawful, for what is intended is not 'peaceful persuasion' but intimidation.

Where picketing oversteps the boundaries of S15 civil action may be taken by those who suffer damage, whether it be the employer picketed or a supplier unable to deliver goods, in respect of civil wrongs committed. However, this will clearly be an effective remedy only if aimed at the union itself; individuals are unlikely to have the means to pay damages and can always be replaced by others if made the subject of an INJUNCTION. Recently injunctions have been granted limiting the number of pickets to six, the maximum number recommended by the 1980 Code of Practice on picketing, even though the Code itself does not have the force of law (see CODES OF PRACTICE).

Piece-work. Piece-work is a form of incentive payment seldom used in its pure form any longer, whereby the pay of the employee is so much per piece produced, without any minimum or maximum. This method (but never the name) still applies in most areas of self-employment, with authors being paid on royalty according to the number of copies sold, barristers receiving fees for cases conducted, and so forth. In the organizational context piece-work continues in an adulterated form as a form of INCENTIVE which is added to the basic rate and rarely exceeds 20 per cent of that basic.

Points rating. This is the most widely used form of JOB EVALUATION. The starting point is a list of job factors to make up the *factor plan*. These are features which all jobs are likely to have in common. To comply with the EQUAL VALUE provisions of the legislation on discrimination, these should not be biased in favour of jobs customarily held by members of one sex only. The next step is *weighting,* deciding the relative value of each factor, and then *degrees,* which act as a multiplier of the weights. These three steps produce a working table like that in table 3.

Such a table is then used to assign points to a JOB DESCRIPTION (not to a job holder), by selecting one of the points figures on the right-hand side for each of the nine factors, so that there is eventually a total points score for the job which can be related to a pay grade. Key features of method are as outlined below:

- factors need to be chosen carefully so that they are appropriate to the JOB FAMILY; those in table 3 are only examples. Factors

Table 3

Factor	Weight (%)	Degrees (points)				
1 Basic knowledge	5	5	10	15	20	25
2 Task Complexity	15	15	30	45	60	75
3 Training	15	15	30	45	60	75
4 Responsibility for people	15	15	30	45	60	
5 Responsibility for materials	15	15	30	45		
6 Mental effort	10	10	20	30	40	50
7 Visual attention	10	10	20	30		
8 Physical activity	10	10	20	30		
9 Working conditions	5	5	10	15	20	25

also need careful description so that those producing job descriptions direct the description to the factors and so that those assigning points can make a sound judgement;

• weights have to be agreed after calculation of their implications;

• degrees are the most effective discrimination – both fair and unfair – so that the number of degrees to be included for each factor has to be considered in the same way as the initial weighting. In the sample table above factors 3 and 5 have the same weight, but the decisions to have five degrees for one and only three for the other makes factor 3 much more significant. Most schemes try to define degree requirement precisely, so that a scheme based on the above table might specify particular stages of training that have to be achieved for each degree, or the number of people for whom a job holder has to be responsible to be assigned each of four degrees available for factor 4;

• assigning points is best done by a small group that includes people having practical experience of the jobs being evaluated and with the final evaluation being an average of their assigned points. Group discussion before scoring the factors produces reasonable closeness of final scores.

Equal Opportunities Commission, *Job Evaluation Schemes Free of Sex Bias* (Manchester: Equal Opportunities Commission, 1982); I. Smith, *The Management of Remuneration: Paying for Effectiveness* (London: Institute of Personnel Management, 1983).

Polytechnics. In 1986 there were 29 polytechnics in England and Wales, all of them designated following the publication in 1966 of a plan to extend the range of higher education by establishing major centres within the maintained sector. Large and strong colleges of further education were upgraded to the status of polytechnic so that there could be a system of higher education which did not depend entirely on universities. Polytechnics differ from universities in that they award degrees of the Council for National Academic Awards (CNAA) to ensure a more consistent standard than is perhaps achieved by universities. They also offer courses that are more vocational in orientation and there is less emphasis on research. Business studies is the largest area of polytechnic work and most of them have incorporated a major college of art and design.

Through an exercise known as Partnership in Validation, the CNAA is steadily handing over increased power to polytechnics to manage their own affairs and become less dependent on the CNAA itself.

Portable pensions. Arrangements for portable pensions were included in the 1986 Social Security Act, allowing employees to contract out of the STATE EARNINGS RELATED PENSION SCHEME, so that people retiring will still receive the basic state pension, but the earnings related element (if not provided by an occupational scheme) will come from a personal, portable pension.

Funding of the portable pension comes first from a rebate of the employer's and employee's National Insurance contributions, representing 5.5 per cent of the employee's earnings. Further regular funding can come from employer and/or employee contributions up to a ceiling of 17.5 per cent of earnings up to the age of 50 and 27.5 per cent for older people. These will attract tax relief at the highest rate. For the first five years there will be an additional 2 per cent National Insurance rebate. The contributions are paid to a building society, insurance company or unit trust who provide a personal pension policy to mature on the retirement of the contributor.

Positive discrimination. Prima facie positive discrimination is unlawful, so an employer sympathetic to the feminist cause or to the problems of ethnic minorities would contravene the SEX

DISCRIMINATION ACT 1975 or the RACE RELATIONS ACT 1976 by, for example, offering a post to a woman because of her sex, or promoting a coloured employee because of colour. In these cases the employer would be discriminating unlawfully against men and white employees respectively.

However, there is limited provision for positive discrimination where employees of a particular sex or racial group have been poorly represented in doing particular work in the preceding 12 months. An employer is then entitled to offer preferential training facilities to those people to enable them to do that work, or to encourage them to take advantage of opportunities to do the work (see S48 of the Sex Discrimination Act and S38 of the Race Relations Act). Thus an employer with no (or very few) female or coloured managers, for example, would be acting within the law in specifically wording a job advertisement so as to encourage women or ethnic minorities to apply for a vacant managerial post. However, all applicants would then have to be treated on an equal footing.

Power. Power is the means whereby managers get things done. Every manager needs to understand the methods of becoming more powerful, which means more influential, having more control and being more effective. The most obvious method is the organization chart, which is an official map of how power is distributed between members of the organization; other official methods include responsibility for making specific decisions and authorizing actions, titles, control of resources, and the power of veto. Individual managers can enhance their personal power in the organization by a range of strategies, including the following.

1 Forming *alliances* enables individuals to collaborate in seeking power by allying themselves to those of similar interests. The production manager might, for example, form an alliance with the personnel manager to block a move by the marketing manager to scale down production in favour of importing more ready-made components. The advantages of all alliances are that you gain the resources, skill and motivation of another person. The problem is that you have to make some reciprocal commitment and lose freedom of movement. If you discard an ally, you may make an enemy.

"We had one or two power cuts while you were away, Gerald. I'm afraid you were one of them."

2 *Doing favours* is a way of ensuring the support of someone you have helped, who appreciates the favour and hopes that more may be provided. That 'hope' binds the giver of the favour to the person on whom it is bestowed by setting up expectations that will need to be fulfilled if resentment (and perhaps sabotage) is to be avoided. One of the most common ways of doing favours is assisting with a promotion, but the favoured person will become a liability if subsequent performance does not justify the promotion.

3 *Being indispensable* is achieved either by being an essential part of the administrative, decision-making procedures (like the person who signs expense claims) or by being a lone expert. It is easier to be a lone expert in something that does not interest many other people (like safety) than in something that interests everyone and in which they all claim to be skilled (like staff selection).

4 *Having a patron* is very similar to MENTORING, except that it is informal and personal rather than explicit. Relatively junior personnel find it useful to 'catch the eye' of someone more

---

Sources of power

1 *Resources:* control what others need whether subordinates, peers or superiors. It includes the following:
- materials;
- information;
- rewards;
- finance;
- time;
- staff.

2 *Skill:* being an expert; having a skill others need or desire.

3 *Motivation:* some seek power more enthusiastically than others.

4 *Debts:* having others under obligation for past favours.

5 *Physical prowess:* being bigger or stronger than opponent; not overtly used in management except as control of resources. However, statistically leaders tend to be taller than the led.

6 *Persuasion skills:* bargaining and personal skills that enable one to make the most of one's other powers, such as resources.

7 *Control of agenda:* coalition and other techniques for managing how the issues are, or are not presented.

8 *Dependence:* where one side depends on the other for willing cooperation the power of removal exists. Strikes or threatening to resign *en bloc* are two examples.

9 *Charismatic:* very rare indeed. Much discussed in management circles as part of leadership qualities. Usually control of resources can account for claims of charismatic power, as many ex-managing directors have found.

---

powerful, who will take an interest in them, mention their work in high places and generally endorse what they are doing. Like all political strategies it is risky: patrons enhance one's power but expect loyalty and assistance.

Many people find this type of political behaviour distasteful and it can destroy effectiveness if taken to extremes. For an organization to operate there has to be a distribution of power among the members in order to get things done, yet that distribution is divisive and stressful. If the stress becomes too great, effectiveness declines. It is for this reason that many programmes of management development advocate behaviours that are 'open'. These mitigate the extremes of politicking.

N. Macchiavelli, *The Prince* (Harmondsworth: Penguin, 1986); H. Mintzberg, *Power in and Around Organisations* (Englewood Cliffs, New Jersey: Prentice-Hall, 1983).

Pregnancy. It is automatically unfair to dismiss an employee because she is pregnant or for a reason connected with her pregnancy (for example, post-natal illness) unless this means she cannot do her job properly or where some statutory restriction would be contravened. Even so, if there is a suitable available vacancy and the employer fails to offer it to her, her DISMISSAL will still be AUTOMATICALLY UNFAIR. It would now seem that a woman may also claim sex DISCRIMINATION. The tribunal should ask themselves whether a man needing time off for some medical condition would be similarly treated. (An earlier case had stated that there could be no claim of sex discrimination because one could not ask whether a man in similar circumstances would be so treated, there being no male equivalent of a pregnant woman!)

See also MATERNITY LEAVE.

Pre-hearing assessment. Where a party to an INDUSTRIAL TRIBUNAL claim feels that the case is so weak it should not be pursued, a pre-hearing assessment may be applied for. Additionally, some tribunal chairmen themselves take the initiative to call for a pre-hearing assessment. At the end of the hearing the party concerned can be warned that costs may be awarded against him or her if the case is subsequently lost at a full hearing. Such a warning clearly deters many applicants from pursuing their case, yet in 1983 13 per cent of 'warned' applicants succeeded at the hearing.

Premium payment. Premia are payments made in addition to the basic or standard rate to reward some additional feature of the work done by the individual (such as acting as supervisor) or to compensate for some inconvenience (such as working shifts or in unpleasant circumstances): for example, dirt money (for working in dirty conditions) or mask money (for doing a job in which wearing a mask is necessary). In the case of *Ministry of Defence* v. *Jeremiah* men were given an 'obnoxious payment' to compensate for the conditions in which they were working.

It is not paying for additional hours of work, for which OVERTIME would be paid.

Procedures. Procedures are the administrative mechanism to turn intention into outcome. They implement POLICY and channel

POWER by specifying the exact sequence of things that people have to do to achieve the required result, like a cookery recipe or a knitting pattern. The main benefits of procedures are:

- they *reduce the need for decisions in the future* by providing a solution to a problem which will work every time that problem occurs;
- they produce *consistency of action* (employee reactions to situations become less capricious since they are able to work together swiftly and harmoniously as long as methods remain unaltered);
- they provide *control for management* as managers know that the system will keep things working correctly so that they can turn their attention to the more uncertain and problematic;
- employees are *freed from supervision* because they know what they are doing, so the benefits of management control are accompanied by the advantages of individual autonomy.

A specialized form of procedure is that used in employee relations to control the behaviour of the two parties to COLLECTIVE BARGAINING, so that specific steps are agreed for handling such issues as GRIEVANCE, DISCIPLINE and REDUNDANCY. In cases of unfair dismissal one of the key determinants of an issue will be procedural fairness, the extent to which the procedure was scrupulously followed. An employer frequently loses a tribunal case because of not meeting all procedural requirements.

With all procedures there is a risk that they inhibit change and can become a straitjacket instead of a framework for action. When they are too rigid, people start to 'cut through the red tape' or 'short circuit the system' so that the benefits of procedure are lost.

N. Singleton, *Industrial Relations Procedures* (London: HMSO, 1975); D. P. Torrington, J. B. Weightman, K. Johns, *Management Methods* (Institute of Personnel Management/Gower, London, 1985), ch. 32.

Professional and Executive Recruitment (PER). This is a specialized arm of the Employment Division of the MANPOWER SERVICES COMMISSION. There is usually a charge to employers for the use of the service, but employees pay no charge. One of the main benefits of PER is that they have a computerized listing of vacancies in all parts of the country.

Profit sharing. One method of incentive payment is to share a part of the profits with the employees. The difficulty is that the connection between cause and effect is not easy for most employees to believe in, and there is considerable frustration for the employee, or group of employees, who work harder, enhance efficiency and reduce costs only to find that profits have been reduced through some factor completely beyond their control, like a change in legislation, a collapse of world prices or the incompetence of other members of the organization. This makes shared profits a pleasant windfall when profits are good, but schemes have little effect on employee attitude and endeavour.

Where profit-related pay (PRP) schemes are registered with the Inland Revenue a part of an employee's pay is linked automatically to the profits of the business and tax relief is available on that proportion, up to a point where PRP is the lower of either 20 per cent of the employee's total pay or £3,000. Half of that sum would be eligible for tax relief, so the person earning £15,000 in a year, of which 10 per cent (£1,500) was PRP, would have £750 on which tax was not payable.

Further particulars of PRP are available from the Profit-Related Pay Office, Inland Revenue, St Mungo's Road, Cumbernauld, Glasgow G67 1YZ.

Protective award. Where an employer fails to comply with the consultation provisions of S99 of the EMPLOYMENT PROTECTION ACT 1975 relating to proposed redundancies (see CONSULTATION), the union concerned (*not* individuals) may ask an INDUSTRIAL TRIBUNAL to make a protective award. This is an order that the employer shall continue to remunerate those employees who were dismissed without the necessary consultation. The remuneration is one week's pay for each week of a 'protected period', which is of such a length as the tribunal considers just and equitable. However, there are upper limits of 90, 38 and 28 days when the number of employees concerned is 100 or more, ten or more, and under ten, respectively. If the employer does not pay, *individual* employees concerned then have the right to ask the tribunal to order payment. Employees are not entitled to a protective award if:

- they unreasonably resign during the period;
- they unreasonably refuse suitable alternative employment;
- they are fairly dismissed for a reason other than redundancy.

In general it would seem that a compensatory approach (that is, compensating employees for the actual loss) is used when determining the protected period. This means, for example, that any contractual payments such as wages in lieu would be deducted from the award. However, a punitive element also appears to be present since the protected period so achieved is sometimes increased or decreased in the light of the seriousness of the employer's default.

Sample questions from a psychological test of numerical ability

1   A party consisted of a man and his wife, their two daughters with their husbands, and four children in each daughter's family. How many people were in the party?

    A. 8   B. 12   C. 14   D. 15   E. 21

2   A man invested £800 and doubled his money at the end of each year. How much did he have at the end of four years?

    A. £3,300   B. £4,000   C. £6,400   D. 12,800   E. None of these

3   Subtract the smaller of the times below from the larger and then select the correct answer from the lettered list.

        5 hours 13 minutes 40 seconds
        3 hours 14 minutes 50 seconds

    A.   1 hour 58 minutes 50 seconds
    B.   1 hour 59 minutes 50 seconds
    C.   2 hours 1 minute   10 seconds
    D.   2 hours 28 minutes 30 seconds
    E.   None of these

Answers 1 C.   2 D.   3 A.

Psychological tests. Psychological tests are used to determine differences between individuals, and their use in employment is based on their diagnostic or predictive value; either they can explain an aspect of a person's performance that was not previously understood, or they can predict how a person will perform in some future situation.

In using tests, managers need to guard against reading too much into the results. If, for instance, there is a best result on a prospective employee showing that person has a level of intelligence higher than 95 per cent of the general population, that is *all* that the result indicates and it should not be used to infer general excellence and effectiveness.

See also APTITUDE TESTS, INTELLIGENCE TESTS, PERSONALITY TESTING.

Q

Qualifying days. Most variants of payment and benefit require an employee to be in service for a minimum length of time before the benefit has been earned. For some of the benefits the minimum length of service is measured in qualifying days, so that payment for a statutory holiday may be withheld if the employee is not in attendance on the day before and the day after the holiday.

See also STATUTORY SICK PAY.

Quality circles. These are probably the best-known of the various techniques used by Japanese management which have been adopted by some British employers, although the essence of the approach has been used in many other ways before. A quality circle is a group of about eight people who meet regularly and voluntarily to discuss current problems in the workplace. By sharing ideas and concentrating responsibility with the people who actually have to do the job, there is a likelihood of generating practical proposals which will be put into operation, rather than 'impractical' management proposals which will be resisted.

Some people regard these circles as a development of employee participation in management, but others feel that the approach undermines collective bargaining and limits discussion to matters concerned with the immediate workplace, only dealing with matters of concern to management, and on the management's terms.

Quality of working life (QWL). QWL is used to cover a range of initiatives taken to improve the quality of life among people at work. The main emphasis is on JOB DESIGN, to improve the non-financial rewards provided by individual jobs, but the idea has also influenced areas of personnel work such as selection and training. Interest in reducing stress is another feature.

Questionnaires. Questionnaires are a means of collecting information that is precise and which can be accurately specified in advance. The best-known example is the opinion poll of voting intentions, where the question to be answered is specific and unambiguous in order that the results can be an accurate reflection of behaviour. Questionnaires are usually used to sample a population, so the replies of 1,000 people can be used to predict the voting intentions of millions.

In personnel-related work questionnaires are sometimes used to determine the reaction of the work-force to a proposed initiative, like the introduction of job evaluation, in which case they are similar to a BALLOT, with no more than one or two questions being asked. Less often they are used to survey attitudes, when a wider range of questions is put and there may be some difficulty about employees inferring too much into the questions and interpreting a question as a statement of management intention.

The response rate will determine the validity of the conclusions which can be drawn from the answers. Response rates of more than 50 per cent can usually be safely interpreted as representative of the whole population sampled, but there is still a need for careful assessment of the response. If, for instance, there is a minority union with one-quarter of the employees in membership, questionnaire results would be misleading if those union members had all withheld their response. Lower response rates can be equally valid, depending on the size of the population and the structure of the sample that has been used. The salient features of questionnaire design are explained below.

1 Type of questions. Precise questions elicit precise answers and therefore produce results that can be easily classified. *Forced choice* questions require the respondent to choose between a limited range of answers, and this can be used not only for the obvious factual information, like age range, but also to classify attitudes or opinions by forcing the respondent to choose from a limited range rather than producing an individual statement that the investigator then has to interpret. *Open-ended* questions enable the respondent to be much more informative, and can be a more accurate way of eliciting views, but the investigators then have to impose their own interpretation on a wide range of such answers in order to produce a meaningful pattern to the results.

2 Sequence of questions. The structure of the questionnaire needs to be logical for the respondent, with question 3 following logically from question 2 and logically preceding question 4, and so on. What is logical to the investigator is not always logical to the respondent.

3 Design of the questionnaire. The respondent is usually a volunteer and the responses have to be won: the respondent has to be motivated to answer accurately and thoughtfully. This is achieved by making the questionnaire worth answering because the questions are interesting and worth thinking about. It must also be easy for respondents to find their way through, with bits of information and explanation cropping up when they are needed and can be assimilated, rather than all being in an indigestible mass at the beginning. *Branching* is where the respondent is told something like this: 'If answer is YES, proceed to question 10; if answer is NO, proceed to question 20.' Instructions like this can be made easier with arrows or lines which 'lead' the respondent's eye to the correct destination.

4 What next? Questionnaire respondents need to know where to send their completed questionnaire and when it is needed. They are also more likely to provide thoughtful replies if the investigator explains how and when they will hear something of the outcome.

Questionnaires should always be *piloted* through a small sample to find out what is misunderstood and what is resented. Investigators have to work hard at getting returns, which often take a lot longer than was anticipated.

Questions procedure. Under the SEX DISCRIMINATION ACT 1975 the burden is on a complainant to prove unlawful discrimination. The questions procedure is designed to help individuals who feel they may have a claim to decide whether or not to commence proceedings and to clarify the facts in issue. A standard form exists (though its use is not obligatory) on which complainants may state the facts of their case and why they consider this treatment unlawful. The employer, or other respondent, may answer by disputing (or agreeing with) the facts, and by giving reasons for the treatment in question. Alternatively the employer may indicate why it was not unlawful.

The questions procedure is admissible before a tribunal. Failure by a respondent to reply within a reasonable time without a good reason, or providing ambiguous or evasive answers, may lead to an inference of unlawful discrimination.

R

Race Relations Act 1976 (RRA). The RRA amends the earlier Act of 1968 and replaces the Race Relations Board by the COMMISSION FOR RACIAL EQUALITY. It closely follows the patterns of the SEX DISCRIMINATION ACT 1975 but outlaws DISCRIMINATION on grounds of race, colour, nationality or ethnic or national origins as opposed to sex or marital discrimination. Religious discrimination as such is not covered, but the term 'ethnic origins' has been interpreted broadly to mean 'a segment of the population distinguished from others by a sufficient combination of shared customs, beliefs, traditions and characteristics derived from a common or presumed common past' (*Mandla* v. *Dowell Lee* [1983] IRLR 209, [1983] ICR 385). On this basis, Sikhs are included, and probably Jews. Segregation on racial grounds is deemed to be discriminatory.

Exceptions to the Act include civil service rules which restrict Crown employment on grounds of birth, nationality, descent or residence, acts done under statutory authority and, as in the case of the Sex Discrimination Act, acts done for the purpose of safeguarding national security.

Range of reasonable responses. Where an employee's conduct or work falls below the accepted standard there is frequently a range of responses which can be made by management, from WARNINGS to FINES, or ultimately dismissal. If dismissal is chosen and a claim of UNFAIR DISMISSAL is made, an INDUSTRIAL TRIBUNAL may be called upon to consider the appropriateness of the sanction. It is not their function to consider what *they* would have done in the circumstances; they must ask whether the *employer's* reaction was reasonable. If they feel that dismissal lies within the range of reasonable responses which could have been made, then on that score the dismissal will be fair. To put it another way, dismissal will only be unfair if the tribunal feels that no reasonable employer would have dismissed in those circumstances.

Rapport. Derived from the French *rapporter,* the term rapport is much used to describe the type of sympathetic relationship or responsive atmosphere which is set up by an interviewer in the first meeting with a respondent. It is regarded as an essential preliminary to enabling interviewees, who may be nervous or suspicious, to relax and be candid in what they want to say.

Standard techniques for establishing rapport are:

- small talk on topics of which the substance does not matter, like the weather, so that the two people can get used to each other without the actual words exchanged having any significance;
- a friendly, easy manner;
- calm attention to what the respondent is saying;
- brief explanation of procedure: what is to happen during the interview.

See also INTERVIEWING, RECRUITMENT.

Recruitment. This refers to the process of obtaining a field of candidates for a vacancy or for an intake. When there is a single vacancy the activity is focused on a job to be done, a gap to be filled. When recruitment is for an intake, then the emphasis is on a type of person to be recruited, like the recruitment of police cadets or student nurses.

"The man we need must have guts, daring and initiative, Mrs Hempson! Is your son that man?"

Methods of recruitment vary according to the vacancy or type of intake. They include:

- internal advertising, which is used more than any other method – even though it may constitute unlawful discrimination – because the majority of people appointed come as a result of personal recommendation by employees;
- local press advertising;
- advertising in professional or trade journals;
- PROFESSIONAL AND EXECUTIVE RECRUITMENT and/or JOB CENTRES;
- YOUTH TRAINING SCHEME, which is regarded by employers as being more significant for recruitment than for training;
- employment agencies;
- list of job seekers kept in the company;
- advertising in national newspapers;
- local authority careers service.

The tightening of LABOUR MARKETS has tended to shift the emphasis for some types of job away from the recruiter towards the job seeker, but there is much greater initiative by recruiters when filling management vacancies. For these recruiters need to think not only of the job that has to be done, but also of the work that is to be offered to the applicant. Increasing the amount of information provided to potential applicants reduces the number of inappropriate applications. The main piece of information is the salary to be offered, although over half of all recruitment advertisements still exclude it. Someone thinking of a job change will take the salary level as the main indicator of whether or not the job will be appropriate. First they will assess whether the change is financially worth while, especially if it involves moving house. Second, they will have a view of their own worth in the job market and will only apply for jobs which they see as being within their scope.

Many employers and recruitment advertising agencies like to make their advertisements fulsome ('Have you the qualities to reach the top?' or 'Self-starting and ambitious professionals needed now'). It is very doubtful that this type of approach achieves more than a warm glow for the employer, especially when the job is over-sold. Frothy advertisements emphasizing vague personal qualities may attract only frothy people with vague personal qualities. Those having substantial qualifications or experience will respond to the advertisement which calls for those qualities.

See also INTERVIEWING.

Recruitment advertising. In placing recruitment advertising most employers will use an advertising agency that will deal with most of the technical aspects, such as booking space, designing the advertisement, checking proofs and conducting all dealings with the journal or newspaper in which the advertisement is to appear. Well-known agencies can also provide the opportunity for the employer to advertise anonymously by using the agency's masthead to provide credibility and drawing power while concealing the identity of the employer.

The agency will advise on the choice of medium for the advertisement but detailed information about the readership of journals and newspapers is provided in *British Rate and Data*.

When drafting the advertisement the main elements to include are:

- name and brief details of the employing organization;
- job and duties of the successful applicant;
- key points of the personnel specification;
- salary;
- how the applicant should respond to the advertisement.

Red circling. In a JOB EVALUATION exercise one of the outcomes is that some jobs are paid too much. The systematic approach of the study suggests a series of grades for jobs and, while some of the grades will be above the prevailing rates of pay, there will be some that fall below the current rate. A common method of dealing with the anomaly is to 'red circle' the current rate by retaining it for the present incumbent but establishing that any successors, or others recruited to identical posts, will be paid at the new, lower grade. In some schemes the job holder keeps the higher grade and any cost of living adjustments that may be awarded in the future, while other schemes freeze the pay rate until cost of living adjustments 'correct' it to the figure produced by job evaluation.

See also GENUINE MATERIAL FACTOR.

Redundancy. An employee will be taken to be dismissed for redundancy if the dismissal is due wholly or mainly to:

• the fact that the employer has ceased, or intends to cease, to carry on business for the purpose of which the employee was employed, or in the place where he was employed (S81(2)(a) of the EMPLOYMENT PROTECTION (CONSOLIDATION) ACT 1978); or
• the requirements of the business for employees to carry out work of a particular kind have ceased or diminished or are expected to cease or diminish (S81(2)(b) of the Employment Protection (Consolidation) Act 1978).

In relation to the first limb of the definition, employees are employed at the place where, under their contracts, they are required to work. If, therefore, under their contracts they may be moved from a site which is closing down to one where work is available, they are not made redundant. A reasonable degree of mobility may also be required by virtue of IMPLIED TERMS. The requirement under S81(2)(b) 'for employees to carry out work of a particular kind' means work which employees can be required to do under their contracts, and not the work they happened to be doing at the time. If there is no reduction in work or the number of employees needed to do it, but the employer reorganizes the business in the interests of efficiency so that, for example, certain shifts are abolished, a redundancy is not created. (See also CONTRACT VARIATION.)

An employee with two years' continuous service who is dismissed for redundancy is entitled to a statutory redundancy payment, though contractual provisions may be more generous. The payment is calculated in a similar way to the basic award of COMPENSATION in unfair dismissal cases, except that years under the age of 18 do not count, and a woman's entitlement ceases on her reaching 60.

The right to a redundancy payment may be lost where:

• the employee is employed on a FIXED TERM CONTRACT for two years or more and agrees in writing to waive his or her right if the contract is not renewed;
• before the ending of the old contract, the employer offers the employee suitable alternative employment and the latter

unreasonably refuses it. If the terms and conditions of the new job differ from those of the old, there is a right to a trial period of four weeks. The employee's CONTINUITY OF EMPLOYMENT is preserved if the new job is accepted;
- the business is sold as a going concern and the new employer takes on the employee, or the employee is transferred by virtue of the TRANSFER OF UNDERTAKINGS (PROTECTION OF EMPLOYMENT) REGULATIONS 1981 (continuity is preserved as in the previous point);
- the employer was entitled to dismiss the employee for gross misconduct.

As a result of the WAGES ACT 1986, an employer has no right to a rebate of the statutory payment unless he or she employs nine or fewer employees.

Dismissal for redundancy is a potentially FAIR REASON FOR DISMISSAL but in the particular circumstances it may be:

- automatically unfair (see AUTOMATICALLY UNFAIR DISMISSAL);
- unfair because the employer did not act reasonably (see UNFAIR DISMISSAL). In general it may be said that a reasonable employer will use a fair, and preferably objective, method of selection, will give employees WARNINGS of impending redundancy, consult with them (see CONSULTATION) to ascertain their views, and consider alternatives before dismissing. However, even where an employer has not followed a fair procedure, the tribunal may conclude that the dismissal is fair because the outcome would inevitably have been the same.

If there is a trade union, then the employer has a duty to consult with union representatives before effecting redundancies (see CONSULTATION, PROTECTIVE AWARD).

See also LAY-OFF, SHORT TIME WORKING.

Re-engagement. If an unfairly dismissed employee does not want REINSTATEMENT, or the INDUSTRIAL TRIBUNAL decides not to order it, re-engagement must be considered. It is an order that the employee be taken back by the employer (or a successor or ASSOCIATED EMPLOYER) in 'employment comparable to that from which he was dismissed or other suitable employment'. The terms of the employment should be, so far as is reasonably practicable, as favourable as if the employee had been reinstated. In deciding whether to order re-engagement the tribunal will take into account the same factors as when considering reinstatement. If neither reinstatement nor re-engagement is ordered COMPENSATION must be awarded.

References. Character references are unreliable as indicators of potential in a new post because the style of reference writers varies greatly, the writers may not be disinterested, and reference readers place more emphasis on reservation than on recommendation as well as assuming there is a meaning hidden behind what the reference actually says.

Extracts from written references

'Mrs A. sets herself very high standards and, in her own judgement, is successful in maintaining them.'

'Mr B. is now coping much better with his problems.'

'There are many things about Miss C. that I do not wish to put in writing, but this is not meant to reflect any discredit on her either as a person or as an employee. I trust that you will take this comment in the spirit in which it is made.'

'Mr D. has very neat handwriting and is always punctual in attending for duty.' [This was the complete reference written on behalf of Mr D.'s application for a senior management position.]

'Mrs E. has not made the progress with us that we had expected, and I am sure that this is as much of a disappointment to her as it is to us. However, I am delighted to recommend her to you without reservation.'

'. . . ready in many ways for advancement . . .'

'When I say that Mr G. would not be able (in my view) to undertake the demanding duties of the post for which he has applied, you may decide that I am doing this merely because I do not want to lose him. I do not think, indeed, that I would like to lose him at the moment, as I might not get a replacement, but it would be quite wrong of me to stand in his way at a time when promotion prospects are so limited, so I leave it to you to make the judgement. If you think he could do the job, so be it, but we must all decide for ourselves where our priorities lie.'

'Having applied for the post myself, and having not received a reply, I find it difficult to write on behalf of Miss H.'

When writing references bear in mind that they should be generally warm and positive. This is such a common practice that a reference written differently would arouse suspicion ('What is the writer trying to hide?'). The most useful feature of references is the inclusion of specific and concrete points about the experience of the candidate in relation to aspects of the post applied for. Reference readers will look for the recommendation in the last sentence: it may even be the only part that is read. The choice lies between:

- unequivocal recommendation ('I recommend without reservation');
- slight reservation ('I recommend for your careful consideration' or 'ready in many ways for advancement');
- definite reservation ('I have some doubts about X's readiness at this stage to take on').

The use of the telephone in taking up references leads to greater candour and more explicit statements, although these may be mistrusted by the candidates ('they have us by the testimonials').

An employer is under no legal obligation to provide a reference for a former employee. If, however, a reference is provided and it is incorrect, then the employer may incur legal liability. Where the reference is defamatory (a false statement which injures a person's reputation) there can be a defence of qualified privilege, unless the employer was motivated by malice. If a false statement is made deliberately with the intention of it being acted upon, then the tort of deceit is committed. In this case the new employer (or any other person) who suffers loss as a result of relying on the statement would be entitled to sue for damages. Furthermore it is highly likely that liability would be incurred even if the false statement were merely made carelessly, though in this case the appropriate claim would be of negligence.

See also REHABILITATION OF OFFENDERS ACT 1974.

Rehabilitation of Offenders Act 1974. This Act provides that a person convicted of a criminal offence is entitled to have the conviction treated as 'spent' after the appropriate rehabilitation period has elapsed. The length of the rehabilitation period is determined by the seriousness of the offence, such seriousness to be reflected in terms of the sentence imposed (see table 4).

Table 4

Sentence	Rehabilitation period
More than 30 months' imprisonment	Cannot become spent
6–30 months' imprisonment	10 years
Not exceeding 6 months' imprisonment	7 years
Fine or other sentence (such as community service order)	5 years
Absolute discharge	6 months
Binding over, conditional discharge, probation	Until end of condition or probation, or for one year (whichever longer)

Under the Act an individual is not obliged to disclose spent convictions, and neither should he or she be asked about them (for example, in an interview or on an application form). It would also be unlawful to exclude that person from a job, or dismiss him or her, because of a spent conviction. However, no remedies are created by the Act and there are no penalties for acting unlawfully. A potential employer cannot therefore be compelled to engage a rehabilitated person complaining of unlawful treatment, and neither would the employer be liable to the latter in damages. However, to dismiss a person on the basis of a spent conviction, or a failure to disclose it, has been held automatically unfair under the provisions of the Employment Protection (Consolidation) Act 1978. An employer who is asked for REFERENCES is under an obligation not to refer in it to any spent conviction, and cannot be liable for that non-disclosure to anyone relying on the reference.

Certain occupations may be exempted from the provisions of the Act by the Secretary of State. Persons currently affected include lawyers, accountants, medical practitioners, dentists, nurses, the police and social service workers.

Reinstatement. Re-employment of an employee found to be unfairly dismissed is rare, though it was intended to be the primary remedy; in 1983 reinstatement and RE-ENGAGEMENT constituted only 3 per cent of tribunal awards (see Lewis, 1986). Reinstatement means restoring employees to their old jobs and in effect treating them as if they had never been dismissed. Thus they must be awarded back pay and benefits such as pay increases or promotion, which they would have received had they not been dismissed.

In deciding whether to award reinstatement the tribunal must take into account:

- the wishes of the employee;
- whether it is practicable (for example, because of opposition from the work-force, or inability to do the job) for the employer to comply with such an order;
- whether the employee caused or contributed to his or her own dismissal and if so whether it would be just to make an order.

An employer who fails to comply with an order for reinstatement may be liable to pay an additional award (see COMPENSATION) unless able to show that it was not practicable to comply with the order.

R. Lewis, *Labour Law in Britain* (Oxford: Basil Blackwell, 1986), p. 559.

Relativities. Relativities in payment are the relationships between different employee groupings, unlike relationships within employee groupings which are called DIFFERENTIALS. *Internal relativities* are relationships between groupings within an organization where the unions and the negotiating machinery are different. Even though the employer is the same for both groups, there is a limit to the coordination of pay arrangements between the groupings. *External relativities* are where the comparison is made with a group that is not only represented by a different union through different negotiating arrangements, but also has a different employer, so there is no coordination at all.

For example, the difference between pay for a teacher on Scale 1 and one on Scale 3 is a differential. The difference between teachers in the school and laboratory technicians in the same school is an internal relativity, but the difference between teachers and barristers is an external relativity.

Relocation. When employees are moved from one part of the country to another, most employers will make some contribution to the financial costs of the move. Arrangements range from flat-rate payments to more elaborate schemes involving payments of removal expenses, solicitors' fees and other payments relating to the employee's house. Less common are schemes to meet the cost of needing to buy a more expensive house by covering the cost of a higher mortgage for a specified number of years, or providing bridging finance to cover the time taken for a house to be sold after the new one has been bought. Some arrangements now operate by actually buying the employee's old house, leaving the employee a free range of choice in the new location.

Some employers offer relocation expenses to new employees joining the organization as well as to existing staff.

Remuneration package. The idea of the remuneration package is, first, to vary and extend the range of benefits the employee receives from employment and, second, to provide some choice between the various components. There is also a small shift away from concentrating on the salary level towards a focus on the cost of employment. The additional benefits (see FRINGE BENEFITS) are less expensive for the employer than they would be for an individual employee and have tax advantages for both. For the employee there is the further advantage that there can be scope for selection between different ways of making up the package within a total cost envelope, so that one person may opt for a more expensive car while another forgoes a car in favour of enhanced pension provision.

Repertory grids. The use of repertory grids is a fairly elaborate method of personality assessment and deciding the important criteria of individual jobs. It was originally developed by G. A. Kelly in the US during the 1950s. Although not widely used, its application is growing in the area of deciding the criteria of individual jobs, so that matching of applicants and jobs in selection is made more accurate.

The technique first requires an interviewee to list ten people. They are usually listed by name, but they could be by role (supervisor, middle manager, researcher, and so on) or by type (such as better with paper than people, and so on). These ten elements make up the horizontal axis of a grid. The next step is for the interviewee to compare three of these people, saying how any two are similar to each other but different from the third. This then provides a range or construct, showing how the interviewee construes his or her environment. If, for example, the intervieweee says that A and B are similar in being enthusiastic about their work, in contrast to C, who is unenthusiastic, then the 'construct' is enthusiastic–unenthusiastic, with a total of ten ticks or crosses being entered on that dimension of the grid. The process is then repeated for three more names to produce more constructs and more assessments. The ultimate array of ticks or crosses produces a 'perceptual map' of the job or of the organization. When this is repeated for a number of different interviewees a coordinated picture emerges of how a range of people see the organization.

This is clearly a difficult and time-consuming technique, which requires the services of a trained psychologist to administer it, but it can greatly improve the quality of job assignments where there is the patience to apply it.

V. and A. Stewart, *Business Application of Repertory Grids* (New York: McGraw-Hill, 1978).

Restraint clause. It is not uncommon for employers to protect themselves against disclosure of trade secrets or misuse of CONFIDENTIAL INFORMATION by an express clause in an employee's contract. They may similarly attempt to prevent damaging competition by an ex-employee or, where they have purchased a business, by the previous owner. Contracts which are in restraint of trade are valid only if reasonable and in the public interest; employers cannot protect themselves against competition by an ex-employee as such, but they may be able to restrain that person from using customer connections acquired during employment. On this basis a milkroundsman and a solicitor's managing clerk have been validly restrained.

The clause must not be excessive as regards area, time of operation or the trades it forbids, but this will depend on the circumstances of individual cases. A worldwide restraint may be valid if in fact the employer operates in world markets; in the case of, say, a hairdresser, a restraint of more than a few miles might be unreasonable.

The courts will not rewrite unreasonable restraint clauses so that, for example, a 25 mile restraint will not be cut down to a more reasonable area; it will simply be declared void. However, if a restraint consists of a number of independent clauses, it may be possible to sever the void restrictions from the valid ones, and allow the latter to stand. Thus on the sale of an imitation jewellery business the vendor covenanted not to deal in real or imitation jewellery in the UK or various other parts of the world, for two years. The restraint on selling imitation jewellery in the UK was held valid since most customers were obtained through adverts in national newspapers. The restraint outside the UK and the restriction on selling real jewellery were unreasonable and therefore void. The courts will not sever a restraint clause if they feel it alters the whole nature of the covenant.

A valid restraint clause is generally enforced by means of an INJUNCTION to prevent its breach, rather than by damages as compensation for the breach.

Restrictive practices. Restrictive practices are ways of working which unduly hinder the efficient use of labour by management. They are imposed by employees in order to increase their bargaining power and the degree of control they have over their own jobs. The main examples are:

- demarcation which requires that certain tasks should only be carried out by specified categories of employee;
- overmanning which specifies a level of manning for an operation, machine or workplace that is greater than necessary;
- using mates, where a skilled craftsman will not work without the support of a craftsman's mate.

Sometimes these are called 'protective practices' as all originally had a logical basis apart from job protection and strengthening bargaining. Demarcation can ensure that work is done only by those competent to do it and a craftsman working with a mate can usually work more efficiently than if working alone.

Retirement. The age at which people retire is steadily becoming lower. Although the age at which one can retire and qualify for state retirement pension remains 60 for women and 65 for men, this is largely to contain the cost of the state pension as the size of the retired population rises. The age at which people actually stop employment is getting lower, especially for men. The Department of Employment now classifies all unemployed men over the age of 55 as retired, many large organizations have official retirement ages of 62 or 60 and the *de facto* age of retirement is in the late 50s for some companies.

The main involvement of employers in the retirement of employees is their contribution to the PENSION SCHEME, but the change from full-time working to full-time unemployment is a change of such magnitude that some preparation is needed. This can partly be achieved by pre-retirement courses, dealing with financial matters, health, leisure pursuits and personal organization, but can be aided by tapering the final period of employment, with the involvement reducing steadily over many months. This not only helps the person retiring but it is also of benefit to the organization in inducting new employees and having advice available from people with great experience, but no longer competing with their colleagues.

Role play. One training method to heighten awareness of issues and to enhance interpersonal communication is role playing, whereby members of a group each take on the character in a case study and make their contribution to the discussion from that standpoint. Sometimes the role players act out a situation, like a management–union negotiation, using closed circuit television as a means of group members learning from the interplay of their own performance with others.

S

Safety. The employer is under a legal obligation not to expose employees to unnecessary risk of injury, which involves selecting staff who are competent for the jobs they have to do and who will not endanger their colleagues, planning systems of work that are safe, and providing safe equipment and premises. (see COMMON LAW DUTY OF CARE).

Although safety is the proper responsibility of all employees, especially all managers, there are some general initiatives which can be taken to make the workplace safer, such as having a safety policy and a safety officer to act as an internal inspector of working practices.

Some occupations, like coal mining, deep sea fishing and nuclear processing, are inherently more hazardous than others and have their own conventions and regulations to limit occupational hazards.

See also HEALTH AND SAFETY AT WORK ACT 1974, SAFETY COMMITTEES AND SAFETY REPRESENTATIVES, SAFETY TRAINING.

Safety committees and safety representatives. Safety committees are a means of ensuring constant vigilance on all safety matters, spreading the responsibility beyond the safety officer. THE HEALTH AND SAFETY AT WORK ACT 1974 specifies that an employer must establish a safety committee if requested to by the safety representatives. Safety representatives can be appointed by an independent recognized trade union from among the existing employees and are empowered to investigate dangerous occurrences and accidents, deal with employees' complaints on safety, and carry out routine inspections. The employer has a legal obligation to consult with safety representatives, provide them with information and allow them time off with pay to carry out their function.

The functions of safety representatives are also the functions of the safety committee as a whole, together with the need to keep and analyse safety records, organize safety training and stimulate safety awareness.

Health and Safety Commission, *Safety Representatives and Safety Committees* (London: HMSO, 1977); Health and Safety Commission, *Time off for the Training of Safety Representatives* (London, undated).

Safety training. This needs to be carried out in three settings: first, at induction so that new employees know the rules and the hazards; second, training on the job is needed to ensure safe working practices as new operations and routines are introduced; third, refresher training overcomes the risk of forgetting and complacency.

Of the various training methods, role playing is one of the most effective in developing changes in behaviour because of the participation in the learning process that is inevitably involved. Strict self-discipline by managers in *always* obeying the rules is an important example, not only in obeying specific rules, but also in demonstrating that all safety rules are always to be obeyed. Poster campaigns have relatively little effect.

Salary and wages. There is no legal distinction between wages and salary, but there are a number of customary differences, such as wages being paid weekly in cash while salaries are paid monthly by cheque or credit transfer. Wages are frequently described in terms of an hourly rate while salaries are invariably described as annual figures. Salary earners also enjoy a much wider range of FRINGE BENEFITS and PERQUISITES.

The significance of these conventions is what they say about the employment relationship and the attitudes of the parties to the employment contract. The nature of wage payment reinforces the idea that the employee is being employed on a short-term basis and that the value of that employee's contribution is closely connected to the number of hours worked. Salary payment reinforces the idea of the employee being a part of the business whose contribution cannot be assessed in the short-term, or in relation to the length of time spent working.

The number of wage earners is declining and the number of salary earners is increasing. This is partly because salary payment is administratively simpler, but it is also in the cause of HARMONIZATION. Entrenched attitudes change, however, very slowly. Salary earners generally have a lower level of sickness absence than wage earners, largely because of the attitudes towards the employment relationship that the two modes of payment engender. When wage earners become salaried it is a long time before the sickness absence level comes down: often it rises in the early stages of the new arrangement.

Salary surveys. An employer wishing to establish the appropriate rate of salary for a new post will want to consider, among other things, comparable salaries for the same position. One means of doing this is to consult a salary survey. The most detailed and comprehensive of these are produced by consultancy firms who restrict publication of the data to their subscribers, who also provide the data for the survey itself. Other comprehensive surveys are carried out by the Department of Employment, with the results appearing in monthly issues of the EMPLOYMENT GAZETTE and the occasional issues of *New Earnings Survey*. Most professional bodies carry out surveys of earnings among their members, as do some trade unions, like TASS.

General guidance on salary levels can be obtained from the *studies* published monthly by Incomes Data Services Ltd, 140 Great Portland Street, London W1N 5TA (01 580 1521) who regularly analyse the salary data relating to a particular group (for example, keyboard personnel, engineers and scientists, clerical staff and supervisors). Each fortnight they also produce a *brief* summarizing the features of recent pay settlements and other items of news relating to salaries.

Secondary action. Primary action is INDUSTRIAL ACTION which is aimed at the employer involved in the dispute:

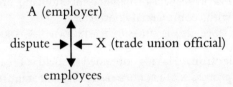

Primary action

A (employer)

dispute → | ← X (trade union official)

employees

X induces the employees to break their contracts of employment with A.

Secondary action, however, is action aimed at an employer who is not a party to the dispute, which occurs, for example, in sympathy strikes and blacking. The result of S17 of the Employment Act 1980 is effectively to limit lawful secondary action to that taken against a first customer or first supplier of the employer in dispute:

Lawful secondary action

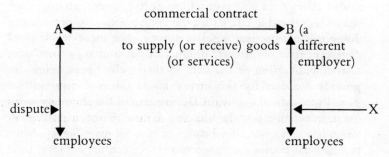

commercial contract

A ◄──────────────────────► B (a

to supply (or receive) goods   different
(or services)   employer)

dispute ►   ◄── X

employees   employees

X induces B's employees to break their contracts of employment, thus inducing a breach of (or interfering with) the commercial contract between A and B.

However, such secondary action will only be lawful if its purpose is directly to prevent the supply of goods (or services), and is likely to achieve that result. If because of the dispute the supply of goods (or services) is switched to an associated employer of A, then secondary action aimed at the associated employer will also be lawful. Permitted secondary action goes no further; thus were X to persuade employees of C (a haulage firm employed by B to deliver goods to A) to break their contracts of employment and induce a breach of the contract between B and C, this would be unlawful.

Where unlawful secondary action is taken, IMMUNITY will be lost in respect of liability for inducing breach of, or interfering with, commercial contracts.

See also ECONOMIC TORTS, GOLDEN FORMULA.

Selection. Having obtained a field of candidates through the processes of RECRUITMENT, the next stage in filling a vacancy is to select the most appropriate of those candidates to be offered the post. The main methods available are assessing the information presented in candidates' APPLICATION FORMS or on the CURRICULUM VITAE, APTITUDE TESTING, GROUP SELECTION METHODS, PSYCHOLOGICAL TESTING, REFERENCES and INTERVIEWING.

The application form and the selection interview are the most popular methods, although not necessarily the most reliable.

In selection candidates are also, of course, making selections as they are deciding whether or not the job on offer provides the opportunities they are seeking. Mainly their selecting takes place earlier, while the employer is recruiting, on the basis of the information provided and the 'image' of the employer created by, for instance, the speed and nature of replies to queries. Selection by candidates of vacancies to pursue or drop is a key determinant of employer selection between candidates as the employer can only select between those who first select him or her. Provision of explicit and appropriate information during recruitment ensures the minimum number of inappropriate candidates.

Selection consultant. Using a consultant to assist in employee selection introduces specialized expertise and an up-to-date knowledge of the labour market, as well as saving a great deal of time and trouble for the employer. There is the further benefit of anonymity in the early stages of recruitment, if this benefit is required.

Where consultants use PSYCHOLOGICAL TESTING they are able to accumulate a bank of test result data that is beyond the scope of any single employer as a basis for establishing vocational norms. Most firms of consultants have some element of specialization in the type of appointments for which they offer their services. This provides up-to-date labour market knowledge as well as extending their expertise in selection. Some, for instance, specialize in vacancies for accountants, others in vacancies for engineers. Another type of specialized expertise is in recruiting to or from an overseas location: few employers would know how to start recruiting someone to work in South-east Asia, for example.

Consultants usually charge a fee of 15–20 per cent of the first year's salary of the appointed person.

See also EXECUTIVE SEARCH.

Selection interview. See INTERVIEWING, INTERVIEW TYPES.

Self-development. Self-development, especially for managers, is an extension of the idea that learning is most effective when the learner is in control of his or her own learning. The employing organization provides resources and suggestions, but the employee decides what to do, how and when to do it, and is the only person to blame if it does not work. It has been much encouraged by the development of COMPUTER BASED TRAINING and distance learning using television and correspondence. There has been a change in the way text books are written, to make them more 'user-friendly', with the assumption that the student will be working alone, rather than the text book being used mainly as an adjunct to a taught course. The tutor's role changes its emphasis with a move towards facilitation, advice and assessment of assignments rather than teaching and directing the student's work. This has the advantage for the learner that it is possible to proceed at the speed which is convenient and to direct the development to the needs of the individual career as well as to the requirements of the employer.

See also LEARNING, MANAGEMENT DEVELOPMENT, ORGANIZATION DEVELOPMENT.

Sensitivity training. This phrase describes a technique for exploring interpersonal behaviour and group dynamics. It is based on the fact that some people lose effectiveness in relationships at work because they do not appreciate the effect of their behaviour on others and lack the ability to respond constructively to the behaviour of others. This form of training heightens the awareness of individuals regarding their impact on others and develops their responses to others.

The best-known method is the T group (T standing for training). A group of 8–12 people are put together in a room without any agenda, structure or leadership and invited to discuss what is happening. The lack of structure deprives group members of the comfortable social conventions which tend to disguise true feelings and they have to work together to find some *modus operandi* for the group. There are bids for leadership and challenges to those bids as group members wrestle with the process of coping with each other. Gradually the veneer of politeness which normally disguises feelings and attitudes towards others is stripped away and individuals become candid with each other and reveal their individual feelings, needs and insecurities. This remorseless process continues in a number of sessions, at the end of which participants have learned more about themselves and have found out new ways of responding to others.

Sensitivity training is a ruthless process which many people find deeply disturbing. Some participants enhance their interpersonal effectiveness by developing new sensitivities and skills to replace previous self-assumptions; others lose the cloak of the self-estimate they had developed over a lifetime and never succeed in replacing it with another framework of self-confidence and engagement with others.

Seven-point plan. Although nearly 40 years old, the seven-point plan is the method of HUMAN ATTRIBUTE CLASSIFICATION used more extensively than any other. Devised by Alec Rodger, the seven points are:

- physical make-up;
- attainments;
- general intelligence;
- special aptitudes;
- interests;
- disposition;
- circumstances.

Candidates for assessment can be considered against each of these points, which may be made more specific by deciding beforehand on essential attributes, desirable attributes and contra-indications.

Sex Discrimination Act 1975 (SDA). The SDA established the EQUAL OPPORTUNITIES COMMISSION, and made it unlawful to discriminate on grounds of sex in the fields of employment, education and the provision of goods, services, facilities and premises. It also proscribed victimization of a person who has, for example, made a claim under the Act or under the EQUAL PAY ACT 1970, or given evidence in connection with such proceedings.

In the employment field discrimination in hiring and firing, or in granting promotion or other benefits, is outlawed, as are discriminatory advertisements. The Act in this area provides protection against discrimination on grounds of marriage as well as on grounds of sex. Liability rests mainly on employers (who may be 'vicariously' liable for unlawful acts of their employees), but the Act also applies to partnerships of six or more partners, trade unions, employment agencies, vocational training bodies, the Manpower Services Commission and bodies which are empowered to confer an authorization or qualification needed in a particular trade or profession. There are certain exclusions from the Act, notably acts done to safeguard national security, certain provisions in relation to death and retirement (but see SEX DISCRIMINATION ACT 1986), special treatment afforded to women in connection with pregnancy or childbirth and discrimination which is necessary to comply with earlier legislation (for instance, the Ionising Radiations Regulations 1985).

Individual complainants must make a claim to a tribunal within three months of the act complained of, and the burden of proving unlawful discrimination lies on them. Claims by employed persons are not restricted to those of EMPLOYEE status, but extend to individuals working under a CONTRACT FOR SERVICES, provided there is an obligation personally to carry out the work. The tribunal has no power to order REINSTATEMENT or RE-ENGAGEMENT, but it can award COMPENSATION up to a maximum of £8,500 (from 1 April 1987), make an order declaring the parties' rights, or make a recommendation of action to remove the effects of the discrimination. Compensation awards are based on the complainant's economic loss, though 'injury to feelings' may also be compensated. In general, awards of compensation are very low and no compensation is payable in respect of 'indirect' discrimination (see DISCRIMINATION) if the employer proves the discrimination was unintentional.

Sex Discrimination Act 1986. The Sex Discrimination Act 1986 amends the 1975 SDA with the result that for example:

- small businesses are no longer exempted from the provisions of the 1975 Act (see SMALL EMPLOYERS);
- the blanket exclusion from the 1975 Act of employment in a private household is replaced by a new GENUINE OCCUPATIONAL QUALIFICATION which permits discrimination on grounds of sex but not marriage in recruitment only where, for example, the job involves nursing duties or physical or social contact with a member of the household;

- the restrictions on women's hours of work (for instance, under the Factories Act 1961) are repealed;
- it is unlawful to require women to retire at an earlier age than men; additionally women, like men, are able to claim unfair dismissal up to the age of 65 (though their entitlement to a redundancy payment ceases at the age of 60) if there is no NORMAL RETIRING AGE or if the normal retiring age is different for women and men (pensionable age is unaffected);
- any term of a collective agreement which is discriminatory is now void.

The provisions of the new Act became operative on a variety of dates up to February 1988.

Sexual harassment. Sexual harassment comprises various kinds of behaviour or words which are easier to recognize than to describe, but clearly includes unwanted physical contact, gestures of a sexual nature and sexist derogatory remarks. Interest currently focuses on the extent to which a woman (or man!) is able to base a claim under the SEX DISCRIMINATION ACT 1975 on such treatment. It now appears to be accepted that sexual harassment does constitute DISCRIMINATION on grounds of sex if the treatment a woman receives is sexually oriented and would not have been meted out to a man. However, it must also be shown that the discrimination took one of the unlawful forms specified in S6(2)(b); namely, that the woman was dismissed or subjected to 'any other detriment'. Thus both the employee who was dismissed for pouring beer over the firm's accountant after he persistently harassed her at a party and the female technician whose male colleagues brushed up against her and made suggestive remarks as part of a campaign to persuade her to leave (which she did) were successful in their claims. As yet it seems that tangible employment repercussions must be proved in order to demonstrate a 'detriment', whereas in America a claim may be brought where the sexual harassment has created a 'hostile working environment'.

In practice, where dismissal is consequent upon harassment, a claim of UNFAIR DISMISSAL would be made where possible since this, unlike a claim under the Sex Discrimination Act, would put the onus on the employer to justify the dismissal. In theory,

"Let's come to an understanding, Miss Garrett. If I sexually harass you, you have the right to sexually harass me right back."

sexual harassment may enable a woman to resign and claim CONSTRUCTIVE DISMISSAL, but this may appear a drastic solution where the chances of REINSTATEMENT being awarded are slight.

See also CONSTRUCTIVE DISMISSAL.

Share ownership. Share ownership by employees in their own companies has been encouraged by the very large privatization flotations of the 1980s and the Finance Acts of 1978 and 1980. The 1978 Act established the Approved Deferred Share Trust (ADST) whereby the company allocates a proportion of the profits to a trust fund which purchases company shares on behalf of employees. The employee shareholder only pays tax when the shares are sold, and this is usually not allowed until they have been held for at least two years. The employee pays tax on disposal, but during the fourth year of ownership it is reduced to three-quarters of what it would have been a year earlier and there is no tax obligation at all if the shares are not sold until after five years of ownership.

The 1980 Act enabled Save As You Earn Schemes to be set up so that employees could purchase shares through monthly deductions from salary.

Shiftworking. A significant minority of the working population are employed on some sort of shiftworking so that their hours of work vary from week to week or from day to day. This is partly due to the nature of the *process,* so that nurses and police officers have to be on duty through the day and night. It can also be due to the nature of the *product or service,* so that bar staff normally work in the evening as well as at weekends and airline personnel run a round-the-clock operation. The third main reason relates to *productivity.* When an item is in strong demand extra shifts may be worked to meet orders and when capital investment is expensive, working shifts is a way of obtaining maximum output from new equipment. The five most usual shiftworking variants are described below.

1 Three shifts. This is where the operation is maintained through 24 hours with shift teams working in spells of 8 hours. The most common arrangement is 6 a.m.–2 p.m., 2 p.m.–10 p.m. and 10 p.m.–6 p.m. Operating for five days a week it is possible to have three shift teams. When operations move to seven days a week, it is usual to establish a fourth team, although some operations run with three teams by lengthening the night shift.
2 'Alternating days and nights' is a form of operating where continuous working is not needed, so that shift hours are, for example, 11 p.m.–7 a.m. and 7 a.m.–3 p.m. (or 4 p.m.) for five days a week.
3 'Double days' is a way of extending the normal working day and is the most common way of dealing with short-term increases in demand. Shift hours are likely to be 6 a.m.–2 p.m. and 2 p.m.–10 p.m., with shifts changing weekly.
4 'Permanent nights' is sometimes used as an adjunct to double days, so that the most unpopular working period is reserved for those who specialize in night working. It is also a way of dealing with maintenance and cleaning operations.
5 Evening shift. Enjoying all sorts of local names, like 'swing shift', 'back shift' and 'housewives' shift', working for four

hours in the evening is a form of employing part-timers – usually temporarily – to meet peaks in demand.

Although these are the main forms of shiftworking employed, many new patterns are being developed as part of making working patterns more flexible.

See also FLEXIBLE WORKING HOURS, SHIFTWORK PREMIA.

J. Atkinson, *Shiftworking* (Brighton, Institute of Manpower Studies, 1982); National Economic Development Council, *Changing Working Patterns: How Companies Achieve Flexibility to Meet New Needs* (National Economic Development Council, 1986).

Shiftwork premia. Shiftwork premia are the additional payments made to employees to compensate for the particular disturbance or inconvenience of having to work varying hours. The traditional method of paying the premium for the shift hours actually worked is gradually being replaced by negotiating a rate for the job which incorporates the premium on the assumption that shifts will be worked. Where premia are still paid the range is typically between 15 per cent, for double days, to 50 per cent, for permanent nights.

Shop steward. Shop stewards have become the bogeymen of our time. A cynical commentator estimated recently that the British population could be put in two groups, half believing that all shop stewards should be shot at sunrise and the other half believing that to be leaving it too late. Yet they are representatives of the trade union in the local place of work, elected by and from the union members in that workplace and remaining employees of the employer. They have the key duties of recruiting and maintaining union membership and communicating with union members. They will represent individual members on matters of grievance and similar queries and usually represent the membership collectively in all negotiations with the management relating to terms and conditions of employment, discipline, manning levels, productivity and innovation. Managements usually prefer dealing with shop stewards rather than with full-time union officials. The working relationship is one that managers need to handle with care. On the one hand they need to develop a constructive level of RAPPORT and trust between themselves and the stewards: on the other hand, they must remember that shop stewards are not managers of the work-force and have different dominant values and objectives from managers. A shop steward is not elected by the membership to agree with what the management wants to do, but to resist some initiatives and to promote what the management often does *not* want to do.

Legislation provides some protection for shop stewards (see AUTOMATICALLY UNFAIR DISMISSAL) that is not available for other employees and makes provision for TIME OFF to discharge both industrial relations and trade union duties.

E. Batstone, I. Boraston and S. Frenkel, *Shop Stewards in Action* (Oxford: Basil Blackwell, 1977).

Short-listing. The short-listing of candidates for selection is a neglected art. It is the process of sifting through a large number of applications and deciding which handful should be placed on a short-list from which the final selection will be made. Managers too readily leave this time-consuming task to consultants or to relatively inexperienced staff, with the senior decision-makers only considering the final listed candidates. Especially when the final decision is to be made by a panel or committee, they should all be involved in short-listing to avoid having to make a final decision between compromise, 'grey' candidates. Their participation in short-listing gives them practice in working together and ensures that full attention is given to the information in the application form rather than too much hanging on the candidates' interview performance. It also improves the prospects of being fair.

The essence of effective short-listing is to compare the APPLICATION FORMS or the CURRICULUM VITAE provided with the PERSONNEL SPECIFICATION and JOB DESCRIPTION that has been prepared. The approach to this should be to see who can be *included* rather than who can be *excluded*. This means that selectors are looking for candidates' strengths as well as simple congruence with the specification. It also inhibits the natural tendency of most selectors to concentrate on why candidates will *not* suit the vacancy instead of concentrating on their positive features. If this process produces a short-list that is too long, then criteria are added to the specification, whilst ensuring that these criteria are relevant to the vacancy and not whimsical.

Short time working. When business is poor some employers retain their employees but reduce the hours of work for a limited period in order to keep the work-force intact in anticipation of a future improvement in demand. If the contract of employment does not make explicit provision for the employer to introduce short time working, then the employee may be entitled to regard it as repudiation of the contract and claim CONSTRUCTIVE DISMISSAL.

By virtue of S87 of the Employment Protection (Consolidation) Act 1978, an employee who is laid off or put on short time working so that he or she receives less than half a week's pay for at least four consecutive weeks, or for at least six weeks within a 13-week period, may give notice to the employer, in accordance with his or her contract, to terminate that employment and claim a redundancy payment. The employer may within seven days issue a counter-notice that within four weeks he or she reasonably expects to be able to provide at least 13 weeks employment without LAY-OFF or short time working. If the counter-notice is disputed, the claim will be referred to an industrial tribunal.

See also GUARANTEE PAYMENTS.

Sick pay. When employees are absent from work through sickness they may soon lose entitlement to their normal salary or wages due to being unable to perform the duties which their contract requires. The main payment basis during sickness absence is STATUTORY SICK PAY (SSP), but most employers make some addition to that, known as occupational sick pay (OSP), which can vary between being a small additional payment to being the maintenance of full earnings throughout the period of sickness absence. As with many other aspects of payment, provision for white collar and management employees tends to be more generous than that for manual employees.

Some employers require a minimum period of service before OSP is paid, usually 3, 6 or 12 months, while others make the payments to all employees. The simplest, and most generous, arrangements for determining the amount of OSP are those where normal earnings are maintained, minus the amount paid via SSP, with this level dropping to maintaining half normal earnings after 3, 6 or 12 months.

Apart from the moral obligation that employers will feel to sustain the employee's income during absence through sickness, there are practical advantages such as maintaining a healthier work-force and being able to attract new employees. All sick pay systems require close monitoring and it is wise to administer OSP and SSP by the same set of administrative procedures and records.

Sit-in. The origin of the sit-in is in the 'stay-down' strikes in 1936 at the South Wales coalfield; it has the effect of the employees immobilizing the employer's plant by occupying it and denying the employer either access or control. In the early 1970s a variant of the sit-in was the 'work-in', when workers asserted not only their defiance of the employer but also sought to demonstrate the viability of a business threatened with closure by maintaining the production operation.

Skill. Skill is used in two ways at the workplace. First it is a learned response that enables an individual to achieve a goal, usually after training, like keyboard skill or analytical ability. Second, it is a classification that confers status on those who possess a range of skills enabling them to carry out a range of duties for which others are not qualified. National agreements regarding the terms and conditions of manual employees frequently have a separate rate of pay for the 'skilled trades'.

The importance in personnel work of understanding the first type of skill is in the approach to training to make sure that the training method is appropriate to the skill to be acquired. Physical or *motor* skills are those requiring the coordination of body movements and sensory perception, like typing, driving or machining. Training methods most likely to be effective are those which enable the trainee to build up skilled performance through working on parts of the process only to acquire competence at segments of the whole before integrating the components. The methods require explanation, demonstration, practice, error-correction, reinforcement of success and target-setting. Intellectual or *conceptual* skills require the trainee to develop competence through holistic methods so that the subject is taught as an entity rather than being split up into bits. Common methods are lecture, reading, discussion, working on assignments and receiving criticism. *Social* skills are developed through the processes of socialization, such as group methods which enable trainees to develop their own self-awareness and social competence through person-to-person exchange. SENSITIVITY TRAINING is an extreme form of this method.

E. and R. M. Belbin, *Problems in Adult Re-training* (London: Heinemann, 1972).

Skills analysis. As a feature of training in skilled tasks, it is sometimes necessary to analyse the skills involved so that they may be effectively taught. Instead of simply showing the trainee what to do, the skills are analysed to determine what contributes to skilled performance and then training methods are derived to develop the skills. The salient feature of this type of analysis is to understand the cues that the experienced worker uses. The skilled typist, for example, is cued by the feel and positioning of the fingers on the keyboard: not by looking at the keys, which is the automatic approach of the tyro.

J. Kenney and M. Reid, *Training Interventions* (London: Institute of Personnel Management, 1986), ch. 6.

Small employers. There is a view that employment legislation has a particularly restricting effect on small businesses. Accordingly small firms have in certain instances been given preferential treatment in relation to statutory requirements, for example:

- the EMPLOYMENT ACT 1980 extended the qualifying period for unfair dismissal claims from one year to two where the number of employees *did not exceed 20* (note: as from 1 June 1985 the qualifying period in every case is two years: see NTINUITY OF EMPLOYMENT);
- an employer with *five or fewer* employees was exempted from the obligation not to discriminate in the field of recruitment, promotion and dismissal under the SEX DISCRIMINATION ACT 1975 (this exclusion was abolished as from 7 February 1987 by the SEX DISCRIMINATION ACT 1986);

- a woman's right to return to work after MATERNITY LEAVE was restricted by the Employment Act 1980 if the firm employed *five or fewer* employees;
- the requirement under the HEALTH AND SAFETY AT WORK ACT 1974 that an employer must prepare and publish a health and safety policy does not apply to a firm with *four or fewer* employees;
- under the Employment Act 1980 a recognized trade union wishing to hold a secret ballot has the right to ask the employer for the use of facilities and not to be unreasonably refused; this provision applies only where the number of employees *exceeds 20*;
- the WAGES ACT 1986 has abolished redundancy rebates for all employers except those employing *nine or fewer* employees.

Spent conviction. See REHABILITATION OF OFFENDERS ACT 1974.

Staff associations. As an alternative to trade union organization a staff association can provide a mechanism for the employer to consult with employees. It is an organization limited in its membership to company employees and often dependent on the company for financial support. Theoretically it provides a body of representative employee opinion with which the management can *bargain*, but dependence on the employer usually means that the association does not have the power to mount any real challenge to employer authority, so that consultation is the limit of its power.

Staff associations are derided by the trade union movement, partly because of their inability to challenge the employer but also because they do not participate in the wider aspects of trade unionism. Managers often prefer staff associations as discussion is limited to matters of internal interest and few managers welcome an independent challenge to their authority. However, a confident, independent challenge can be very useful – if not welcome – and recognizing a staff association that is not accepted by the CERTIFICATION OFFICER as *independent* (see INDEPENDENT TRADE UNION) does not avoid the possibility of a trade union seeking recognition in its place.

State Earnings Related Pension Scheme (SERPS). In addition to the flat-rate state retirement pension, an additional pension is payable to people who have completed 20 years of contributions related to their earnings. Most occupational pension schemes contract their members out of SERPS, which can be done provided that the benefits of the occupational scheme are at least as good as those provided by SERPS.

The potential cost of SERPS to the Exchequer is considerable and the government has made various moves to try and reduce this cost. Legislation has been introduced to encourage personal pensions as one alternative which individual employees might prefer.

Status quo. The strict translation from Latin is 'the state in which', but it is used in employee relations to describe 'the existing state of affairs' and its significance is that many agreements include a clause that prevents the management from making a change in working practice which is resisted by the employees until PROCEDURE is exhausted; they are obliged to maintain the status quo.

Statutory notice periods. Certain minimum notice periods are laid down in S49 of the Employment Protection (Consolidation) Act. For an employee with under two years' continuous employment the period is one week (the right does not apply to a casual worker employed on a specific task for less than three months); where there is over two years' continuous employment the period is one week's notice for each year worked up to a maximum of 12 weeks. However, the employer retains the right of SUMMARY DISMISSAL for certain misconduct.

Employees must give one week's notice once they have been employed for four weeks. The statutory provisions do not prevent them waiving their right to notice, or to receiving wages in lieu of notice. It is not clear whether the employer has a right to give wages in lieu if the employee wishes to work out the period of notice.

Statutory Sick Pay (SSP) Until April 1983, an employee who was absent from work through sickness would normally be entitled to sick pay via the state sickness benefit scheme, which operated independently of any contractual provisions. The Social Security and Housing Benefits Act 1982 introduced a scheme of statutory sick pay, which was revised in April 1986 by the Social Security Act 1985. The effect of the scheme is to transfer to the employer the obligation to pay sick pay for a maximum period of 28 weeks for any one period of an employee's incapacity for work.

For the first three days of sickness, SSP is not payable; from the fourth day onwards it is payable only for 'QUALIFYING DAYS', which will usually be the employee's normal working days. Within limits, however, 'qualifying days' may be the subject of agreement between employer and employee. Employers are entitled to make their own rules about notification of illness (for example, that it must be in writing) but they cannot demand evidence of incapacity by means of a doctor's statement unless the illness lasts more than seven days. Reasonable steps should be taken to make the notification rules known to the employee. If an employer decides that SSP is not payable, the employee can ask for a formal decision from the adjudication officer, by applying to his or her local social security office.

There are two weekly rates of SSP dependent on the employee's average earnings. The rates change each April, but in 1987 were as follows:

- £47.20 per week where normal weekly earnings are greater than £76.50;
- £32.85 per week where normal weekly earnings are less than £76.50.

No SSP is payable to employees whose average earnings are below the lower lower weekly limit for National Insurance contribution liability; otherwise employees in general are eligible immediately they begin work for an employer. The employer must deduct tax and National Insurance contributions from payments of SSP, and is then entitled to recoup the SSP paid by deducting it from National Insurance contributions.

A contractual payment made to an employee under the provision of an occupational sick pay scheme will offset any SSP liability in respect of a particular day. However, employers may, for example, use their own scheme to 'top up' SSP to the level of the employee's actual earnings.

Employer's Guide to Statutory Sick Pay, NI 227, available from local offices of DHSS.

Stereotyping. Experience and folklore both make us tend to develop stereotyped assumptions about people: gentlemen prefer blondes, Scots are mean, red-haired people are bad-tempered, small people are aggressive, and so forth. Some of these may be reliable indicators of how the next person you meet will behave, but they are at best very rough and ready indicators and at worst are misleading and damning of those who are stereotyped.

"Miss Huntswell. I'd like some paper clips, staples, glue, pencils, erasers, memo paper – all arranged in an atmosphere of creative clutter."

At one level stereotyping is a useful method of dealing with some of life's situations. 'Never take sweets from a stranger' is regarded by most parents as sound advice to give to children, despite the fact that it categorizes large numbers of people as dangerous when they are innocent. When stopping the car to ask a passer-by for travel directions, drivers typically pick the person to ask on the basis of a quick assessment of appearance, rather than making a random choice. In the workplace similar rough and ready judgements can be sensible for individuals when dealing with everyday situations, especially in situations leading to possible unjustified or unlawful DISCRIMINATION. All men with beards are not lacking in self-confidence; all negroes are not less intelligent than all Asians; all married women in their mid-twenties are not going to take maternity leave in the next 12 months; and all graduates of the university of X are not as obdurate and intractable as the one you had to dismiss last week.

Strikes/striking. There is no general statutory definition of a strike but it plainly connotes a concerted stoppage of work by employees during a dispute, used as a lever against an employer. In this country there is no legal right to strike; on the contrary stiking would normally be regarded as a repudiation by employees of their contract of employment for which they could be summarily dismissed (or sued for damages for breach of contract, but this is unlikely to happen). Even if not dismissed they are not entitled to be paid whilst striking. A week during which employees are on strike cannot be counted as a week of employment, but their CONTINUITY OF EMPLOYMENT is not broken.

See also ECONOMIC TORTS, IMMUNITY, INDUSTRIAL ACTION, SUMMARY DISMISSAL, TRADE UNION ACT 1984.

Subsistence allowance. The employee required to be away from home through working commitments is normally entitled to a subsistence allowance to cover food and accommodation during the absence. There are three broad approaches to containing the expenditure: the first is meeting reasonable expenditure. There are no rules or guidelines, but the employer will compensate the employee for reasonable expenditure incurred. The only difficulty comes in the interpretation of 'reasonable'. The second method is meeting expenditure within limits, which is more common. It entails setting ceiling figures for standard items, such as bed and breakfast, lunch and dinner, and agreeing to compensate for expenditure within those limits. The third type is set allowances. Employees claim a pre-determined amount of money for specified items, regardless of the actual expenditure incurred. Receipts will be required for those items of expenditure where the employer can claim a refund of VAT, as well as to justify the expenditure itself.

Summary dismissal. Summary dismissal means dismissal without notice, and would normally constitute a WRONGFUL DISMISSAL. However, at COMMON LAW summary dismissal is lawful in the case of an employee who commits an act of gross misconduct amounting to a repudiation of his or her contract of employment. Examples of such misconduct have been dishonesty, striking and taking secret commissions. Nevertheless an employer who intends to dismiss summarily for specific offences would be well advised to make clear to employees the consequences of their behaviour. Failure to do so may result in a successful claim of UNFAIR DISMISSAL, unless it must have been obvious that summary dismissal would follow from such conduct. Furthermore, whether a particular act of misconduct is sufficiently 'gross' to justify summary dismissal is for a court or tribunal to decide as a question of fact; the view of the employer is not necessarily decisive.

Suspension. A sanction commonly resorted to as a disciplinary measure is the suspension of an employee from work. Suspension with pay is generally lawful, and may be desirable as a temporary measure where, for example, management wishes to investigate an alleged offence. Suspension without pay would be unlawful unless specifically provided for in the contract of employment; an employee suspended unlawfully would be entitled to sue for damages for breach of contract, or resign and claim CONSTRUCTIVE DISMISSAL.

Under certain health and safety legislation an employer may be required to suspend employees on 'medical grounds'. Such medical grounds relate not to the condition of the employees, but to dangers which may arise in, for example, the handling of certain chemicals. The suspended employees are entitled to be paid a week's pay for each week of the suspension up to a maximum of 26 weeks provided that they are in fact medically fit for work (the qualifying conditions and loss of entitlement are similar to those for a GUARANTEE PAYMENT). It should be noted that the statutory remuneration provisions apply only where the employer has a contractual right to suspend without pay.

T

Technical and Vocational Education Initiative (TVEI). As an attempt to improve what is seen as inadequacy in the preparation by schools of young people for entry to employment, the TVEI was established in 1983 under the auspices of the MANPOWER SERVICES COMMISSION. Programmes are run within schools but usually with some time spent in a local technical college during the early stages and almost entirely based in the college towards the end. Students take the courses from the age of 14 until 18. The criteria for the programmes are:

- to prepare the students for employment in a situation of rapid change;
- to develop problem-solving capacities;
- technical and vocational features;
- planned work experience;
- regular counselling and written assessments;
- equal opportunities for both sexes.

Theory X/Theory Y. A simple formulation by the American Douglas McGregor suggests that many managers adopt Theory X as their personal explanation of human behaviour; the elements of Theory X are that people dislike work, will avoid it whenever possible and have to be coerced and blackmailed by their employers to do what is needed. McGregor's alternative Theory Y is that work is as natural as play and rest, that people will exercise self-control and direction towards objectives towards which they are committed, that the potential to be imaginative, creative and ingenious in seeking solutions to the organization's problems is widely, not narrowly, distributed among the employees of organizations, and that the intellectual potential of most employees is only partially utilized.

The simplicity and clarity of this classification has appealed to many managers and it now is almost axiomatic.

D. McGregor, *The Human Side of Enterprise* (New York: McGraw-Hill, 1960).

Time off. Employers may be sympathetic to reasonable requests by employees for time off work; indeed, time off for specified purposes may be the subject of contractual provisions. However, even in the absence of contractual entitlement, employees may be able to rely on various statutory rights, principally to be found in the EMPLOYMENT PROTECTION (CONSOLIDATION) ACT 1978, namely:

- ante-natal time off: a pregnant employee has the right not to be unreasonably refused time off to keep ante-natal appointments (the employer may require her to produce a certificate of pregnancy and her appointment card);
- MATERNITY LEAVE;
- trade union *officials* are entitled to reasonable time off *with pay* to carry out duties concerned with industrial relations between their employer and his employees. The ACAS Code of Practice on Time Off for Trade Union Duties and Activities (1977) envisages these duties including collective bargaining, consultations with management, meetings with other officials and so on. The Code also gives guidance on what is 'reasonable', including considerations of any previous time off, the size of the work-force and the particular demands of the business. Reasonable time off must also be provided for approved (by the TUC or the union) training relevant to the duties;
- trade union *members* have a right to reasonable time off *without pay* to take part in the activities of an independent trade union recognized by the employer (the ACAS Code of Practice provides similar guidance to this right, but it should be noted that industrial action is not included as a trade union 'activity');
- public duties: reasonable time off, not necessarily with pay, must be granted to an employee who is, for example, a magistrate, a member of a tribunal, local authority or regional health authority, or a school governor (under S29 of the Employment Protection (Consolidation) Act, the criteria of 'reasonableness' include how much time is needed and how much has already been taken, the circumstances of the business and the effect on it of the employee's absence);
- redundancy time off: an employee with at least two years' service (see CONTINUITY OF EMPLOYMENT) who is dismissed for REDUNDANCY is entitled to time off with pay during the period of notice in order to look for work or make arrangements for training;
- safety representatives: under the HEALTH AND SAFETY AT WORK ACT 1974 a recognized trade union may appoint safety representatives. The Safety Representative and Safety Committee

Regulations 1977 provide that such individuals have a right to time off with pay to perform their statutory functions and undergo training in relation to them.

Though the third, fourth and fifth rights listed do not depend on the employees concerned establishing any particular period of continuous employment, they are available only to those who work more than 16 hours per week.

Time span theory of discretion. In attempting to create a radically new method of job evaluation, Elliott Jaques propounded the theory that the time span of discretion in a job is the longest period of time over which the job holder exercises discretion without being checked by a superior. He also argued that this time span could be equated with a salary level that the job holder regarded as fair, so that the establishment of a time span of discretion for a job could be used to rank jobs for JOB EVALUATION purposes.

This technique has been adopted rarely and now ranks as of little more than historical interest, although the idea of FELT-FAIR has taken deeper root.

Trades Union Congress (TUC). Established in 1868, the TUC is a body with great influence and little power, even though the influence has waned in the 1980s. It is a body to which unions seek affiliation so that the TUC may act as a coordinating body and speak on behalf of the union movement through the medium of its General Council or its General Secretary. The General Council has 51 members elected from 33 trade groups within the union movement. The General Secretary is a full-time official, who is initially elected to the office but then remains in it without need for re-election. There is an annual meeting of the Congress itself, which ranks with party political conferences as one of the major political gatherings of the autumn.

The influence of the TUC is largely outside itself, as it provides representative members on a wide range of bodies, such as the National Economic Development Council, ACAS, the Council for Racial Equality and the EQUAL OPPORTUNITIES COMMISSION. There is no other body to represent the labour movement outside Parliament, so the TUC is the automatic source, operating in the same way as the Confederation of British Industry. The TUC's lack of power derives from its lack of sanctions in relation to individual unions. If the TUC were able to impose sanctions on unions to bring them into line with Congress policy, then the TUC would lose its nature as a voluntary body and contradict the basic tenet of trade union philosophy: that a union exists to serve its membership.

Trade union. A trade union exists for three main purposes:

- to further the economic and social interests of its members;
- to provide an independent challenge to the authority of management in relation to employees;
- to provide a representative element within the framework of a political democracy.

Unless one regards mediaeval craft guilds as the forerunners of trade unions, the beginnings can be traced back to the friendly societies and journeymen's clubs of the late eighteenth and early nineteenth centuries. By 1910 there were 2,600,000 trade union members in Britain, and this number grew steadily until 1979, when the number reached 13,500,000: over half of the working population. There has since been a steep decline, due to the increase in unemployment, legislation and a weakening of union effectivness in negotiation with managements. The number of unions has also decreased, over 1,000 unions in 1939 dwindling to under 400 in 1983, with 80 per cent of all members being in only 22 unions.

Trade Union Act 1984. The aim of the Trade Union Act 1984 is to achieve a greater degree of trade union democracy, principally by the use of secret ballots on issues affecting union members.

1 Voting members of the principal executive committee must be elected by a ballot, and re-elected every five years. Every member has the right to vote, and may complain to the High Court or to the CERTIFICATION OFFICER if the right is denied.
2 The union is required to ballot all members as to whether or not it shall have a political fund. A resolution to that effect

needs only a simple majority to be carried, but it will cease to have effect after ten years unless a new ballot is held. Where a majority in favour is not obtained, or a resolution ceases to have effect, members cannot be required to contribute to the fund. Even where a political fund is approved, individual members have the right not to contribute.

3 Where official INDUSTRIAL ACTION is contemplated a ballot must be held, otherwise IMMUNITY from liability for certain ECONOMIC TORTS will be lost. Authorization for the action must be obtained not more than four weeks before it is taken; all those whom it is reasonably believed may be called on to take part must be balloted (and no one else!). A question must be included on the ballot paper asking members whether they are prepared to take part in a strike (or whatever form the industrial action is to take) involving them in a breach of their contracts of employment – which may be seen by some as an intimidatory question. If no ballot is held, or a majority is not obtained, anyone who suffers loss as a result of the action, whether the employer, a supplier, a customer, a worker prevented from working, or even a member of the public, may sue for damages and/or apply for an INJUNCTION. There is growing evidence that persons affected by unlawful action are prepared to use the law in this area.

Workplace ballots are not prohibited, though postal ballots are preferred in electing committee members. What is essential is that they should be in secret, and free from interference.

See also BALLOTS.

Trade Union and Labour Relations Act 1974/Trade Union and Labour Relations (Amendment) Act 1976. The Trade Union and Labour Relations Act (TULRA) was the result of the Labour Government's commitment to repeal the ill-fated Industrial Relations Act of 1971. The effect was to restore the pre-1971 tradition of minimum legal interference in collective industrial relations and the legal unenforceability of collective agreements. However, the provisions of the 1971 Act relating to the right not to be unfairly dismissed were retained and strengthened by widening the definition of dismissal to include

'CONSTRUCTIVE DISMISSAL' and by reducing the service qualification from two years to 26 weeks. Where a closed shop existed the combined effect of the 1974 Act and its 1976 amendment was that dismissal of an employee for non-membership of the union would be fair unless the employee objected to membership on religious grounds.

Trade union facilities. Where an employer recognizes a trade union for purposes of collective bargaining, it is usual for the employer to provide facilities for union representatives to discharge their representative functions. This applies principally to TIME OFF work for industrial relations and trade union duties. Other facilities which the employer may provide include:

- access to new employees to explain about union membership and procedures;
- noticeboards and opportunities to distribute union literature;
- facilities for typing, photocopying and similar clerical assistance;
- the use of a telephone;
- a place for meetings and discussion with individual union members.

Trade union membership and activities. In the UK collective freedom is protected largely by means of statutory rights bestowed on individual employees. Thus, for example, trade union officials and members have rights to TIME OFF for trade union duties and activities. The right to belong to a union and the corresponding right not to belong operate largely through the UNFAIR DISMISSAL legislation, making it automatically unfair to dismiss an employee for membership or non-membership of the union (but see CLOSED SHOP). However, discrimination against, for example, union activists may take more subtle forms than dismissal. Employees therefore have the right not to have action *short* of dismissal taken against them as individuals in order to compel them to join the union (or a particular union), or to deter them from, or penalize them for, being members of an INDEPENDENT TRADE UNION, or taking part in its activities at an appropriate time (S23 of the EMPLOYMENT PROTECTION (CONSOLIDATION) ACT 1978).

The rights given in S23 are not without limitations. Where a CLOSED SHOP exists they relate only to the union(s) specified in the UNION MEMBERSHIP AGREEMENT, and employers may lawfully take action to compel employees to belong if it would have been fair to dismiss them for non-membership of the union in those circumstances. Trade union activities are protected only 'at an appropriate time', and this means outside working hours off the employer's premises, or when employees are on the premises with the employer's express or implied consent but not actually working (for example, during meal breaks). During working hours the employer's consent is needed. Activities of a trade union are not necessarily to be equated with activities carried on by trade union members; thus the section was held inapplicable where employees who happened to be trade union members presented a petition about safety at work. Furthermore the section only protects against action taken against individuals, and this requirement has been restrictively interpreted. Thus the employer who sacked employees as a response to the union's request for recognition was held to be taking action against *the union*, as opposed to individual members.

There are some surprising omissions in the legislation: no protection is given against an employer's refusal to recruit on the basis of union activity, and neither is it automatically unfair to dismiss an employee for union activities in a previous job (though the employer would have to justify dismissal in the usual way: see UNFAIR DISMISSAL).

Trade union recognition. When employers recognize a trade union they are undertaking at least to consult with union representatives and to listen to representations on behalf of individual employees who are union members. The employer may agree to recognize the union for dealings on a wider range of issues, such as negotiating terms and conditions of employment, establishing joint committees, procedures for dealing with DISCIPLINE, DISPUTES, GRIEVANCES, REDUNDANCY, manning levels and employee deployment.

As one of the main purposes of trade unions is to challenge management authority (see TRADE UNION) it at first seems strange that any employer should contemplate recognition at all, if it can be avoided, as it appears to be nurturing a viper in one's bosom.

This undoubtedly is the view that many members of management take, but there are some practical reasons for considering recognition, apart from reluctantly yielding to pressure:

- if employees want union representation, they will not readily cooperate with an employer who refuses it;
- union representatives provide a focus for discussion and consultation on matters affecting the work-force, so that communication and working relationships can be improved and so that management plans can be modified before implementation if the process of consultation shows them to be misconceived;
- union recognition provides a mechanism for employee representation in ways advocated by legislation, like PENSION FUND TRUSTEES and SAFETY REPRESENTATIVES;
- union channels provide a means of employees directing their worries or frustrations towards a possible resolution.

Union membership remains high for all categories of employee, although it is highest for manual workers and those in the public sector of employment where union recognition by management is often a requirement of the statute that set up the undertaking.

Trade unions only enjoy a number of their statutory rights as long as they are recognized by the employer. If the recognition is withdrawn, they lose the rights that are dependent on that employer's recognition, such as being consulted about proposed redundancies (see CONSULTATION).

Training. There is widespread acceptance among employers that more training needs to be provided for people at work and contemplating work, but there is also a lack of enthusiasm to make the provision. The 1980s – a time of increasing anxiety about the need to keep up to date with technological advance – has been a time of declining employer provision of training for employees. One of the main reasons for this is the intangibility of the results that training presents, so a need to reduce costs frequently is translated into a need to cut training. The MANPOWER SERVICES COMMISSION has calculated that British employer investment in training represents 0.15 per cent of the average firm's turnover, which is one-seventh of the level in the US and one-fourteenth of the best in West Germany. Despite this generally disturbing figure, a vigorous minority of companies invest heavily in employee training and development, regarding it as a key to their continuing commercial success.

The training process can be summed up in a mnemonic devised by John Chapman, ASDICE:

- *A*ssessment of training needs, through training needs analysis, JOB ANALYSIS;
- *S*pecification of training objectives, and development of criteria for evaluating the training when complete;
- *D*esign of the training programme;
- *I*nstruction methods selection, and deciding between OFF-THE-JOB TRAINING and ON-THE-JOB TRAINING;
- *C*onduct of the training, including MOTIVATION, INSTRUCTION and FEEDBACK;
- *E*valuation of the training programme, perhaps through PERFORMANCE APPRAISAL.

D. P. Torrington and J. B. Chapman, *Personnel Management*, 2nd edn (Englewood Cliffs, New Jersey: Prentice-Hall, 1983), ch. 9.

Training methods. Methods of training have to be selected according to the SKILLS that are to be developed, although it is less important to select the right method than to ensure the motivation and interest of the trainee in what is being learned.

1 Assignments or projects are increasingly used in schools and colleges as ways in which the learner uses a number of different types of learning, mainly organizing the study and selecting approaches on his or her own initiative. It is especially appropriate in management development, where there can be the invaluable aspect of the outcome being practically useful beyond the value of the training itself.

2 Lectures or talks are the standard way of conveying information and are appropriate where the trainee has to comprehend and remember information.

3 Discussion groups are a development of the lecture approach, except that the emphasis quickly shifts away from what the lecturer has to say towards what the trainee has not yet understood. It is still directed at what the trainee has to comprehend and remember, but is better for reinforcement and dealing with misunderstandings.

4 Distance learning is the method long used by correspondence schools and used more extensively since the advent of television and computers. It has the merits of the discussion group in that the focus is on what the trainee has yet to understand, but it lacks the social support that discussion provides.

5 Experimental methods include a range of techniques such as ROLE PLAY and SENSITIVITY TRAINING, where the experience of the trainee is the route to understanding. They are the preferred methods for social skills training and for attitude development.

6 Part methods are where the task to be performed is broken down into components for the trainee to learn how to do each bit before gradually putting the various bits together in an integrated performance. This is the main method of developing motor skills.

Transactional analysis. Transactional analysis was originally developed as a form of therapy by Eric Berne, based on the theory that there are three ego states of the individual. The *parent* state is one of authority and superiority and a person in this state is likely to be dominant and scolding. The *child* state is one of childlikeness: tantrum and charm, obedience and defiance, sulks and joy. The *adult* is objective and rational, analysing situations as realistically as possible. All of us have all three states and spend our day moving between them. The manager trying to win someone round will discern the ego state of the other person and respond appropriately.

There are basically three types of transaction: *complementary, crossed* and *ulterior.* Where the participants are in the ego state appropriate to the transaction, then it will be complementary, as when a 'parent' speaks to a 'child' and the 'child' responds as would a child to a parent. Two people speaking to each other as 'adults' is also a complementary transaction.

The crossed transaction is where the opening comment produces an inappropriate response, such as when an 'adult to adult' opening produces a 'parent to child' reaction. Rather more complex is the ulterior transaction where the real message is disguised under a more socially acceptable, apparent transaction. A manager who wanted a subordinate to apply for promotion feared that the subordinate would not be keen to change his job, so he said, 'I believe there is a good job coming up in Oxted, but I am not sure whether you are quite ready for it yet.' That is apparently adult to adult. If the reply is, 'Yes, I suppose you are right and I had better wait a bit longer,' then it is an adult to adult response and the manager has failed in his manoevre. If, however, there is a child to adult response of, 'Why shouldn't I stand as good a chance as everyone else? I'll certainly have a damned good try,' then the manager has succeeded with his ulterior transaction.

Central to transactional analysis is another idea of stroking: we all need attention, recognition and approval. *Positive conditional strokes* are signs of approval or recognition that are bestowed on behaviour with the implicit condition that the stroking will continue as long as the behaviour continues: 'We are delighted with your progress', or 'The customer appreciated the trouble you were taking.' *Positive unconditional strokes* are given for some feature of who you are rather than what you have done, 'I like you', or 'It's good to have you around.' *Negative conditional strokes* respond to behaviour that is not like, with the implication that the disapproval will be removed if the behaviour changes: 'You still make too many errors of detail', or 'The committee are not yet convinced . . . ' Although negative, this form of stroking is still useful. The fourth possibility of *negative unconditional stroking,* as in 'I can't stand the sight of you', may enable the speaker to let off steam but does nothing for the working relationship.

Managers who understand the nature of the three ego states and their interaction will be able to analyse what is being said and decide how to respond. If they can build a strong adult ego state, and encourage others to do the same, they will conduct transactions in a forthright and constructive manner. They concentrate on complementary transactions, use ulterior transactions sparingly and avoid negative unconditional strokes while developing effective use of the other three.

E. Berne, *Games People Play* (London: André Deutsch, 1966).

Transfer of Undertakings (Protection of Employment) Regulations 1981. The aim of the Transfer of Undertakings Regulations, which are the UK's implementation of obligations cast on it by EEC Directive 77/187, is to protect the rights of employees when a business or other undertaking is transferred as a going concern. Prior to the Regulations such employees would have been entitled to a redundancy payment from their employer, unless the purchaser made an offer to employ them which they accepted. The present position is that employees whose contracts are subsisting at the time of the transfer are automatically transferred with the business. Their CONTINUITY OF EMPLOYMENT is preserved, and all their contractual and statutory rights become enforceable against the new owner.

Where an employee is dismissed by the vendor before the transfer, or by the purchaser after the transfer, the regulations provide that if the dismissal occurs because of the transfer it will be automatically unfair. However, the employer in question has a defence if able to show that the reason for the dismissal was an economic, technical or organizational one entailing changes in the work-force. A finding of fair dismisssal will then ensue provided that the tribunal is satisfied, as in an ordinary case of unfair dismissal, that the employer acted reasonably in the circumstances. A common occurrence is that the purchaser makes some of the new work-force redundant. This would normally be accepted as an 'economic' or 'organizational' reason, but would not preclude the dismissed employees from claiming a redundancy payment. However, where the purchaser attempts, for example, to cut the transferred employees' wages to bring them into line with his or her own employees, the former may resign and claim CONSTRUCTIVE DISMISSAL. In this case the 'economic, technical or organizational' defence will not apply because, although the reasons for dismissal may be described as economic (or organizational), it does not 'entail changes in the *work-force*', but merely their terms and conditions. Furthermore, although a vendor may be able to rely on the defence if the purchaser insisted on dismissal of the work-force as a pre-condition to the sale (an economic reason entailing changes in the work-force), this may not be so where no such pre-condition existed.

Where either of the employers concerned recognizes a trade union he or she has a duty to give certain information to the union representatives and to consult with them (see CONSULTATION).

See also AUTOMATICALLY UNFAIR DISMISSAL, REDUNDANCY, UNFAIR DISMISSAL.

Truck legislation. The word 'truck' stems from the French *trouquer*, meaning to barter (not, as may be thought, from legislation for lorry drivers) and indicates one of the abuses outlawed by the Truck Act 1831: that of payment by tokens or vouchers which could be exchanged for goods at the company's store. As the Act obliged employers to pay the wages of manual workers in the current coin of the realm, payments in kind were also prohibited. The Truck Act 1896 regulated lawful fines and deductions which could be made from the wages of manual workers and shop assistants. The legislation was in much need of reform and has now been repealed and updated by the WAGES ACT 1986.

U

Unemployment. The main concern about unemployment is as a social ill, and evidence is accumulating about its corrosive effect on individuals' health, family life and social cohesion. For this reason most discussion is directed at how to reduce the level of unemployment, although it has considerable influence on what happens *within* organizations.

1 Apprehension about unemployment makes most employees anxious to retain the jobs they have. This anxiety may generate loyalty, hard work and commitment, but it can also make people unduly cautious and more concerned to avoid mistakes than to make a positive contribution.

2 Difficulty in finding alternative employment means that some people continue in jobs they dislike and working with colleagues they have come to mistrust. Older employees may resent the promotion of young people over their heads, and so lose enthusiasm and hamper change and initiative within the organization.

3 New recruits may have been out of work for months or years and some may be working for the first time some years after they have finished school, which is their only other experience of organized life. INDUCTION can then be a lengthy process until they acquire the routine of working and its associated SELF-DISCIPLINE.

4 Unemployment is the plight of certain types of employee: those with few skills, those in the northern part of the country, those at the top and bottom of the age range and – to some extent – those who are male. The effects of this for the employer are that there are still many jobs which are very difficult to fill and the organization's employees tend to divided into two groups: those whose working behaviour *is* adversely affected by unemployment and those who are unaffected.

Unfair dismissal. The concept of 'unfair' dismissal as opposed to WRONGFUL DISMISSAL was first introduced by the Industrial Relations Act 1971, and its provisions are now contained in Part V of the Employment Protection (Consolidation) Act 1978. Every EMPLOYEE who has been continuously employed for two years at the EFFECTIVE DATE OF TERMINATION (see CONTINUITY OF EMPLOYMENT) is entitled not to be unfairly dismissed. However, the right will not apply if the employee falls within certain categories, for instance:

- the police;
- employees ordinarily working outside Great Britain;
- employees on FIXED TERM CONTRACTS for one year or more who waive their right;
- employees whose claims are settled by ACAS;
- employees who have reached the NORMAL RETIRING AGE;
- employees dismissed whilst taking part in INDUSTRIAL ACTION.

Employees who allege they have been unfairly dismissed must make a claim to an INDUSTRIAL TRIBUNAL (a form, IT 1, is provided for this purpose, but its use is not essential) within three months of the effective date of termination unless the tribunal grants an extension because it feels it was not 'reasonably practicable' to bring the claim in time.

Legally, an unfair dismissal claim has three stages:

- employees must show that they have been dismissed (see DISMISSAL);
- in order to defend the claim the *employer* must establish the reason for the dismissal and that it was one of the potentially FAIR REASONS FOR DISMISSAL;
- the tribunal must decide whether in the circumstances (including the size and administrative resources of the employer's undertaking) the employer acted reasonably or unreasonably in treating the reason as sufficient to dismiss the employee; the question must be decided 'in accordance with equity and the substantial merits of the case' (S57(3)).

Under S57(3), the tribunal's task is to judge the reasonableness of the *employer's* decision, and not to substitute its own (see RANGE OF REASONABLE RESPONSES). No statutory guidance is given to tribunals as to what constitutes 'reasonableness', but in relation to a particular reason for dismissal certain considerations will invariably be relevant. For example, in cases of *misconduct* the following questions may be studied:

- was a fair procedure followed;

- were there clear rules consistently applied;
- were the sanctions brought home to those concerned (see WARNINGS);
- was the employee allowed to give an explanation;
- was a reasonable investigation undertaken?

Procedural unfairness, however, will not *automatically* result in a finding of unfair dismissal; the tribunal occasionally concludes that a fair procedure would have made no difference to the result. It should be noted that acquittal in subsequent criminal proceedings is not a relevant consideration.

In cases of *incompetence*:

- was the employee given adequate support and supervision;
- was it made clear to that person in what way he or she was failing to meet the required standard and how he or she could improve (see also WARNINGS);
- could an alternative job have been found?

In cases of dismissal on *medical* grounds:

- did management investigate the employee's condition and the prognosis;
- was there CONSULTATION with the employee before a decision was reached;
- could an alternative job have been found (perhaps temporarily if the condition was expected to improve)?

The decision to dismiss is nevertheless a managerial one, not a medical one.

In general terms employees should be treated with regard to their individual circumstances, such as length of service and past record, even if this means an apparent lack of consistency. Where unfair dismissal is established the tribunal must grant the appropriate remedy, whether REINSTATEMENT, RE-ENGAGEMENT or, much more commonly, COMPENSATION.

See also AUTOMATICALLY UNFAIR DISMISSAL, REDUNDANCY.

S. D. Anderman, *The Law of Unfair Dismissal* (London: Butterworths, 1985).

Union Membership Agreements. (UMAs). A union membership agreement is defined by S30(1) of the Trade Union and Labour Relations Act 1974 as an agreement or arrangement which:

- is made by an independent trade union and an employer or employer's association; and
- relates to employees of an indentifiable class; and
- has the effect in practice of requiring that the employees for the time being of the class to which it relates (whether or not there is a condition to that effect in their contract of employment) be or become a member of the union which is a party to the agreement or of another specified independent trade union.

Where it is the practice in accordance with the UMA for employees to be union members, dismissal for non-membership may be fair (see CLOSED SHOP).

V

Value added schemes. A development of incentive schemes (see INCENTIVES) includes arrangements where the incentive payment to the employee is linked to an assessment of the value added to the product through the work of the group of which the employee is a member. Schemes are usually based on an index of performance over previous years with an agreed payment to employees which are triggered by pre-determined improvements in the index.

I. Smith, *The Management of Remuneration* (London: Institute of Personnel Management, 1983), ch. 7.

Visual aids. 'What I hear, I forget: what I see, I remember' explains why visual aids to learning are used. The blackboard has been partly replaced by the white board and flip chart, a white background being clearer than a black one. The overhead projector has the further benefit of providing an illuminated white background, with the presenter able to produce material prepared beforehand rather than having to write it up on a blackboard during the lesson, facing away from the audience.

Other visual aids include models, displays, charts and demonstrations. It is difficult for any communicator who is not highly skilled to hold the attention of an audience and communicate effectively for more than a few minutes without some form of visual display to reinforce the message, but the aids are not the message itself, so they have to be selected and used to *aid* communication, not to replace it.

W

Wages Act 1986. The controversial Wages Act 1986 repeals all TRUCK LEGISLATION and a variety of other statutes such as the Payment of Wages Act 1960. The law governing pay is amended in four main areas:

1 REDUNDANCY rebates: from 1 August 1986 the right to claim a rebate from the Redundancy Rebate Fund was restricted to those employers who, together with any ASSOCIATED EMPLOYER, employ nine or fewer employees at the date the employee's contract terminates.
2 The existing protection against unlawful FINES and deductions from wages is replaced by new provisions.
3 The requirement that certain workers should be paid in 'coin of the realm' unless they requested in writing some form of 'cashless pay' is removed. So far as employees taken on after 1 January 1987 are concerned, there is nothing to prevent an employer making it a term of an employee's contract that wages should be paid by cheque or credit transfer. In the case of existing employees who can show that they have a *contractual* right to be paid in cash (as opposed simply to a right under the Truck Act 1831), the employer may not be able to switch unilaterally to 'cashless pay' without committing a breach of contract. Such breach, if considered sufficiently serious, would entitle an employee to resign and claim CONSTRUCTIVE DISMISSAL. However, the employer may argue that the administrative convenience of cashless pay amounted to 'some other substantial reason of a kind to justify dismissal' (see FAIR REASONS FOR DISMISSAL).
4 The powers of WAGES COUNCILS are severely curtailed.

F. P. Davidson, *A Guide to the Wages Act 1986* (Financial Training Publications, London, 1986).

Wages Councils. Wages councils are the successors to the Trade Boards set up in sweated labour jobs under the Trade Boards Act 1909. They were established to regulate terms and conditions of employment in industries where COLLECTIVE BARGAINING was weak, typically industries dominated by women workers, or where employers were geographically widely spread, or where employees worked from home. Presently wages councils cover some 43 industries, ranging from agriculture and catering to retailing (including the 'Pin, Hook and Eye and Snap Fastener' and 'Ostrich and Fancy Feather and Artificial Flower' industries). Each council consists of an equal number of employer and employee representatives and up to three independent members chosen by the Secretary of State for Employment.

The WAGES ACT 1986 reformed wages councils and restricted their powers, so that in future:

- young persons under the age of 21 are excluded from the scope of protection;
- there is a limit on the charge which employers can make for living accommodation they provide;
- councils are restricted to setting a *single* minimum hourly rate of pay and a single overtime rate (for piece-workers the appropriate piece-rate is such that a worker of ordinary competence would have earned those minimum rates).

The Act requires councils to consider the impact on employment levels of the rates which they set 'in particular on workers in areas where the level of remuneration is lower than the normal average for such workers'. It is believed that by enabling employers to pay lower wages to under-21-year-olds, the provisions of the Act will create job opportunities.

Employers who pay below the rate specified are liable to be sued for breach of contract by the workers concerned (since the statutory rate prevails over any lower rate as a term in the contract). Moreover it is a criminal offence punishable by a fine of up to £400 to pay less than the statutory minimum. Should the wages inspectorate bring a prosecution in respect of such an offence, the court is further empowered to order payment of up to two years' arrears of wages to workers affected by the underpayment.

Waiting time. Waiting time is that period when an employee employed under a traditional incentive scheme is available for work but is prevented from working through lack of materials, lack of work or while awaiting instructions. In calculating the amount of incentive to be paid, these periods are deducted so that the payment is assessed on the basis of the time actually spent working.

See also INCENTIVES.

Warnings. Warnings will generally be an integral feature of management's disciplinary procedure. Where dismissal for misconduct may be contemplated, the ACAS Code of Practice 'Disciplinary Practice and Procedure in Employment' (see CODES OF PRACTICE) recommends an oral or written warning to be followed by a final written warning, and then by dismissal (or other sanction).

It is important that the consequences of failure to comply with any warning are clearly spelled out. An employer who does not follow the recommendations of the Code takes the risk of losing a subsequent unfair dismissal claim in that he or she has not acted 'reasonably' (see UNFAIR DISMISSAL). However, there may be instances of gross misconduct (see SUMMARY DISMISSAL) where warnings are clearly inappropriate. It is generally wise to make clear to employees the sort of conduct which will trigger the warning procedure, and that which will be regarded as serious enough for dismissal without warning to be justified.

Employees who may ultimately be dismissed for incapacity (see point 1 under FAIR REASONS FOR DISMISSAL) should be warned that their performance is not adequate, additionally making it clear how they can improve and giving them sufficient supervision and support. In this area a warning is a matter of substance rather than procedure, so that where an employee is hopelessly incompetent or where the consequences of error are very serious, a warning may be unnecessary. Where, for example, bad workmanship results from mere laziness, the use of the disciplinary procedure may be more appropriate.

A 'reasonable' employer will generally consult employees (see CONSULTATION) and give them as much warning as possible of impending redundancies. The 1972 Industrial Relations Code of Practice includes this recommendation (see also REDUNDANCY).

Weighted application form. The APPLICATION FORM contains a great deal of information about a candidate for appointment, yet the form is often used in only a superficial way in SHORT-LISTING and as a basis for the SELECTION INTERVIEW. Where the employer has a great deal of experience in recruiting for a particular type of vacancy, it can be useful to develop the detail of questions posed on the form and to weight the answers given. Pre-selection is then carried out in a systematic way by adding the points score of the form and short-listing the highest scorers. If, for instance, a company has found that employees with A level German have made more effective systems analysts than those with A level biology, that might be a method of discriminating between applicants at an early stage by weighting application form data.

This is not yet a widely used technique and can only be valid when there is extensive historical evidence over a large number of factors.

Welfare. Contemporary PERSONNEL MANAGEMENT grew from the industrial welfare movement of the early twentieth century and 'looking after the employees' remains a significant activity for most employers. Apart from matters relating to health and sickness absence, welfare activities are mainly:

- running sports and social clubs for the employees, together with a range of associated activities (such as holidays, outings and reunions for pensioners);
- advising employees on personal matters in much the same way as a Citizens' Advice Bureau, but with the additional element of sometimes being able to offer either financial assistance or the provision of a service (such as paying for a spouse to fly out to an employee in hospital abroad);
- providing personal services at work, like chiropody and hairdressing.

White collar workers. White collar workers are those who, metaphorically, wear the white collar associated with clean and comfortable office work instead of the blue collar associated with dirty and uncomfortable manual work. This is a distinction of great import in relation to the attitudes of both employer and employee (see SALARY AND WAGES). The proportion of the British working population in white collar employment had risen from 20 per cent at the beginning of the century to over 50 per cent by the 1980s. This proportion continues to increase so that the white collar employee is now the norm.

Women. Over the last 15 years the number of women in the labour market has steadily increased. The greatest rise has been in the employment of married women, largely in part-time jobs. In excess of five million individuals are now part-time workers, but only 1.9 per cent of men were employed part-time in 1986 as opposed to 23.7 per cent of women (see Central Statistical Office, *Social Trends* No. 17, 1987 edition, HMSO). Women's jobs are unevenly spread throughout the labour market and tend to be concentrated in many which attract low pay: thus the majority of homeworkers are married women, and women manual workers tend to be found in the personal service occupations such as catering, cleaning and hairdressing. Despite equal pay legislation, women's average weekly earnings remain only 66 per cent of men's (*Employment Gazette,* March 1987).

There is, in general, nothing special about employing women; in fact to afford them different treatment from that afforded to men, whether it be preferential or less favourable, may contravene the SEX DISCRIMINATION ACT 1975 or the EQUAL PAY ACT 1970. The protective legislation which previously limited women's hours of work has been repealed by the SEX DISCRIMINATION ACT 1986.

However, employers should be aware of certain matters pertaining specifically to women, namely:

* women are not entitled to a redundancy payment after the age of 60;
* women over the age of 60 can be exempt from paying National Insurance contributions (but the employer would not be exempt);
* it is automatically unfair to dismiss a woman because of pregnancy or a reason connected with it. It may also constitute sex discrimination. However, preferential treatment afforded to a pregnant employee would not constitute discrimination against a male employee;
* those employing women need to be aware of statutory MATERNITY RIGHTS;
* employers should be wary of affording less favourable treatment to part-timers (for example, by excluding them from pension schemes or making them redundant first) as this may constitute unlawful indirect DISCRIMINATION.

Works rules. In the case of *Secretary of State for Employment* v. *Aslef,* the railway union, Lord Denning said of British Rail's rules, 'these rules are in no way terms of the contract of employment. They are only instructions to a man as to how he is to do his work' ([1972] 2 QB 455). On this view rules may be changed unilaterally by management and, provided they are reasonable, an employee is under a duty to obey them. However, it is generally accepted that some rules become part of an individual's contract of employment, either because they are expressly incorporated into it by an acknowledgement to that effect which was signed on commencing employment, or via the appropriate COLLECTIVE AGREEMENT. Similarly works rules may take effect as IMPLIED TERMS of the contract by, for example, CUSTOM AND PRACTICE.

Disciplinary rules should be clearly laid down and drawn to the attention of employees, especially where their breach will attract the sanction of dismissal. However, even where such sanction is stipulated, a claim of UNFAIR DISMISSAL may still succeed if the INDUSTRIAL TRIBUNAL feels it was unduly severe or where employees have been led to believe that a breach of the rule would be overlooked, or at least would not have led to dismissal.

Work to rule. The work to rule is one of the most extraordinary forms of industrial action, as the employees frustrate employers by obeying the *employers'* rules. The effectiveness of the sanction rests on the obsolescence of many working PROCEDURES and the inflexibility of many COLLECTIVE AGREEMENTS, whereby aspects of how work should be done are enshrined in documents which are no longer accurate guides on what to do and they are sensibly ignored until the time comes when the employees are looking for some leverage. There is also frequent disagreement about what the rules are.

Written reasons for dismissal. An employee who has worked for at least six months for an employer is entitled to ask for a written statement of the reasons for dismissal. In providing such a statement there is no obligation on the employer to use any particular technicalities or form; a straightforward statement of why the employee was dismissed suffices. The employee is entitled to be given the statement within 14 days of making the request; if the employer unreasonably refuses or gives untrue or inadequate particulars in the statement, the employee may (within three months of the EFFECTIVE DATE OF TERMINATION) complain to an industrial tribunal. Where the complaint is upheld, the tribunal will award the employee two weeks' pay, and may make a declaration as to the reasons for the dismissal.

The written statement is admissible in later tribunal proceedings, but this would normally be of significance only to employees with two years' continuous service (see UNFAIR DISMISSAL).

Wrongful dismissal. A dismissal in breach of the CONTRACT OF EMPLOYMENT is said to be 'wrongful'. Most frequently, wrongful dismissal occurs where employees are dismissed without notice or with less than the notice to which they are entitled contractually or by statute (see STATUTORY NOTICE PERIODS). A dismissal carried out other than in accordance with a stated contractual procedure, or where the contract was for a fixed term, would also be wrongful.

Wrongful dismissal claims are brought in the County Court (or the High Court if the amount claimed is more than £5,000) where the usual remedy is an award of damages. In assessing the damages, the aim is to compensate the employee for what has been lost, which will generally be the wages that would have been earned during the period in respect of which notice was not given. Where a FIXED TERM CONTRACT is wrongfully terminated, damages are payable over the unexpired period of the contract, and may therefore be considerable. An employee is, however, under a duty to 'mitigate' the loss by taking reasonable steps to find other suitable employment. Wages earned in a new job during the period in question must be deducted from damages, as must income tax (unless damages are more than £25,000, in which case the amount over £25,000 is subject to tax by the Revenue) and any unemployment benefit, supplementary benefit or unfair dismissal compensation awarded for loss of earnings. A redundancy payment is not deducted.

Very occasionally the court has granted an injunction to prevent a dismissal in breach of a specified procedure from taking effect. However, this is done only where the relationship of 'trust and confidence' between employer and employee remains, and where damages would not be an adequate remedy.

Wrongful dismissal has no relationship to UNFAIR DISMISSAL.

Y

Youth Training Scheme. This scheme is widely known as YTS. It represents one of the largest investments in training undertaken by central government. Its objective is to remedy the problem of youth unemployment and to improve the stock of useful vocational skills available to employers. It is available to all school-leavers of 16 and 17 who wish to join, and runs for two years.

"We got him from the Youth Opportunities Programme."

The core of the scheme is the *managing agent* who may be an employer, a college or a specialist business. The managing agent organizes a YTS scheme in exchange for a management and administration fee geared to the number of YTS trainees covered. The managing agent also passes on to trainees a *training allowance* which is a weekly subsistence payment at a level slightly above that of supplementary benefit. The scheme has to include both work experience and OFF-THE-JOB TRAINING, alongside regular assessment and feedback on progress.

YTS trainees are to be found in all types of undertaking as there are many more employers who provide work experience than act as managing agents. The quality of the training inevitably varies, but many employers now use YTS as their main recruitment channel for school-leavers.

Appendix I:
The Basic Tool Kit

If about to employ people for the first time, you need the following basics:

1 Free Leaflets

From your local Post Office
Leaflets on National Insurance contributions and PAYE.

From ACAS
No. 2 Introduction to Payment Systems
No. 3 Personnel Records
No. 6 Recruitment and Selection
No. 7 Induction of New Employees
No. 10 Employment Policies

From Commission on Racial Equality
Code of Practice

From Department of Employment
PL700 Written Statement of Main Terms and Conditions of Employment
PL704 Itemized Pay Statement
PL724 Guarantee Payments
PL711 Rules Governing Continuous Employment and a Week's Pay

From Equal Opportunities Commission
Code of Practice

From Health and Safety Executive
Securing Compliance with Health and Safety Legislation at Work

2 Free Advice

From ACAS Advisory Service and Department of Industry Small Firms Advisory Service.

3 A Book

Employing People: The ACAS Handbook for Small Firms. An excellent publication available from ACAS offices.

Appendix II:
Upgrading the Tool Kit

After a few months your tool kit will need up-grading. You may need:

1 More Free Leaflets

From ACAS
No. 1 Job Evaluation
No. 5 Absence
No. 8 Workplace Communications
Code of Practice: Disciplinary Practice and Procedures in Employment

From Data Protection Registrar
Guideline No. 1. An Introduction and Guide to the Act

From Department of Employment
PL710 Employment Rights for the Expectant Mother
PL705 Suspension on Medical Grounds Under Health and Safety
    Regulations
PL702 Time Off For Public Duties
PL754 Union Membership Rights and the Closed Shop
Fair and Unfair Dismissal: A Guide for Employers
Individual Rights of Employees: A Guide for Employers
The Law on Unfair Dismissal: Guidance for Small Firms

From Health and Safety Executive
Writing a Safety Policy Statement: Advice to Employers
Safety Committees

2 Another Book

Michael Armstrong, *A Handbook of Personnel Management Practice*, 2nd edn (London: Kogan Page, 1984).